The VIETNAMESE SOCIAL SCIENCES at a FORK in the ROAD

Editors
Quan-Hoang Vuong, Trung Tran

Contributors
Viet-Phuong La, Manh-Tung Ho, Thu-Trang Vuong, Manh-Toan Ho, Hong-Kong T. Nguyen, Thu-Hien T. Le, Tien-Trung Nguyen, Phuong-Thao T. Trinh, Xuan-Hung Doan, Thu-Hang T. Nguyen, Phuong-Tram T. Nguyen, Khanh-Linh Hoang, Phuong-Hanh Hoang, Thi-Hanh Vu, Hung-Hiep Pham, Minh-Hoang Nguyen.

Hanoi, Vietnam

We would like to express our sincere gratitude towards all organizations that have supported us in writing this book.

The Vietnamese Social Sciences and Humanities at a Fork in the Road

The *Vietnamese Social Sciences and Humanities at a Fork in the Road*, utilizing an object-oriented structured database on the productivity of Vietnamese researchers, seeks to provide a comprehensive overview of the development of Social Sciences and Humanities in Vietnam from 2008 to 2018.

Quan-Hoang Vuong (Ph.D., Université Libre de Bruxelles) is the director of Centre for Interdisciplinary Social Research, Phenikaa University in Hanoi, Vietnam. He is chairman of the Vietnam chapter of the European Association of Science Editors and serves in the NAFOSTED Scientific Council on Basic Research in the Social Sciences and Humanities (2019-2021). Dr. Vuong has published more than 120 academic articles, and book chapters in about 50 refereed journals and books by such publishers as Elsevier, Inderscience, Nature Publishing Group, Springer, Praeger, Wiley, World Scientific, etc.

Trung Tran is an Associate Professor of Mathematics Education and works at Vietnam Academy for Ethnic Minorities. He is a member of the Vietnam chapter of The European Association of Science Editors (EASE), a leader of the Vietnamese Science Editors (VSE) Team, and a chairman of Editor's Board of Journal of Ethnic Minorities Research (ISSN: 0866-773X).

ISBN: 978-3-11-068607-4

DOI: 10.2478/9783110686081

© 2019 Quan-Hoang Vuong, Trung Tran, and Chapters' Contributors

Published by Sciendo, part of Walter de Gruyter GmbH, Berlin/Boston

Cover Illustration: © Thu-Trang Vuong, Ha-My Vuong

Preface

The book has been in our preparation for about two years, emerging from our research project on the research productivity of Vietnamese scholars in the social sciences and humanities (SSH), the first of its kind in Vietnam. The project continues to involve a dozen research workers taking on different responsibilities, from collecting data and structuring our exclusive, in-house developed database — Social Sciences and Humanities Peer Awards (SSHPA), to writing script and programming the tools to manipulate such data, to performing statistical investigations and writing research papers based thereon.

Analyzing the increasingly larger database and datasets extracted therefrom, we will be presenting the main insights in eight chapters, with the following considerations in mind.

Our first consideration is the intense demand for changes we have witnessed with respect to the national social sciences and humanities. Over the past five years, the public, the Vietnamese SSH's community itself, and several government agencies have been involved in a heated discussion on how to reform Vietnam's SSH and integrate it into the world's dialogue. Many high-quality media reports, as well as research papers, have pointed out the lack of international publications among many leading research institutions and universities. Politicians, researchers, and education managers have engaged in a heated discussion over how SSH in Vietnam should be reformed: timeline, subject areas, process, etc. To address the situation, the government finally issued Circular 08 on April 04, 2017, which makes it mandatory for Ph.D. supervisors to have at least two peer-reviewed articles in Scopus-indexed or Web-of-Science-index journals/book chapters, among other things. Clearly lifting the humble position of the social sciences and humanities, especially compared to the natural sciences and technology, remains a challenging task ahead. On the one hand, the Vietnamese SSH community must overcome barriers such as the complexity of organizational structures of Vietnamese institutions, the lack of incentives, and the absence of research culture. On the other hand, it is important to be cautioned against the "inferiority by default" mindset, which seems to have made a majority of scholars in SSH content with their mediocre performance.

Second, the rising importance of, and hence the emphasis on, SSH is inevitable, following the growing complexities and interaction of different, but integral parts, of the emerging economy of Vietnam. More often a long-standing impasse creates persistent pessimism among the public, industry leaders, or even policymakers. This is unfortunate and unnecessary since life has its own upbeat sentiment, even right when one is most pessimistic. Therefore, the book will make the case for our built-in hope and optimism even though Vietnam's SSH performance has thus far been lagging.

Our final consideration is the bigger game out there to participate. Research productivity has become a major weapon in the upcoming competition – or, dare we even say, battle – between economic rivals. The developing world suddenly realized, in 2016, that they might have some chance —no matter how slim it is—of seeing China's research output exceeding that of the United States for the first time in its entire history. Our general conception of knowledge and the scholarly world, our epistemology and our vision toward an actionable program of changes, based on improved productivity, has since been transformed.

The book, thus, seeks to present a vibrant and changing picture of international publishing in Vietnam's SSH in the 2008-2018 period. In Chapter 1, we will touch on some major policy changes that paved the way for increases in both quantity and quality of scientific publishing. Moving forward, Chapter 2 will delve further into the bigger picture, showing a clear growth in the population of SSH researchers as well as an expansion of collaboration networks at home and abroad. In Chapter 3, in breaking down the publication output by year and by field, we zoom in on two fields in SSH—namely Health Care, and Education—that which are among the top 3 in terms of productivity in the ten years period. Chapter 4 dedicates to the Economics field, the most interdisciplinary and productive fields according to the data. The analysis in both chapter 3 and 4 hints at a rise in interdisciplinary research, an approach that could connect more researchers across disciplines and facilitate the move toward open access in academia. Next, in Chapter 5 we will turn to the profiles of productive researchers in Vietnam SSH during the decade, highlighting some eminent figures, the rising achievements of female researchers, and the expansive collaborative networks of high-output groups. It is indeed astounding that 10 Vietnamese authors produced nearly one-fourth of the articles published in Scopus-indexed journals during the period. The force of a strong individual researcher is to be reckoned with.

Following a review of scientific publishing in Vietnamese SSH in 2008-2018, the next section of the book covers policy implications, the finance of scientific publishing, and the emerging business of science. In particular, Chapter 6 discusses the question of quality and the latest developments in academic publishing, including the open access movement and increased financial funding for scientific research and publishing. In Chapter 7, we examine the impact of Circular 08 of the Ministry of Education and Training on the doctoral research and training programs, a policy that serves as the milestone in pushing international scientific publishing in Vietnam forward. Last but not least, Chapter 8 gives room for an in-depth discussion of the prospects for academic entrepreneurship and the business of science in Vietnam.

Browsing through the chapters, you will see numerous charts, tables, figures, and snippets of our interviews with 28 Vietnamese experts, all about research productivity and how we can move forward. We want to let the data speak, and for that sole reason, this book is more of a data book. And, we believe that eleven years' worth of data should be sufficient for us to attain some substantial level of understanding. This book serves as a thumbnail sketch of an immense artwork painted by at least 1,300 scholars through 2,270 published research items during 2008-2018.

Acknowledgment: This research is funded by the Vietnam National Foundation for Science and Technology Development (NAFOSTED) under the National Research Grant No. 502.01-2018.19. We are also grateful to research staff at A.I. Social Data

Lab (Vuong & Associates, Hanoi, Vietnam) for their assistance and participation in the data project, especially Dam Thu Ha and Nghiem Phu Kien Cuong. We would also want to show our appreciation to Nguyen Pham Muoi for his continued support for this project. We would like to thank Phenikaa University, Hanoi, Vietnam for their support. We are deeply grateful for Ho Xuan Nang Science Foundation for their generous philanthropic contribution for science. We are also grateful for Dr. Jakub Gąsior of Sciendo (De Gruyter), who has provided truly generous support during the publication process.

We are truly thankful for the constructive comments and criticisms of our reviewers: Giang Thanh Long (National Economics University, Hanoi, Vietnam), Tran Quang Tuyen (University of Economics and Business, Vietnam National University, Hanoi, Vietnam), Joseph Progler (Ritsumeikan Asia Pacific University, Beppu, Japan), Nancy K. Napier (Boise State University, Boise, Idaho, USA).

As part of our research for this book, we have reached out and interviewed 28 Vietnamese researchers in social sciences and humanities. We would like to take this opportunity to express our deepest gratitude for the generous support of Bui Thanh Huong, Bui Thi Minh Hong, Giang Thanh Long, Ho Huu Loc, Huynh The Du, Khuat Thu Hong, Le Quan, Le Quang Thanh, Le Van Canh, Nguyen Cao Nam, Luu Trong Tuan, Nguyen Trong Chuan, Nguyen Tai Dong, Nguyen Thi Hien, Nguyen Thi Thuy Minh, Nguyen Thu Thuy, Nguyen Viet Cuong, Pham Si Cong, Pham Van Ha, Tran Dinh Phong, Tran Duc Vien, Tran Huu Tuan, Tran Nam Binh, Tran Quang Tuyen, Tran Tuan Phong, Tran Van Kham, Truong Dinh Thang, Tran Thi Ly.

Authors
August 2019, Hanoi, Vietnam

Abbreviations and acronyms

ADB	The Asian Development Bank
GDP	Gross Domestic Product
ICOR	Incremental Capital-Output Ratio
ISI	Institute of Scientific Information
JCR	Journal Citation Reports
JIF	Journal Impact Factor (also, IF – Impact Factor)
LMIC	Low- and Middle-Income Countries
NAFOSTED	National Foundation for Science and Technology Development
OA	Open-Access
OSF	Open Science Framework
SSH	The Social Sciences and Humanities
US$	The United State dollar
VND	Vietnamese Dong (local currency)
WB	The World Bank
WOS	Web of Science

About the authors

Quan-Hoang Vuong (PhD, Université Libre de Bruxelles) is the director of Centre for Interdisciplinary Social Research, Phenikaa University in Hanoi, Vietnam. He is chairman of the Vietnam chapter of the European Association of Science Editors, and serves on the NAFOSTED Scientific Council on Basic Research in the Social Sciences and Humanities, Economics Section (2019-2021). Dr. Vuong has published more than 120 academic articles, and book chapters in more than 50 refereed journals and books by such publishers as Elsevier, Inderscience, Nature Publishing Group, Praeger, Springer, Wiley, World Scientific, etc.

Trung Tran is an Associate Professor of Mathematics Education and works at Vietnam Academy for Ethnic Minorities, Hanoi, Vietnam. He is a member of the Vietnam chapter of The European Association of Science Editors (EASE), a leader of the Vietnamese Science Editors (VSE) Team, and a chairman of Editor's Board of Journal of Ethnic Minorities Research (ISSN: 0866-773X).

Thu-Hien Thi Le works as a full-time Associate Professor of Education at the University of Education - Vietnam National University, Hanoi, Vietnam.

Tien-Trung Nguyen holds a PhD degree in Mathematics Education. He works as a senior editor at Vietnam Journal of Education, Vietnam's Ministry of Education and Training, and a guest lecture for leading universities in Vietnam.

Phuong-Thao Thi Trinh holds a PhD in Mathematics Education, and works as a lecturer at Thai Nguyen University of Education, Thai Nguyen, Vietnam.

Xuan-Hung Doan (PhD) works as a senior lecturer of the People's Police Academy, Ministry of Public Security, Hanoi, Vietnam. He participates in the board panel of a journal in the People's Police Academy.

Thu-Hang Thi Nguyen is working at the Faculty of Basic Sciences at Thai Nguyen University of Agriculture and Forestry, Thai

Nguyen, Vietnam. She is a PhD candidate at Thai Nguyen University of Education, Thai Nguyen, Vietnam.

Phuong-Tram Thuy Nguyen holds a PhD in Mathematics Education, and works as a high school teacher in Lam Dong, Vietnam.

Khanh-Linh Hoang is working at the Institute of Theoretical and Applied Research at Duy Tan University, Vietnam. She is studying at Faculty of Political Theory – Civic Education at Hanoi National University of Education, Hanoi, Vietnam.

Thi-Hanh Vu received her PhD in Economics and Management in 2015 from the Université Libre de Bruxelles, Belgium. She is currently a lecturer of International Business at the School of Economics and International Business of the Foreign Trade University, Hanoi, Vietnam.

Phuong-Hanh Hoang is a researcher at National Center for Sustainable Development of General Education Quality, Vietnam National Institute of Educational Science, Ministry of Education and Training, Hanoi, Vietnam. She holds a BSc in Psychology from University College London and an MA in Linguistics from School of Oriental and African Studies, UK.

Hung-Hiep Pham earned his PhD in International Business Administration from Chinese Culture University, Taiwan ROC. Currently, he is the director of Center for Research and Practice on Education, Phu Xuan University, Hue, Vietnam. His research interests include education management, scientometrics, and consumer behavior.

Viet-Phuong La is a researcher at the Centre for Interdisciplinary Social Research, Phenikaa University, Hanoi, Vietnam and also is a software engineer for A.I. for Social Data Lab, Vuong & Associates, Hanoi, Vietnam.

Manh-Toan Ho holds a BA in social sciences from Ritsumeikan Asia Pacific University, Beppu, Japan, and is an MA candidate at the National Economics University in Hanoi, Vietnam. He is working as a researcher in the Centre for Interdisciplinary Social Research, Phenikaa University, Hanoi, Vietnam; and a science communicator for EASE Vietnam SciComm/SSHPA (https://sc.sshpa.com/), in addition to other media outlets in Vietnam.

Hong-Kong To Nguyen holds a BA in philosophy and political science from Columbia University and is currently pursuing an MA in International Relations at Ritsumeikan Asia Pacific University in Beppu, Japan. She is also a Japanese government (MEXT) scholar and an active member of the Vietnam chapter of The European Association of Science Editors.

Thu-Trang Vuong is a graduate student at *École doctorale* of Sciences Po Paris. She has worked on a varied range of topics, including entrepreneurship in emerging countries, public health, education, political analyses of culture and religion, with the aim of providing insights for policy-making.

Minh-Hoang Nguyen holds an MSc in Sustainability Science from Ritsumeikan Asia Pacific University, Beppu, Japan, where he now continues with his PhD track.

Manh-Tung Ho is affiliated with the Centre for Interdisciplinary Social Research, Phenikaa University, Vietnam and the Institute of Philosophy, Vietnam Academy of Social Sciences. He is an MA candidate in society and culture at Ritsumeikan Asia Pacific University in Beppu, Japan.

List of Figures

Figure 2.1. All article output in Vietnamese SSH from 2008 to 2018 34
Figure 2.2. All Vietnamese authors with published articles in SSH from 2008 to 2018..35
Figure 2.3. The total number of new authors by year, 2008-2018..36
Figure 2.4. Female and male new authors from 2008 to 2018........37
Figure 2.5. The age of 'new' authors by year in 2008-2018. The central line denotes the average age of 'new' authors that year while the other two lines denote the oldest and youngest age of a 'new' author that year. 39
Figure 2.6. A comparison of international publication output at three Economics institutions, namely NEU, UEB-VNUH, and UOEHCM, 2008-2018. 44
Figure 2.7. The collaboration networks in academic publishing from Vietnam to the rest of the world in (a) 2008, and (b) 2018. ...46
Figure 2.8. The ratio of Vietnamese to foreign in terms of authors and articles, 2008-2018...48
Figure 2.9. The number of lead authors by Vietnamese versus foreign authors, 2008-2018. 48
Figure 3.1. The total number of articles across all fields published in 2008-2018 in international journals. 53
Figure 3.2. (a) The total number of authors and (b)The total number of articles across all fields, both categorized by publications' Impact Factor (IF), during the 2008-2018 period. The data labels refer to the highest impact factor recorded for each color-coded category. 54
Figure 3.3. Publication differences across research fields, categorized by male and female authors, 2008-2018. 55
Figure 3.4. A visual comparison of total articles published in Health Care versus all fields in 2008-2018. 58
Figure 3.5. The total number of articles in Health Care, both categorized by publications' Impact Factor (IF), during the 2008-2018 period. The data labels refer to the highest impact factor recorded for each color-coded category..59
Figure 3.6. The trend in co-authorship within the field of Health Care in 2008-2018..66
Figure 3.7. A visual comparison of total articles published in Education versus all fields in 2008-2018...68

Figure 3.8. The total number of articles in Education, both categorized by publications' Impact Factor (IF), during the 2008-2018 period. The data labels refer to the highest impact factor recorded for each color-coded category. 74

Figure 3.9. The trend in co-authorship within the field of Education in 2008-2018. 75

Figure 3.10. A comparison of the number of new authors each year in (a) Economics, (b) Health Care, and (c) Education in 2008-2018. 76

Figure 4.1. A visual comparison of total articles published in Economics versus all fields in 2008-2018. 82

Figure 4.2. (a) The total number of authors in Economics and (b) The total number of articles in Economics, both categorized by publications' Impact Factor (IF), during the 2008-2018 period. The data labels refer to the highest impact factor recorded for each color-coded category. 83

Figure 4.3. The trend in co-authorship within the field of Economics in 2008-2018. 86

Figure 4.4. The interdisciplinary network of all 32 fields in Vietnam's SSH, 2008-2018. 87

Figure 4.5. A comparison between the interdisciplinary networks of (a) Economics and (b) International Relations, 2008-2018. 88

Figure 4.6. Targets publishers in economics fields during 2008-2018. 91

Figure 5.1. The highest count of publications by an individual researcher by year, 2008-2018. 99

Figure 5.2. The number of authors with solo articles in 2008-2018. 102

Figure 5.3. (a) The number of authors with published articles in 2008-2018, categorized by gender. (b) The number of new authors in SSH by year in 2008-2018, categorized by gender. 104

Figure 5.4. The number of articles in relation to the number of authors, 2008-2018. 107

Figure 5.5. The number of articles with co-authorship by count of authors in (a) 2008 and (b) 2018. 109

Figure 5.6. The network of (vm.4) Nguyen Viet Cuong in three years, 2010, 2014, and 2018. 112

Figure 5.7. The number of lead authors in relation to the number of articles published, 2008-2018. 113

Figure 5.8. (a) A co-authorship network of all Vietnamese social scientists and their international collaborators in the period 2008-2011. (b) A co-authorship network of all Vietnamese social scientists and their international collaborators in the period 2008-2015. 117

Figure 5.9. A co-authorship network of all Vietnamese social scientists from 2008-2018. 117

Figure 7.1. The number of new authors aged 20-35 by year and its percentage to the total number of new authors by year, 2008-2018. 144

Figure 7.2. The year-on-year increases (percent) of the total numbers of authors and articles, 2008-2018. 146

Figure 7.3. The number of articles published fully by Vietnamese authors versus the total number of published articles, 2008-2018. The dashed red line marks 2016 as 'the point of no return' 148

Figure 7.4. The ratio of Vietnamese to foreign in terms of total articles and lead articles, 2008-2018. 150

Figure 7.5. The number of articles claimed by higher education institutions in Vietnam, 2008-2018.**Błąd! Nie zdefiniowano zakładki.**

Figure 7.6. The transformation of author group networks over the years, (a) 2008, (b) 2015, and (c) 2018. 154

Figure 7.7. A count of news items in Vietnamese fetched by Google News on the keywords *"công bố quốc tế"* (international publications), 2008-2018. 158

List of Tables

Table 2.1. The list of institutions with the highest number of published articles by year, 2008-2018. 40

Table 2.2. The list of institutions with 20 or more published articles in ISI/Scopus-indexed journals in 2008-2018. All publications from member units have been accounted for 41

Table 2.3. Top ten institutions with higher productivity in 2016-2018 42

Table 3.1. The total number of SSH articles, categorized by fields, published by Vietnamese authors in international journals in 2008-2018 57

Table 3.2. The 20 articles in the field of Health Care published by Vietnamese authors in journals with the highest impact factors (JIF) in 2008-2018 65

Table 3.3. The 20 articles in the field of Education published by Vietnamese authors in journals with the highest impact factors (JIF) in 2008-2018 73

Table 4.1. The leading fields in international publication within Vietnamese SSH in three recent years, 2016-2018 81

Table 4.2. The top ten articles in the field of Economics published by Vietnamese authors in journals with the highest impact factors (JIF) in 2008-2018 85

Table 4.3. Top 15 academic institutions in Vietnam having the largest number of publications in economics in 2018 94

Table 5.1. Researchers with the highest count of publications in a year, 2008-2018 99

Table 5.2. Researchers with the highest count of solo publications in a year, 2008-2018 101

Table 5.3. The publication output of the top ten female and male authors, 2008-2018. 105

Table 5.4. Top 50 authors who have led at least five articles (excluding solo publications), 2008-2018 115

Table 6.1. Top ten SSH publications with the highest JIF in Vietnam from 2008 to 2018 132

Chapter 1
The debates and the long-awaited reform
Trung Tran, Phuong-Thao T. Trinh,
Thu-Trang Vuong, Hiep-Hung Pham

Economic reforms and growth in Vietnam

With a *per capita* GDP of USD2,343 in 2017, Vietnam has since become a lower-middle-income country (LMIC). Official statistics for 2018 indicate that Vietnam's nominal GDP expanded at an on-year rate of 7.08% to hit USD240.5 billion (VND5,555 trillion), putting its *per capita* income at USD2,587 (Vuong, 2019b). The strong and continuous growth of the economy over the past 33 years has brought the country's poverty rate down to just 5.8% out of its population of 96.5 million. This economic reality alone represents a spectacular development, especially considering the fact that merely two decades prior, in 1993, the economy produced as little as USD36 billion (Vuong, 2019a).

The rapid economic development of Vietnam implies profound changes for the public and the government, as well as the nation's academics. On the one hand, just as a well-known Vietnamese proverb goes, *"có thực mới vực được đạo"* (lit., only with food can one achieve enlightenment), improved socioeconomic conditions have enabled more people to move beyond the day-to-day concerns to pursue scientific and intellectual careers. On the other hand, such pursuits, while laudable, have not yielded many remarkable results at the international level. The field of social sciences and humanities (SSH) in Vietnam, in particular, presents multiple issues that require systemic and comprehensive reforms.

Scientific standards: Vietnamese versus international

One of the biggest debates when it comes to academic publishing in Vietnam is the adoption of international scientific standards (Vuong, 2019c). Many social scientists are reluctant to embrace publishing their articles in international journals because of the language barrier, the lack of knowledge about international publishing practices, and most importantly, the absence of proper incentive, whether that be financial or professional promotions.

For these scholars, their main publication outlets are the 356 domestic scientific journals (as of 2016), all of which are listed in the index used by the Vietnamese State Council for Professorship to evaluate the qualifications of candidates for the state honorary titles (Kim Ngoc, 2016).

The list includes less than a handful of journals indexed in reputable international databases, namely ISI Web of Science and Scopus. Notably, these journals are all in the field of natural sciences and managed by foreign publishing houses even as they retain their host organizations. For instance, *Advances in Natural Sciences: Nanoscience and Nanotechnology* is a journal of the Vietnam Academy of Science and Technology (VAST) but published by the United Kingdom-based Institute of Physics (IOP) Publishing. *Vietnam Journal of Mathematics* is established by VAST and Vietnam Mathematical Society but published by the Switzerland-based Springer. Similarly, *Acta Mathematica Vietnamica* is created by VAST and now published by Springer.

> "In my experience, most of the theses and dissertations in Vietnam are not qualified for international publications, especially in terms of methodologies. Professors and associate professors of social sciences in Vietnam, who are the direct supervisors for master's students and PhD candidates, do not have updated knowledge of the most recent scientific trends, which results in low-quality social science research." *Dr. Truong Dinh Thang, Quang Ngai Teacher Training College, Quang Ngai, Vietnam.*

> "Because of the nature of the field, social science in Vietnam is less globalized than hard science. Therefore, many Vietnam Social scientists are still not entirely familiar with the modern format of presentation, citation, review, and methodology." *Dr. Tran Nam Binh, RMIT University Vietnam*

A comparison with other countries in the Association of the Southeast Asian Nations (ASEAN) highlights the degree to which SSH publishing in Vietnam has lagged behind: Malaysia has 77 journals (UKM, 2015) while Thailand has 30 journals (TCI, 2019) indexed in Scopus. Even as the regional countries team up to create their own academic publishing standards, known as the

ASEAN Citation Index (ACI), only 12 journals from Vietnam are included here (ACI, 2019). Of these journals, two are in the realm of social sciences, namely the *Journal of Asian Business and Economic Studies* and the *Journal of Economics and Development*, and are both published by the UK-based Emerald Publishing Services.

The other hundreds of Vietnamese journals on social sciences and humanities are absent in the ACI as well as the Web of Science and Scopus indexes. In a quality assessment of 100 SSH journals in Vietnam, Kim Ngoc (2016) pointed out four major shortcomings. First, with the exception of six journals published in English, the majority is in Vietnamese but is published infrequently, not in accordance with the publishing schedule. Second, many widely-practiced publishing standards are not embraced, such setting an official English translation of the journal title, listing the academic credentials of the Editorial Board, or fixing the content and structure of the article in conformity with international practices. Third, only two journals have its board comprised of both credible domestic and foreign scientists while the majority is made up solely of Vietnamese scientists, signaling a lack of international collaboration in the publishing front. Fourth, a large number of Vietnamese SSH journals do not implement a peer review process – which marks the biggest difference between Vietnamese and international journals.

> "The experience of international publication usually stays within small research teams, and it does not get standardized. I think conducting research based on international qualifications is neglected in our country. The number of funding agencies that require research projects to be qualified for international publication is limited. Other than NAFOSTED, I rarely see other funds setting international publications as one of their criteria for applicants, this is even true for scientific promotion."
> *Dr. Nguyen Viet Cuong, National Economics University, Hanoi, Vietnam*

Given that the Vietnamese academic publishing industry still falls short of acceptable international standards, social scientists inevitably have to turn to international journals in order to make their research reach a larger audience, and hence, bigger impact (Vuong, 2019c). Nevertheless, to the "old guards" of Vietnamese academia, the ones who have attained seniority in age, career age, and institutional status, the constant urge to publish papers in international journals has turned into a sensitive issue. Some defensively argued that social sciences and humanities in Vietnam carry a kind of "local typicality" that makes it difficult, and even unfit, for international publications. Others expressed acceptance of the new norms but suggested gradual reforms, citing many publishing practices as unsuitable in Vietnam.

As the debates rage on, changes are underway. Publications by Vietnamese social scientists on the international stage have grown in quantity and quality. The government has taken a more proactive approach toward lifting research standards. Private education institutions and corporates are eyeing opportunities in academia to expand their influence. This chapter introduces two milestones in science policymaking in Vietnam, one in 2008 and the other in 2017, and discusses the importance of building a transparent and comprehensive database on scientific productivity.

Top-down reform

March 2008 marks the first milestone in the development of science and academia in Vietnam: it was the starting operation date of the National Foundation for Science and Technology (NAFOSTED) – the first national scientific funding agency of Vietnam. The Foundation was established five years earlier, under the Government's Circular no. 122/2003/ND-CP dated October 22, 2003. Six years into its run, NAFOSTED underwent major changes in terms of organization and operations. In particular, according to Circular no. 23/2014/ND-CP issued by the Government on April 3, 2014, the Foundation is responsible for funding and sponsoring scientific projects in line with international standards – a criterion that was not listed in the previous circular. Following up on the initial reform in 2014, NAFOSTED has made various efforts to raise the bar for international publications across disciplines.

The grants provided by NAFOSTED, whose exact number is not publicized, have had a tremendous effect in promoting scientific research in multiple disciplines, spanning natural sciences and technology (NST) as well as social sciences and humanities (SSH). In its initial years of operation, the Foundation prioritized funding for basic research in the field of NST, aiming to promote scientific quality and international integration through science and technology development. On average, the Foundation claims to fund more than 300 science-technology projects a year, through which thousands of scientists benefit (NAFOSTED, 2018). The period from 2015 to 2018 witnessed some significant changes in NAFOSTED funding for projects in both NST and SSH disciplines as well as for supporting strong research groups. As of end-2018, funding from NAFOSTED had been poured in to more than 2,700 research projects that involved over 10,000 scientists and 2,400 doctorate degree holders (NAFOSTED, 2018). The result was the international publication of over 4,000 articles in journals indexed in ISI/Web of Science database.

The majority of scholars in Vietnam consider the *modus operandi* of NAFOSTED to be mindful of global trends, open-minded and generally considerate of the capacity of grantees to achieve their goals in a timely manner with quality results. Given the key role of NAFOSTED in shaping the national scientific research landscape, we have chosen 2008 as the beginning year for the scope of our dataset.

April 2017 marks the second milestone in Vietnam's science policymaking: it was when the Government issued Circular 08/2017/TT-BGDDT to revamp the standards for doctoral training programs. The Circular went into effect from May 20, 2017, replacing the rules issued in 2009 and amended in 2012. The new standards now specify additional conditions for doctorate students and mentors. Accordingly, for a thesis to qualify for defense, the research results must be published in the form of at least two journal articles, one out of which must be indexed by ISI/Scopus; or as two reports in a peer-reviewed international conference; or as two other international peer-reviewed journals.

In the same vein, the most important qualification of a research mentor is to have published at least once in an ISI/Scopus-indexed journal, or in a reference manual with a standard ISBN. The qualification, however, could be substituted by two peer-reviewed journal articles, whose content must be related to the subject of their mentee's thesis in terms of discipline.

Bottom-up responses

Bombarded by constant talks about international integration and international scientific standards, the Vietnamese academic sphere in general and SSH in particular now face two very pressing demands: to increase productivity and to raise quality. For SSH, these challenges imply significant changes to improve the effectiveness of science funding policies, optimizing education strategies, and forming the future generations of scholars.

There has recently been an increasing focus on research quality – which is most often reflected through the quality of publications. The case of AIST, as reported in *Tia Sang Magazine* issue January 29, 2018, illustrates this new inclination: researchers working on the project have insisted on conducting additional research at the price of missing the NAFOSTED deadline, in order to bring forth a manuscript – and subsequently, a publication – of the highest quality possible. This tendency is not limited to natural sciences and technology (NST) but extends to SSH disciplines, both as a natural process and as the result of conscious efforts by research and education experts in promoting SSH research.

> "The biggest challenge for Vietnam's social sciences is, without doubt, the training of researchers. Vietnam has a large number of social scientists with high doctorate degrees but only a few of them can do research per international standards. The majority lack foreign languages and cannot access non-Vietnamese materials nor exchange information with international colleagues. Even the exchange and discussion of ideas within the domestic social scientist community remain limited. Those who do not know how to do research make up the dominant group and wield power, thus, the academic spirit of learning and criticizing in a professional manner is not truly encouraged. For this reason, a genuine academic space does not exist, or if it does, it is rather fragile and fragmented." *Dr. Khuat Thu Hong, Institute for Social Development Studies (ISDS), Hanoi, Vietnam*

The concern of raising both the quantity and quality of research is not confined within developing countries such as Vietnam. The global scientific community is also witnessing the silent yet vigorous competition between three large world centers of scientific research: the United States, Europe, and China. Already being a leading world economic power does not mean the United States would not aim for the same position in academia as well; American research centers keep their eyes on all competitors, in particular China. Their concerns encompass both aspects of scientific research: productivity and quality. This was evidenced by the heated reaction on *Nature* journal in 2018, when the National Science Foundation (NSF), using Scopus database, reported that, for the first time in history, China had surpassed the United States in scientific publication counts (Tollefson, 2018). The NSF report stated in 2016 that China churned out 426,000 publications recorded in Scopus database, while the US had 409,000 studies. This difference of 17,000 studies reflects the sheer efforts of China in stepping up its investment in science and technology: as noted by Tollefson (2018), China's spending on Research and Development (R&D) as a share of the country's economy had increased proportionally in recent years, while US spending had remained level.

These examples highlight the fact that increasing the volume as well as the quality of a country's scientific innovation could propel a country's productivity growth and prosperity. For a developing country such as Vietnam, institutionalizing the international standards in scientific publishing and requiring international publications in indexed journals, books, and conferences for Ph.D. candidates and supervisors are only the start. However, these first steps mark a truly important milestone in the international integration of the nascent SSH academic community in Vietnam.

The urgent need for studying scientific productivity

The international integration of Vietnamese SSH community means the adoption of standard scientific practices such as the peer-review process, the ethical consideration when dealing with human subjects, or the declaration of conflict of interests. With the growing number of international publications (Manh, 2015; Nguyen, Ho, et al., 2017), to some extent, one can be sure this integration process is taking place. However, to what extent this whole enterprise may achieve maturity is, indeed, a more difficult question to answer. Perhaps, this question would only find satisfactory answers in concrete numbers and statistics. This is the reason why in February 2017 we launched the SSHPA project, which enables, for the first time, multidimensional visualizations of the networks of Vietnamese researchers in social sciences and humanities. This is a significant contribution, as the network data allow for more potential in terms of statistical approaches, such as the usage of Bayesian techniques for analysis.

The project fills in the gap of research on scientific productivity in Vietnam, a topic that has in fact attracted attention at the international level from as far back as the 1960s. J.D. Price had pioneered some early works such as "Science since Babylon" (1961) or "Little Science, Big Science" (1963). While the subject has remained a heated topic not only in academia but also to governments, legislatures, and the general public, all around the

"Output/input density can be another measure [of scientific productivity]. This is the measure of scientific production based on the extent of investment (in terms of grant/facilities/ human resources) that the laboratory/researcher owned or received. To determine the appropriate quantity, we should be referring to international standards. When the output does not have any breakthrough and the investment is big, we might say that labor productivity of the project in question is low. Consequently, it translates to low investment efficiency. This assessment is especially important for policymakers and science and technology leaders. It is absurd to ask a Vietnamese scientist to work as productively as a Singaporean scientist, who receives ten times the amount of investment." *Dr. Tran Dinh Phong, University of Science and Technology of Hanoi (USTH), Hanoi, Vietnam* world, it had shown little signs of interest in Vietnam even during the 2000s.

The year 2010 marked the first journal article on the subject of productivity in academia, by Pham Duy Hien (Pham, 2010). Another publication in the same area of research followed suit in 2011 (Nguyen & Pham, 2011). After this, it took four years for a third publication (Manh, 2015) and then another two years for the fourth paper on academic productivity to be published (Nguyen, Ho, & Le, 2017). New papers remained few and far between. However, all results observed so far have concluded on common findings that are worth pointing out:

- Vietnam has a relatively low scientific productivity among ASEAN countries (Nguyen & Pham, 2011; Pham, 2010);

- Productivity has however been rising steadily every year for the past five years (Manh, 2015; Nguyen, Ho, et al., 2017);

- The number of international collaboration is quite high (Nguyen, Ho, et al., 2017).

These characteristics showed that the scientific community of Vietnam was still in the process of developing its research capacity to meet international standards.

The above results have been reached using data from reputable databases such as ISI Web of Science (which was previously owned by Thompson Reuters but has been managed by Clarivate Analytics since 2017) and Scopus (by Elsevier). However, there is a risk that the full picture of the state of Vietnamese research has not been represented accurately, as there are several other drawbacks of using the ISI and Scopus databases for productivity monitoring. First, these databases – ISI/WoS and Scopus – very often have duplicates. Valderrama-Zurián, Aguilar-Moya, Melero-Fuentes, and Aleixandre-Benavent (2015) have found duplicates in about 12% articles just by studying seven journals in Scopus.

Second, journals could be eliminated from ISI and Scopus indexing, which meant articles published in these journals would fall into a blind spot. Moreover, the databases take quite an amount of time, up to several months, to update themselves on new publications. Lastly, when it comes to the attributes of scientific papers, ISI and Scopus mainly record large-scale characteristics such as general discipline and country of origin. As such, specific information that might be of use in the case of Vietnam, such as geographic-administrative region, affiliated institution, or even information on the individual author, are lacking when these databases are used.

In 2017, a series of research papers had been released by the NVSS (Network of Vietnamese Social Scientists) research team, to fill this gap and better monitoring Vietnamese scientific productivity. The papers were based on a publicly released dataset, which later becomes Social Sciences and Humanities Peer Awards or SSHPA (http://sshpa.com/), of 412 Vietnamese authors who have published papers in Scopus-indexed journals from 2008 through 2017. The two main research directions have been international collaborations by Vietnamese authors in social sciences and humanities (SSH), and the relationship between demographic elements and scientific productivity. The studies in the series mainly employed network analysis (Ho, Nguyen, Vuong, & Vuong, 2017; Ho, Nguyen, Vuong, Dam, et al., 2017) and cross-sectional dataset analysis (Vuong, Ho, Vuong, Napier, et al., 2017; Vuong, Napier, et al., 2018; Vuong, Nguyen, Ho, Ho, & Vuong, 2018).

Through network analysis, we were able to observe a disparity in influence among leading authors in the SSH research community. These scholars assembled around them clusters of less influential authors, yet their influence showed low coverage when considering the entire community as a whole (Ho, Nguyen, Vuong, Dam, et al., 2017). While this, for the time being, is a weakness, it would serve as a good starting ground for future collaboration and extension of the network. In addition, another network data-based publication had pointed out that there is a lack of attention on the robustness of sub-networks of academics, despite the fact that sub-networks play an important role in bringing together scholars in research work (Ho, Nguyen, Vuong, & Vuong, 2017).

Other results have shown that over 90% of researchers in SSH in Vietnam have co-authored with both domestic and foreign colleagues (Vuong, Ho, Vuong, Nguyen, et al., 2017); however, the number of publications in which Vietnamese researchers were first authors remained modest, with the average researcher only leading 2 papers during the entire decade.

Demographic factors such as age, gender, and geographic residence also have a significant influence on scientific productivity. A publication on *European Science Editing* provides certain insights into the correlation between an author's productivity and their age, as well as the number of their first-authored papers. Gender, however, does not seem to be associated with productivity, which refutes the conventional stereotype of masculine superiority in scientific productivity, even when the number of female academics was lower (Vuong, Ho, Vuong, Napier, et al., 2017). Another study using the same dataset, published in early 2018, yields similar findings on the lack of correlation between gender and scientific productivity, as well as the significant influence of the geographic residence of the author. This study uses the 'sequence-determines-credit' method to calculate the productivity of the author based on their position in the list of authors, called 'contribution point' (CP). The method is then used as the indicator of productivity instead of the absolute number of publications. The most striking result, perhaps, is the fact that 88% of authors have a CP of under 5 (meaning that they have first-authored for than five times) throughout their entire career. Authors in the 40-50 age range have a higher CP compared to younger authors; however, they still only scored about 3 in average CP. Note that this amount of contribution has been counted over a period of 10 years: this means that even authors in the age group with the highest average CP out of all (40-50 years) have yearly relative productivity of about 0.3 (Vuong, Nguyen, et al., 2018).

Regarding the effects of the work environment and collaboration on research productivity, another study found that international collaboration could help boost general research output; however, when only high-performing researchers are concerned, this effect disappears. The study also showed that authors affiliated with universities have higher research output than authors affiliated with research institutes. This effect is highly contradictory with common beliefs, as in the mind of most people in Vietnam until now, the university only prioritizes teaching (Vuong, Napier, et al., 2018).

These findings show that the field of SSH in Vietnam is still in the nascent stages of its development and shows optimistic prospects of future growth. Unlocking this potential requires thorough policy-planning, and the collaboration of all parties involved: government, institutes, universities, and the researchers themselves.

Against this context, the SSHPA project has always endeavored to achieve the following goals: (1) to find all Vietnamese social scientists who have international publications in indexed journals; and (2) to make sure that our database is tidy, reliable, and accurate. The details of how we have reached these goals have been described and verified in a data descriptor published in *Scientific Data*, a journal under the wing of Nature Publishing Group.

Our database includes not only journal articles but also book chapters, conference papers and other publications that are indexed in Scopus, Web of Science and other journals/conferences approved by NAFOSTED (Vuong, La et al., 2018). This database is continually updated and forms the basis for the statistics provided in this book, with hopes that it will provide much more comprehensive understanding of all facets of the growing Vietnamese SSH academic community: the questions of quantity and quality, the story of interdisciplinary research, the eminent role of senior researchers, the rise of young scientists, the turning-point for Vietnamese SSH in 2017.

References

ACI Secretariat. (2019). List of ACI journals (587 Journals). ASEAN Citation Index. Retrieved July 31, 2019, from http://www.asean-cites.org/index.php?r=contents%2Findex&id=9

Ho, M.-T., Nguyen, H.-K. T., Vuong, T.-T., & Vuong, Q.-H. (2017). On the sustainability of co-authoring behaviors in Vietnamese social sciences: A preliminary analysis of network data. *Sustainability, 9*(11). doi:10.3390/su9112142

Ho, M.-T., Nguyen, V.-H. T., Vuong, T.-T., Dam, Q.-M., Pham, H.-H., & Vuong, Q.-H. (2017). Exploring Vietnamese co-authorship patterns in social sciences with basic network measures of 2008-2017 Scopus data. *F1000 Research, 6*, 1559.

Manh, H. D. (2015). Scientific publications in Vietnam as seen from Scopus during 1996–2013. *Scientometrics, 105*(1), 83-95.

NAFOSTED. (2018, November 23). Quỹ Phát triển khoa học và công nghệ Quốc gia – 10 năm hình thành và phát triển [The National Foundation for Science and Technology Development (NAFOSTED) - 10 years of establishment and development]. Retrieved August 1, 2019, from https://nafosted.gov.vn/quy-phat-trien-khoa-hoc-va-cong-nghe-quoc-gia-10-nam-hinh-thanh-va-phat-trien/

Nguyen, V. T., Ho, L. P. T., & Le, V. U. (2017). International collaboration in scientific research in Vietnam: an analysis of patterns and impact. *Scientometrics, 110*(2), 1035-1051.

Nguyen, V. T., & Pham, T. L. (2011). Scientific output and its relationship to knowledge economy: an analysis of ASEAN countries. *Scientometrics, 89*(1), 107-117.

Pham, D.-H. (2010). A comparative study of research capabilities of East Asian countries and implications for Vietnam. *Higher Education, 60*(6), 615-625.

Price, D. d. S. (1961). *Science Since Babylon*. New Haven: Yale University Press.

Price, D. d. S. (1963). *Little Science, Big Science* New York: Columbia University Press.

Tollefson, J. (2018). China declared world's largest producer of scientific articles. *Nature News*. Retrieved from https://www.nature.com/articles/d41586-018-00927-4

Valderrama-Zurián, J.-C., Aguilar-Moya, R., Melero-Fuentes, D., & Aleixandre-Benavent, R. (2015). A systematic analysis of duplicate records in Scopus. *Journal of Informetrics, 9*(3), 570-576.

Kim Ngoc. (2016). Tiêu chuẩn quốc tế của tạp chí khoa học và việc áp dụng tại Việt Nam [International standards for scientific journals and their adoption in Vietnam]. *Vietnam Social Science Review. 8*(105).

TCI. (2019). List of journals accepted in Scopus. Thai-Journal Citation Index Centre. Retrieved July 31, 2019, from http://www.kmutt.ac.th/jif/TCI_Collaboration/?page_id=1368.

UKM. (2015). List of Malaysian Journal Indexed by ISI Web of Science, Scopus and ERA. Universiti Kebangsaan Malaysia. Retrieved July 31, 2019, from http://www.ukm.my/ptsl/wp-content/uploads/2015/06/Malaysian-journal-indexed-in-ISI-WOS-Scopus-and-ERA_24.3.2015.pdf

Vuong, Q.-H. (2019a). Computational entrepreneurship: from economic complexities to interdisciplinary research. *Problems and Perspectives in Management, 17*(1), 117-129.

Vuong, Q.-H. (2019b). The financial economy of Viet Nam in an age of reform, 1986-2016. In U. Volz, P. Morgan, & N. Yoshino (Eds.), *Routledge Handbook of Banking and Finance in Asia* (pp. 201-222). London, UK: Routledge.

Vuong, Q-H. (2019c). The harsh world of publishing in emerging regions and implications for editors and publishers: The case of Vietnam. *Learned Publishing* 32. doi:10.1002/leap.1255

Vuong, Q.-H., Ho, M.-T., Vuong, T.-T., Napier, N. K., Pham, H.-H., & Nguyen, V.-H. T. (2017). Gender, age, research experience, leading role and academic productivity of Vietnamese researchers in the social sciences and humanities: exploring a 2008-2017 Scopus dataset. *European Science Editing, 43*(3), 51-55.

Vuong, Q.-H., Ho, M.-T., Vuong, T.-T., Nguyen, V.-H. T., Napier, N. K., & Pham, H.-H. (2017). Nemo solus satis sapit: Trends of research collaborations in the Vietnamese social sciences, observing 2008–2017 Scopus Data. *Publications, 5*(4). doi:10.3390/publications5040024

Vuong, Q.-H., La, V.-P., Vuong, T.-T., Ho, M.-T., Nguyen, H.-K. T., Nguyen, V.-H., . . . Ho, M.-T. (2018). An open database of productivity in Vietnam's social sciences and humanities for public use. *Scientific Data, 5,* 180188. doi:10.1038/sdata.2018.188

Vuong, Q.-H., Napier, N. K., Ho, M.-T., Nguyen, V.-H. T., Vuong, T.-T., Pham, H. H., & Nguyen, H.-K. T. (2018). Effects of work environment and collaboration on research productivity in Vietnamese social sciences: evidence from 2008 to 2017 Scopus data. *Studies in Higher Education,* 1-16. doi:10.1080/03075079.2018.1479845

Vuong, T.-T., Nguyen, H.-K. T., Ho, M.-T., Ho, M.-T., & Vuong, Q.-H. (2018). The (in)significance of socio-demographic factors as possible determinants of Vietnamese social scientists' contribution-adjusted productivity: Preliminary results from 2008–2017 Scopus data. *Societies, 8*(1). doi:10.3390/soc8010003

Chapter 2
Scientific publishing: a slow but steady rise
Tien-Trung Nguyen, Viet-Phuong La,
Manh-Toan Ho, Hong Kong T. Nguyen

International scientific publishing is transforming from a mere recommendation to a standard practice of Vietnamese social sciences and humanities (SSH) researchers. This chapter will utilize the latest evidence from our database (as of March 2019) to discuss the connection between scientific productivity and quality of Vietnamese SSH international publications. This chapter will set out the context for the in-depth discussions in the following chapters.

The national scientific production during 2008-2018

In the period from 2008 to 2018, the database, SSHPA, recorded 1,374 Vietnamese authors who have produced 2,363 research articles. If we assume that all these articles are single-authored, then an average Vietnamese author has produced 1.7 articles during this period. These Vietnamese authors collaborated with 1,636 foreign researchers, altogether being affiliated with a total of 1,311 Vietnamese and international organizations. Most of these organizations are research institutes and universities, but the data also show some contributions from business organizations.

Figure 2.1 shows the total number of research articles published by Vietnamese SSH researchers from 2008 to 2018. The number climbs steadily in this period from 88 in 2008 to 391 by the end of 2018. Notably, the fast-growing period started sometime in 2014.

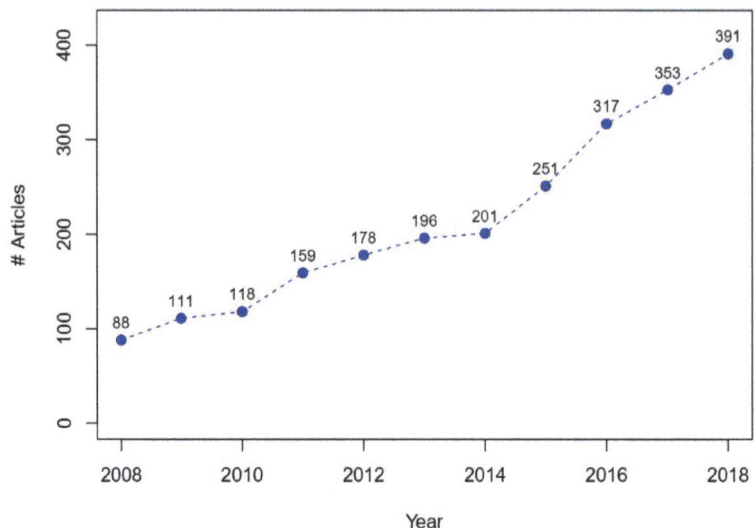

Figure 2.1. All article output in Vietnamese SSH from 2008 to 2018

The growing population of researchers in SSH

The number of Vietnamese authors in each year is shown in Figure 2.2. Similar to the rise in publication output, the number of Vietnamese authors who participated in scientific publishing also surged by 6.78-fold from 136 authors in 2008 to 923 in 2018. The rise in authors helps push the scientific productivity between 2014 and 2018 to a record high.

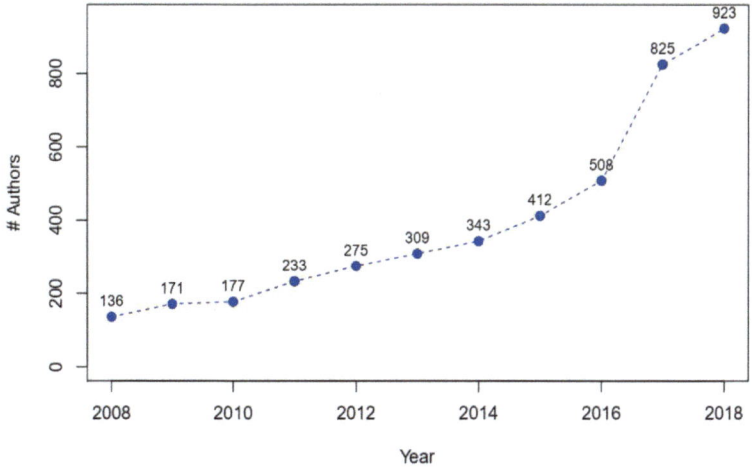

Figure 2.2. All Vietnamese authors with published articles in SSH from 2008 to 2018

One of the explanations for the growing output in Vietnamese SSH is the steady stream of new authors over the years. Our team has made extensive efforts to validate the mathematics and statistics behind our calculation of the number of new authors each year, as shown in Figure 2.3. The assignment of 'new author' is relative; someone is 'new' in our database upon comparison to data of the previous year(s). The implication is clear: An author might have published decades before and stopped for some time before returning to the academic publishing world in the post-2008 period. According to our database, this author would be counted as 'new', though not 'new' in the sense of his or her involvement in academia.

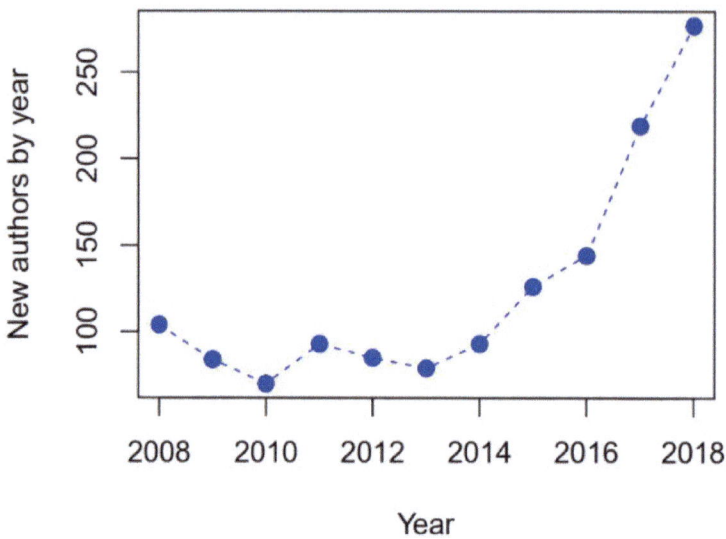

Figure 2.3. The total number of new authors by year, 2008-2018.

In Figure 2.3, the number of new authors by year hovers consistently around or below 100 from 2008 to 2014 before spiking up to over 200 and 250 between 2016 and 2018. When broken down by gender, as in Figure 2.4, the numbers highlight a trend previously touched on: the dominance of male authors in 2008-2017 and the sudden increase in female authors in 2018. Meanwhile, in 2018, not only did the number of published articles peak at 391 in 2018 (Figure 2.1), the number of new authors with international publications also reached its all-time high at 277. The rise of new authors highlights the impact of Circular 08 that was issued in 2017 to improve the standard of doctoral training in Vietnam. The new standards for doctorate students have simultaneously motivated and pressured young researchers to publish internationally. We will cover this aspect in more details in Chapter 6. Here, we note that the dynamic starts in 2016 and continues to grow strongly.

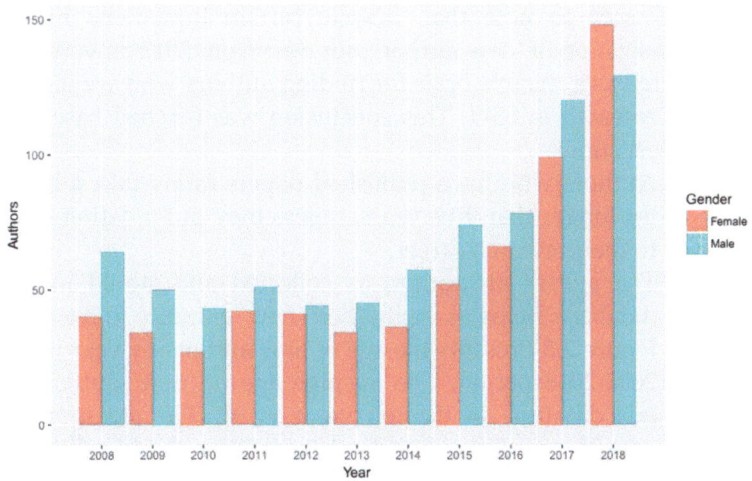

Figure 2.4. Female and male new authors from 2008 to 2018

The data on scientific output also show that during 2015-2018, the rate of female authors newly joining the scholarly publishing world stood as high as 35% year-over-year on average each year. This figure is substantially higher than that of their male counterparts, which averages at about 20% year-over-year, per year. Vietnamese women with published articles today account for 42% of the total number of authors in SSH, compared to 30% ten years ago, refuting the impression that research is a typically male job in the country.

Similar to China, Japan, and South Korea, Vietnam is mostly characterized as a typical Confucian society where unequal relationships—which favor men in both society and family—have been preserved over thousands of years by socio-cultural ties, power hierarchies, life functions, and jobs (Frederickson, 2002; Gao, 2003). Nonetheless, societal transformations brought about by recent reforms have helped women in Vietnam break the barriers to SSH jobs and excel. In the special case of education research, the top two Vietnamese female authors contribute more than 36% of all research output over the past ten years (65/178 publications). We will further discuss the gender gap in publishing in Chapter 4 of this book.

It is necessary to note that, despite certain limitations in the conceptualization of 'new author', our data from 2012 onward can be regarded as a reliable basis for finding authors who are indeed 'new' to research in SSH. This conclusion was reached based on three observations:

    i. Authors who have published papers rarely take a break for longer than five years, unless they put a definite end to their research career.

    ii. The age of an author, as collected and stored in our database, helps us verify their 'new' entrance to the field. Figure 2.5 presents the age of new authors by year in the 2008-2018 period. The average age of 'new' authors in our database in the ten years is 38. The oldest 'new' author recorded in our database is 79 years old, while the youngest 'new' author is 18 years old.

    iii. When the volume of data increases, the longer the database is maintained, especially after 2017, any disparities between our estimation and the actual numbers will be increasingly small; this means the level of data accuracy and reliability will rise.

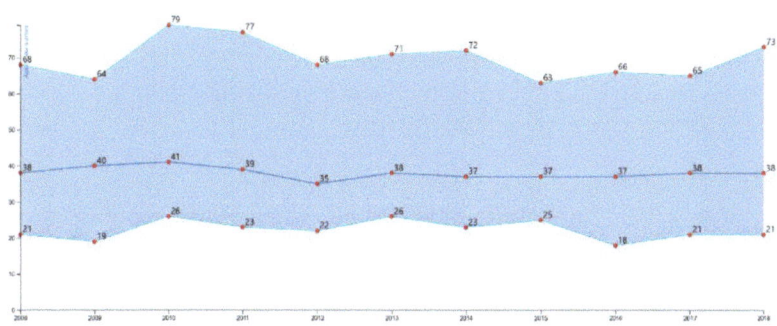

Figure 2.5. The age of 'new' authors by year in 2008-2018. The central line denotes the average age of 'new' authors that year while the other two lines denote the oldest and youngest age of a 'new' author that year.

The institutional landscape

Up to 29% of the published articles in 2008-2018 were produced by seven institutions in Vietnam. This number alone speaks volumes about the unequal distribution of productivity in SSH in Vietnam, in the past decade. To understand how an author is able to work efficiently and publish papers regularly, it is imperative to grasp the working environment of the author (Nguyen & Meek, 2016; Vuong, Napier, et al., 2018).

The biggest names by year

Table 2.1 shows that in the ten years in question, the most significant contributors to the total output by year came down to two big names, of which Vietnam National University Hanoi holds the title for the highest number of published papers in a year for eight consecutive years from 2012 to 2018.

Institutions	Year	Articles
Vietnam Academy of Social Sciences	2008	17
National Economics University Hanoi	2009	17
Vietnam National University Ho Chi Minh City	2010	11
Vietnam National University Hanoi & Ho Chi Minh City	2011	18; 18
Vietnam National University Hanoi	2012	19
Vietnam National University Hanoi	2013	28

Vietnam National University Hanoi	2014	25
Vietnam National University Hanoi	2015	32
Vietnam National University Hanoi	2016	41
Vietnam National University Hanoi	2017	40
Vietnam National University Hanoi	2018	45

Table 2.1. The list of institutions with the highest number of published articles by year, 2008-2018.

One of the explanations for VNU's persisting leading position is the significant contributions of its unit members. For instance, two schools under VNU Hanoi, namely University of Social Sciences and Humanities Hanoi and University of Economics have many authors with papers published in ISI/Scopus-indexed journals.

At the same time, from a comparative data point of view, the annual output of these institutions is, in fact, low when compared with the output of a strong individual researcher. For instance, Luu Trong Tuan (coded vm.16) published as a single author 12 articles in 2009, 14 articles in 2011, and 16 articles in 2012 (as we will explore in details in Chapter 4, see Table 4.1. and Figure 4.1.). His output alone is nearly as high as that of a large national university that employs thousands of lecturers and trains hundreds of doctoral candidates.

Institutions with more than 20 publications in 2008-2018
Table 2.2 presents a list of 19 Vietnamese institutions that have published 20 or more articles during the ten years. The data includes all publications from member units under the count of the parent unit; for example, the number of articles recorded for Vietnam National University Hanoi already includes output from its school units such as the University of Social Sciences and Humanities and the School of Medicine and Pharmacy. This is also the case for the Vietnam Academy of Social Sciences and institutions of similar scale. Notably, the list includes some private research and educational institutions such as Duy Tan University, FPT University, and Phenikaa University.

	Institution	Article
1	Vietnam National University Hanoi	268
2	National Economics University Hanoi	160
3	Hanoi Medical University	141
4	University of Economics Ho Chi Minh City	106
5	Vietnam National University Ho Chi Minh City	105
6	Vietnam Academy of Social Sciences	101
7	Ministry of Health	69
8	Duy Tan University	63
9	Hanoi University of Public Health	46
10	Research and Training Centre for Community Development	46
11	Can Tho University	41
12	RMIT University Vietnam	40
13	Hue University	39
14	Nha Trang University	32
15	Foreign Trade University	29
16	Thuongmai University	29
17	French-Vietnamese Center for Management Education Ho Chi Minh	26
18	Phenikaa University	25
19	Ho Chi Minh City Open University	20

Table 2.2. The list of institutions with 20 or more published articles in ISI/Scopus-indexed journals in 2008-2018. All publications from member units have been accounted for.

According to the accumulative count of Table 2.2, the five institutions with outstanding output in the 2008-2018 period were Vietnam National University Hanoi, National Economics University Hanoi, Hanoi Medical University, University of Economics Ho Chi Minh City, and Vietnam National University Ho Chi Minh City.

High-productivity institutions in recent years
While Table 2.2 provides useful information on the output over a long period of time, it does not show the changes in institutional

output each year. Table 2.3 corrects this shortcoming by listing the top ten institutions in the 2016-2018 period.

	2018			2017			2016	
	Inst.	Art.		Inst.	Art.		Inst.	Art.
1	VNU Hanoi	45	1	VNU Hanoi	40	1	VNU Hanoi	41
2	Hanoi Med U	40	2	Hanoi Med U	29	2	UOE HCM	21
3	Duy Tan U	35	3	NEU Hanoi	26	3	NEU Hanoi	13
4	NEU Hanoi	34	4	Duy Tan U	20	4	VNU HCM	13
5	UOE HCMC	25	5	VASS	18	5	VASS	12
6	VASS	23	6	Hanoi U of Public Health	17	6	Hanoi Med U	10
7	Phenikaa U	17	7	UOE HCM	17	7	FTU Hanoi	9
8	VYPA	16	8	MOH	16	8	Duy Tan U	8
9	FVCME HCM	14	9	Viet Duc H	14	9	FPT Uni	8
10	VNU HCMC	12	10	National Otolar H	12	10	MOH	8

Table 2.3. Top ten institutions with higher productivity in 2016-2018.

It is easy to see the stability in leading publication output of VNU Hanoi, followed by a number of other higher education institutions in HCM City. One can also notice the rise of newly established private universities such as FPT University or Phenikaa University. The first private university in Vietnam – Duy Tan University (Tran & Thanh-Tam, 2014) – has a truly impressive record: It ranked No.8 in 2016, No.4 in 2017 and No.3 in 2018.

Another noticeable feature of Table 2.3 is the fact that the positions of the institutions have changed dramatically over the year, with exception to the No.1 position of VNU. This indicates the nascent state of Vietnam's SSH: As the conjuncture has yet to stabilize, there are indeed opportunities for young institutions and universities to catch up and even create major changes in the field.

Comparing the scientific output of three institutions in Economics
Among the fields of SSH that are most productive in international publications, our database shows that Economics is leading (see Chapter 3). In this chapter, we would like to suggest looking at the publication output of three institutions in the field of Economics to see the differences in scientific publications at the institutional level. Figure 2.6 shows the international publications from 2008 to 2018 of three well-known higher education institutions in Economics in Vietnam, namely National Economics University Hanoi (NEU), University of Economics Ho Chi Minh City (UOEHCM), and University of Economics and Business - Vietnam National University Hanoi (UEB-VNUH).

The figure highlights the leading position of NEU over the other two institutions in terms of published articles. In fact, except for 2011, 2015 and 2016, NEU has always recorded more publications than the remaining two schools. The breakthrough in output for NEU happened in 2017-2018, likely because of the recruitment of new researchers and authors at the university, adding to the already prolific pool of researchers such as Nguyen Viet Cuong and Giang Thanh Long.

The case study here emphasizes, first of all, the importance of having both excellent individual researchers leading as well as a unified group of researchers. More importantly, given the not so wide gap in publications among these institutions, it is possible that this landscape will continue to change in the

> "My prioritized criterion is the attitude of a potential research partner: whether they truly want to work on the research project or not. Once we find the common ground, the problems of finding a shared topic, distributing resources can be solved easily. Hence, in the current context, it is necessary to build a network of researchers who shared a vision."
> *Dr. Giang Thanh Long, National Economics University, Hanoi, Vietnam*

foreseeable future. One prolific author would be enough to move the school's output up.

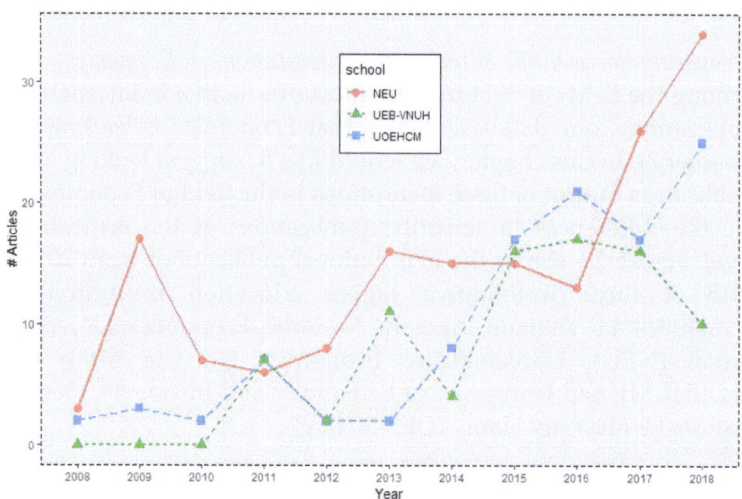

Figure 2.6. A comparison of international publication output at three Economics institutions, namely NEU, UEB-VNUH, and UOEHCM, 2008-2018.

The international collaboration networks
Another major characteristic of international publications in Vietnam's SSH during the past ten years is the prevalence of collaboration with foreign researchers. The branching out of collaboration networks at both the domestic and international levels reflects the global integration and economic transformation of Vietnam, which officially joined the World Trade Organization in January 2007 (Vuong, 2019b).

Numerous research articles have pointed out that international scientific collaboration may help boost citations, including higher self-citation rates (Goldfinch, Dale, & DeRouen, 2003; Katz & Hicks, 1997; Koricheva & Leimu, 2005; Narin, Stevens, & Whitlow, 1991; Van Raan, 1998). Within the context of Vietnam, one study has noted that 77% of Vietnam's scientific output between 2001 and 2015, as indexed in the Thomson Reuters' Web of Science database, involved international collaborations (Nguyen, Ho-Le, & Le, 2017). Similar to findings elsewhere, internationally coauthored papers in Vietnam also received twice the average citation as domestic papers; articles with an overseas corresponding author also had a higher citation rate than those with the domestic corresponding author (Nguyen, Ho-Le, et al., 2017). Such findings suggest that international collaboration has indeed contributed to improving the quality and quantity of Vietnam science.

> "I think international collaboration in Vietnam is still a mere façade and does not result in a ready product such as international publications. The main reason is the level of expertise. To have a fruitful collaboration, both sides should have a similar level of expertise, or at least each side possesses certain skills or resources that can complement each other. Currently, Vietnam's advantage is that we can offer many new interesting topics, but the Vietnamese authors lack writing and editing skills, and credibility in scientific publishing to convince the reviewers and editors of high-ranking journals. Therefore, most of the international collaborations that resulted in scientific publications are usually from personal efforts and connection." *Dr. Bui Thanh Huong, Ritsumeikan Asia Pacific University, Oita, Japan*

The expansion of international collaboration networks is best visualized in Figure 2.7. As the images show, not only are there more connections made in 2018 than in 2008, the connections are also thicker, reflecting a higher density in the international collaboration networks.

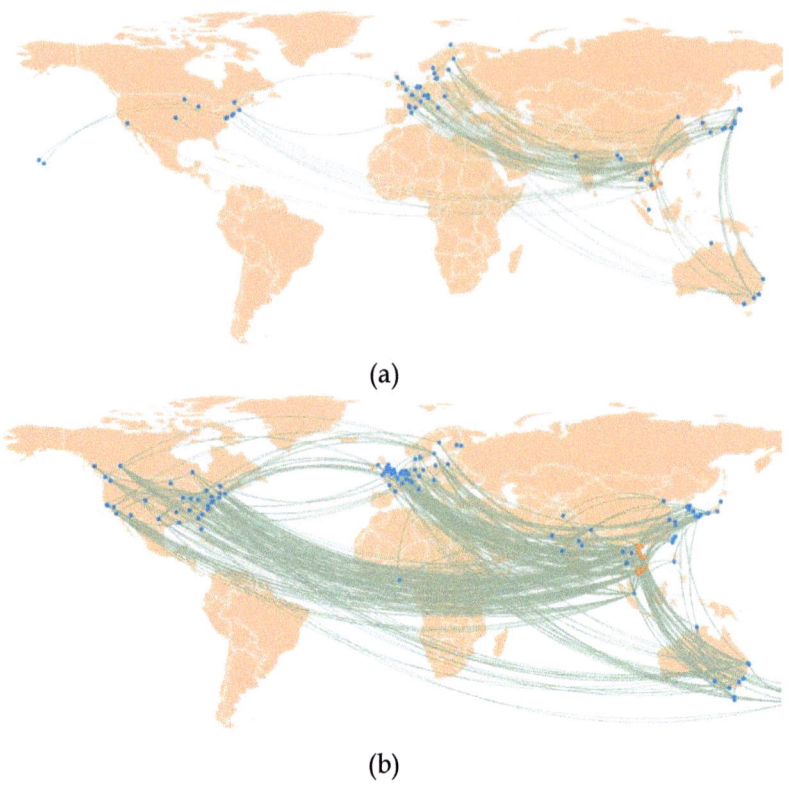

Figure 2.7. The collaboration networks in academic publishing from Vietnam to the rest of the world in (a) 2008, and (b) 2018.

> "I believe that international collaboration, especially in research and training, is an inevitable and irreversible trend today. We all know that to have an international publication, especially in high-ranking journals, is not easy at all. Given that many universities and research institutes in Vietnam still lack basic infrastructure such as laboratories, research equipment, e-library, etc., international collaboration will help us overcome such shortcomings. Additionally, international researchers could help us see more clearly where we stand in the global research landscape, thereby allowing us to catch up faster with the world." *Dr. Le Quang Thanh, Flinders University, Australia*

Yet, these images do not spell out the explicit proportion of foreign involvement in these publications. Given that our database offers a focused look into the scientific productivity of Vietnam's SSH in 2008-2018, we were able to extract more specified data on international collaborations during the period. In Figure 2.8 from 2008 to 2010, the rate of Vietnamese to foreign authors slightly dropped but picked up again in 2011-2013, staying at above 65%. In 2014-2015, this rate fell again to below 65%. The period from 2016 to 2018 witnessed a breakthrough as the proportion of Vietnamese authors in the total published papers rose to above 70%, peaking at nearly 74% in 2017. Overall, the trend is optimistic: the number of Vietnamese authors has consistently accounted for more than half of the total number of authors in one published collaboration.

Meanwhile, in terms of article, the ratio of full-on Vietnamese authored articles to those involving foreign authors consistently hovered below or near 40% from 2008 to 2015. The proportion of Vietnamese-authored articles only rose from 2016, staying above or near 45% as of end-2018. This finding is in line with previous observations on a higher number of new Vietnamese authors after 2016 and the increased involvement of Vietnamese researchers in a published paper.

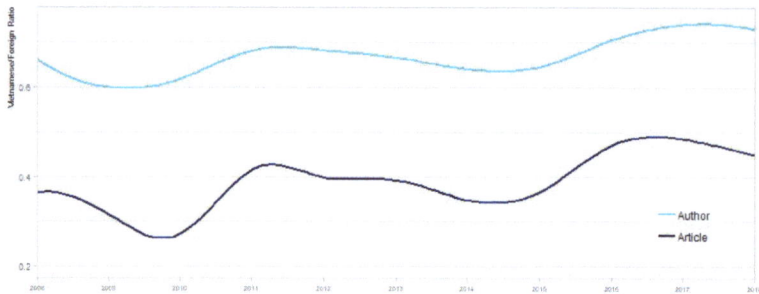

Figure 2.8. The ratio of Vietnamese to foreign in terms of authors and articles, 2008-2018.

In terms of the number of lead authors over the ten years, Figure 2.9 shows once again that the number of Vietnamese authors taking the helm in a published work has climbed 5.64-fold from 59 in 2008 to 333 in 2018. These numbers speak volumes about the growing ability and determination of Vietnamese social scientists in getting their research published in international journals. While international collaboration is an inevitable part, the domestic researchers themselves are also gaining ground and moving forward.

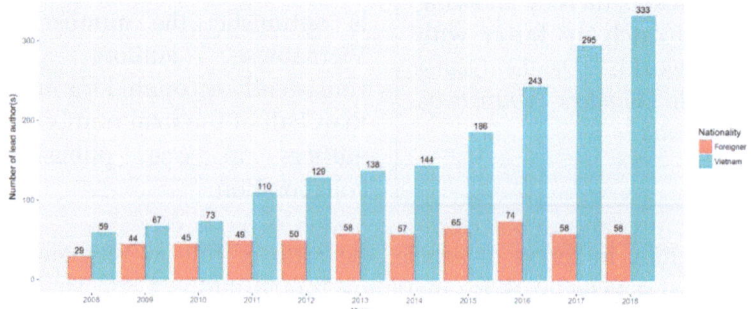

Figure 2.9. The number of lead authors by Vietnamese versus foreign authors, 2008-2018.

This chapter has revealed a steady rise in research output of the Vietnamese SSH community. Most notably, the rise was driven by increasing involvement of Vietnamese researchers, as shown in the continuous increase of the number of publications done by only Vietnamese researchers and the number of lead authors

(Figure 2.8 and 2.9). With the pressure from the public, the focus of the government (VnExpress, 2018) and the learning-by-doing effects, it is expected that this trend will continue long into the future. Scientific publishing in social sciences and humanities in Vietnam will become increasingly integrated into the international community.

References

Frederickson, H. G. (2002). Confucius and the moral basis of bureaucracy. *Administration & Society, 33*(6), 610-628.

Gao, X. (2003). Women existing for men: Confucianism and social injustice against women in China. *Race, Gender & Class, 10*(3), 114-125.

Goldfinch, S., Dale, T., & DeRouen, K. (2003). Science from the periphery: Collaboration, networks and 'periphery effects' in the citation of New Zealand Crown Research Institutes articles, 1995-2000. *Scientometrics, 57*(3), 321-337. doi:10.1023/A:1025048516769

Ho, M.-T., Nguyen, H.-K. T., Vuong, T.-T., & Vuong, Q.-H. (2017). On the sustainability of co-authoring behaviors in Vietnamese social sciences: A preliminary analysis of network data. *Sustainability, 9*(11). doi:10.3390/su9112142

Ho, M.-T., Nguyen, V.-H. T., Vuong, T.-T., Dam, Q.-M., Pham, H.-H., & Vuong, Q.-H. (2017). Exploring Vietnamese co-authorship patterns in social sciences with basic network measures of 2008-2017 Scopus data. *F1000 Research, 6*, 1559.

Katz, J. S., & Hicks, D. (1997). How much is a collaboration worth? A calibrated bibliometric model. *Scientometrics, 40*(3), 541-554. doi:10.1007/BF02459299

Koricheva, J., & Leimu, R. (2005). Does scientific collaboration increase the impact of ecological articles? *BioScience, 55*(5), 438-443. doi:10.1641/0006-3568(2005)055[0438:DSCITI]2.0.CO;2

Manh, H. D. (2015). Scientific publications in Vietnam as seen from Scopus during 1996–2013. *Scientometrics, 105*(1), 83-95.

Narin, F., Stevens, K., & Whitlow, E. S. (1991). Scientific co-operation in Europe and the citation of multinationally authored papers. *Scientometrics, 21*(3), 313-323. doi:10.1007/BF02093973

Nguyen, H. T. L., & Meek, V. L. (2016). Key problems in organizing and structuring university research in Vietnam: The lack of an effective research "behaviour formalization" system. *Minerva, 54*(1), 45-73.

Nguyen, T. V., Ho-Le, T. P., & Le, U. V. (2017). International collaboration in scientific research in Vietnam: an analysis of patterns and impact. *Scientometrics, 110*(2), 1035-1051. doi:10.1007/s11192-016-2201-1

Nguyen, V. T., Ho, L. P. T., & Le, V. U. (2017). International collaboration in scientific research in Vietnam: an analysis of patterns and impact. *Scientometrics, 110*(2), 1035-1051.

Nguyen, V. T., & Pham, T. L. (2011). Scientific output and its relationship to knowledge economy: an analysis of ASEAN countries. *Scientometrics, 89*(1), 107-117.

Pham, D.-H. (2010). A comparative study of research capabilities of East Asian countries and implications for Vietnam. *Higher Education, 60*(6), 615-625.

Price, D. d. S. (1961). *Science Since Babylon*. New Haven: Yale University Press.

Price, D. d. S. (1963). *Little Science, Big Science* New York: Columbia University Press.

Tollefson, J. (2018). China declared world's largest producer of scientific articles. *Nature News*. Retrieved from https://www.nature.com/articles/d41586-018-00927-4

Tran, D. L., & Thanh-Tam. (2014). Kể về ngôi trường Đại học dân lập đầu tiên [Talk about the first people-founded university]. *Nhan Dan*. Retrieved from http://www.nhandan.com.vn/giaoduc/item/24780102-ke-ve-ngoi-truong-dai-hoc-dan-lap-dau-tien.html

Valderrama-Zurián, J.-C., Aguilar-Moya, R., Melero-Fuentes, D., & Aleixandre-Benavent, R. (2015). A systematic analysis of duplicate records in Scopus. *Journal of Informetrics, 9*(3), 570-576.

Van Raan, A. F. J. (1998). The influence of international collaboration on the impact of research results. *Scientometrics, 42*(3), 423-428. doi:10.1007/BF02458380

VnExpress. (2018). Quỹ Nafosted áp chuẩn bắt buộc, công bố quốc tế Việt Nam tăng mạnh [NAFOSTED increases the pressure, Vietnamese international publications increase rapidly]. *VnExpress.* Retrieved from https://vnexpress.net/khoa-hoc/quy-nafosted-ap-chuan-bat-buoc-cong-bo-quoc-te-viet-nam-tang-manh-3849565.html

Vuong, Q.-H. (2019a). Computational entrepreneurship: from economic complexities to interdisciplinary research. *Problems and Perspectives in Management, 17*(1), 117-129.

Vuong, Q.-H. (2019b). The financial economy of Viet Nam in an age of reform, 1986-2016. In U. Volz, P. Morgan, & N. Yoshino (Eds.), *Routledge Handbook of Banking and Finance in Asia* (pp. 201-222). London, UK: Routledge.

Vuong, Q.-H., Ho, M.-T., Vuong, T.-T., Napier, N. K., Pham, H.-H., & Nguyen, V.-H. T. (2017). Gender, age, research experience, leading role and academic productivity of Vietnamese researchers in the social sciences and humanities: exploring a 2008-2017 Scopus dataset. *European Science Editing, 43*(3), 51-55.

Vuong, Q.-H., Ho, M.-T., Vuong, T.-T., Nguyen, V.-H. T., Napier, N. K., & Pham, H.-H. (2017). Nemo solus satis sapit: Trends of research collaborations in the Vietnamese social sciences, observing 2008–2017 Scopus data. *Publications, 5*(4). doi:10.3390/publications5040024

Vuong, Q.-H., La, V.-P., Vuong, T.-T., Ho, M.-T., Nguyen, H.-K. T., Nguyen, V.-H., . . . Ho, M.-T. (2018). An open database of productivity in Vietnam's social sciences and humanities for public use. *Scientific Data, 5*, 180188. doi:10.1038/sdata.2018.188

Vuong, Q.-H., Napier, N. K., Ho, M.-T., Nguyen, V.-H. T., Vuong, T.-T., Pham, H. H., & Nguyen, H.-K. T. (2018). Effects of work environment and collaboration on research productivity in Vietnamese social sciences: evidence from 2008 to 2017 scopus data. *Studies in Higher Education*, 1-16. doi:10.1080/03075079.2018.1479845

Vuong, T.-T., Nguyen, H.-K. T., Ho, M.-T., Ho, M.-T., & Vuong, Q.-H. (2018). The (in)significance of socio-demographic factors as possible determinants of Vietnamese social scientists' contribution-adjusted productivity: Preliminary results from 2008–2017 Scopus data. *Societies, 8*(1). doi:10.3390/soc8010003

Chapter 3
The faster-growing fields
Thu-Hien T. Le, Hiep-Hung Pham,
Viet-Phuong La, Quan-Hoang Vuong

This chapter focuses on the growth of 32 fields of research studies and explores some of the lessons from the growth of research studies in healthcare and education, which are among the top 3 productive fields in social sciences and humanities in Vietnam.

'Ploughing' every field

Our database shows that 32 fields have recorded international publications from 2008 to 2018. This number alone, however, does not highlight the trend nor the disparity in publication outputs among the fields—some of which are clear winners, some lagging far behind, and a few rapidly catching up. Before delving into the details of the publication landscape by fields in Vietnam, this chapter will summarize some outstanding statistics and trends.

First, while research productivity of Vietnamese authors in SSH still has room for improvement both in quality and quantity, it is clear that research quantity has been increasing steadily in the past decade. Figure 3.1 is a lucid illustration of the rising number of articles, across all research fields, published by Vietnamese researchers in SSH in the documented period. In 2008, all SSH fields saw fewer than 100 articles published in international journals, a modest number reflected by the lack of awareness about international research publication as well as official policies promoting such work. Over the following years, research output has gradually picked up, with the number of articles more than doubling by 2014. The rate of publication output also almost doubles from 2014 to 2018, attesting to the ever-growing determination of Vietnamese SSH researchers in getting their works known internationally.

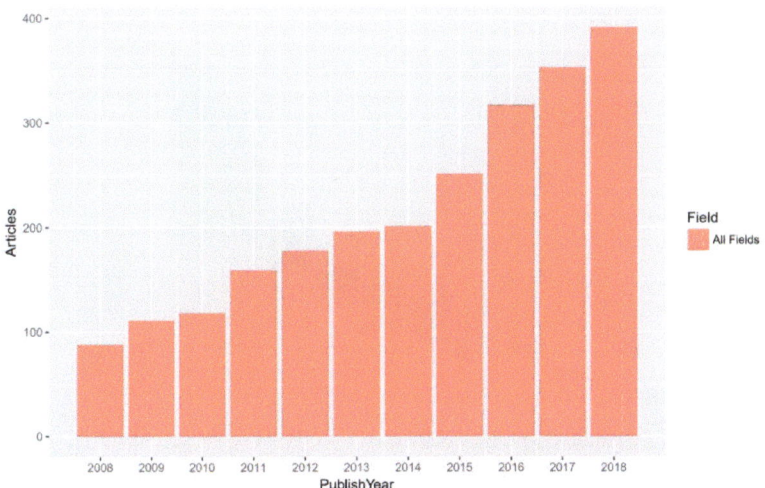

Figure 3.1. The total number of articles across all fields published in 2008-2018 in international journals.

Second, in terms of quality, just as the hike in the number of articles, both the numbers of authors and articles in journals having impact factor (IF) have also surged dramatically over the ten years. In Figure 3.2, our database presents a unique visualization of the publication quality, as measured by a journal's IF (See Chapter 5, section 3, for more details on JIF). Not only has the absolute number of authors publishing in journals with IF skyrocketed by more than 15-fold to approximately 1,750, the share of publications with IF ranging between two and three has also increased vividly in the 2013-2018 period (Figure 3.2a). The same trend is observed when looking at the absolute number of articles published in journals with IF in the ten years: the proportion of articles in journals with IF higher than two and three is on the rise (Figure 3.2).

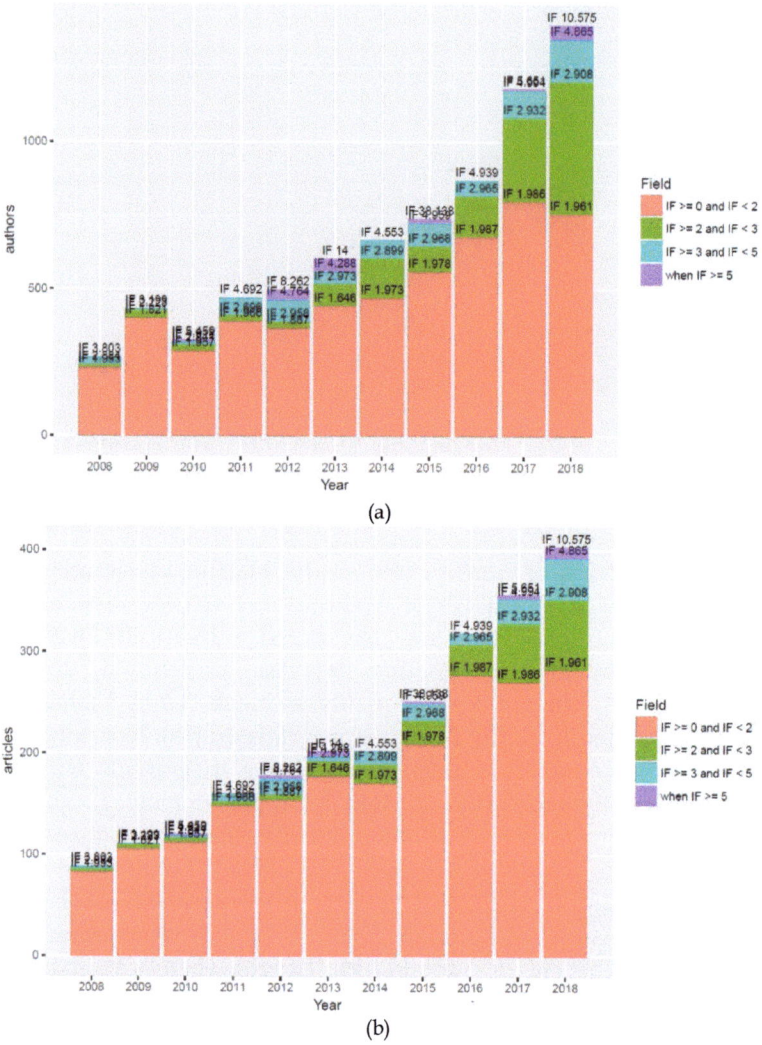

Figure 3.2. (a) The total number of authors and (b)The total number of articles across all fields, both categorized by publications' Impact Factor (IF), during the 2008-2018 period. The data labels refer to the highest impact factor recorded for each color-coded category.

Third, in terms of gender differences by fields, Figure 3.3 presents a remarkable visualization of the varying research fields between male and female Vietnamese authors. The majority of male authors are involved in articles in the fields of Economics, Health Care, Business, and Environment/Sustainability Science, whereas the majority of female authors have written and published papers in the fields of Health Care, Education, Sociology, and Economics. Here, the two fields of Economics and Health Care share two properties: large numbers of publications and authors.

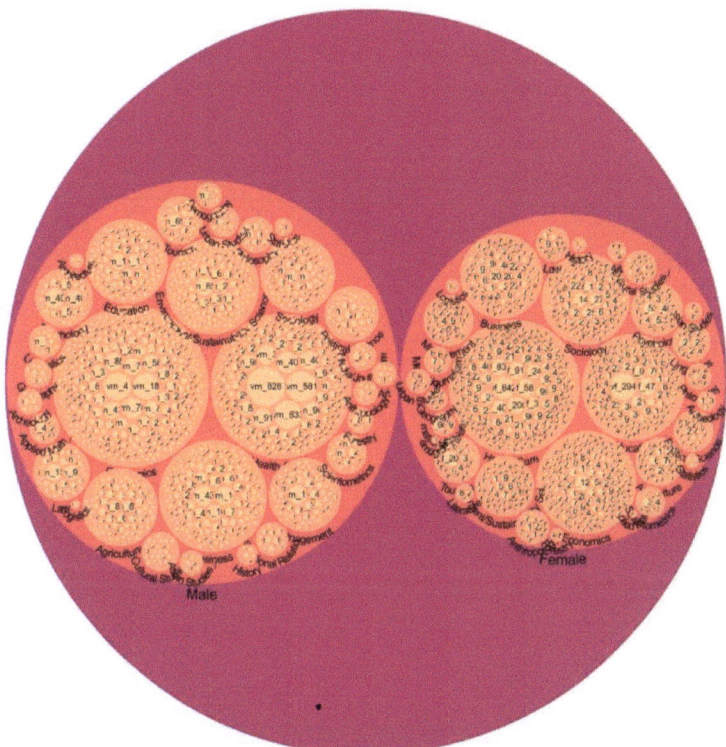

Figure 3.3. Publication differences across research fields, categorized by male and female authors, 2008-2018.

All fields are born unequal

With regard to the exact number of publications across all 32 fields, Table 3.1 captures both the diversity and disparity in some succinct numbers: the field of Economics alone leads the total output with 620 articles, accounting for 22.70% of the total number of articles published by Vietnamese SSH authors. For the sake of comparison, the number of articles for each field averages at 85.

Field	Article	Percentage
Economics	620	22.70%
Education	338	12.38%
Health Care	313	11.46%
Business	308	11.28%
Sociology	179	6.55%
Environment/Sustainability Science	149	5.46%
Management	121	4.43%
Agriculture	115	4.21%
Law	88	3.22%
Political Science	74	2.71%
Tourism	72	2.64%
Psychology	52	1.90%
Linguistics	38	1.39%
International Relations	36	1.32%
Philosophy	29	1.06%
Media/Journalism	26	0.95%
Cultural Studies	26	0.95%
Anthropology	20	0.73%
Scientometrics	18	0.66%
Urban Studies	16	0.59%
Applied Math	14	0.51%
Geography	13	0.48%
Forestry	12	0.44%
Demography	9	0.33%
Art	8	0.29%
History	8	0.29%

Archeology	7	0.26%
Asian Studies	6	0.22%
Literature	6	0.22%
Logistics	4	0.15%
Statistics	4	0.15%
Architecture	2	0.07%

Table 3.1. The total number of SSH articles, categorized by fields, published by Vietnamese authors in international journals in 2008-2018.

These talking numbers go so far as revealing an unequal distribution of publication output among SSH fields in Vietnam. How wide the publication gaps are, we will take a closer look below.

Health care and social medicine: collaborating and open access publishing

An upcoming field in terms of publication output within the Vietnamese SSH is Health Care, which saw the number of articles published in international journals jumped 6.8-fold from 9 in 2008 to 61 in 2018. Table 3.1 also confirms that the Health Care field is only second or third, behind Economics and Education, in terms of publication output in 2017-2018. The first surge in publication happened in 2009 with 20 articles, the second one was in 2012 with 25 articles, and the last and most recent spike was in 2017 with 59 articles, as can be seen in Figure 3.4.

The high number of articles published in 2009 was attributed to the publication of papers that have been done as part of bigger research projects. For instance, out of the 20 articles recorded in this field in 2009, Hoang Van Minh from the Filabavi Health and Demographic Surveillance System, Vietnam was the lead author in 11 collaborated articles. What was more remarkable was the fact that all these articles were published in the same journal, *Global Health Action* of Taylor & Francis, most likely because they presented findings sourced from one multi-site cross-sectional study that was conducted in 2005 in nine Health and

Demographic Surveillance System (HDSS) sites in five Asian countries, all part of the INDEPTH Network.

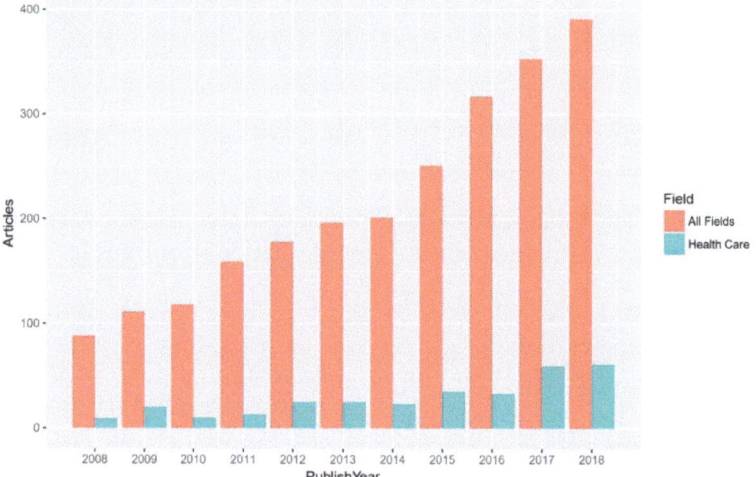

Figure 3.4. A visual comparison of total articles published in Health Care versus all fields in 2008-2018.

Given that the sudden increase in publication output was the product of one research team, it is understandable that this result does not hold for the next years. As noted previously, output in Health Care did not pick up again until 2012, which exhibited some signs of more sustainable productivity for the field. Particularly, of the 25 publications recorded this year, three were published by a single author and four with two authors. Of the Vietnamese authors most prolific in 2012, Tran Xuan Bach from Hanoi Medical University, Vietnam was either the sole author or co-authors in 13 published articles, followed by his colleague Nguyen Thanh Long from the Administration of HIV/AIDS Control, Ministry of Health, Hanoi, Vietnam with seven articles.

The year 2012 saw a clear emergence of some productive research teams in the field of Health Care in Vietnam. Data on 2017 publications confirm this observation: of the 59 articles recorded this year, Tran Xuan Bach was again leading in terms of output with 22 articles, followed by two non-collaborated authors, namely Hoang Van Minh with 14 articles and Vuong Quan Hoang (then affiliated with Université Libre de Bruxelles (ULB) - Solvay Brussels School of Economics and Management) with 9 articles.

These are some glimpses into the research activities and collaboration in Health Care. Chapter 5 of this book will discuss further the emergence of leading researchers and the formation of productive research groups in Vietnamese SSH.

Turning to the quality of publications in Health Care, we once again review the JIF of these publications. According to Figure 3.5, the proportions of articles in journals with IF between 2 and 3 increased dramatically in 2017-2018, compared to the previous year.

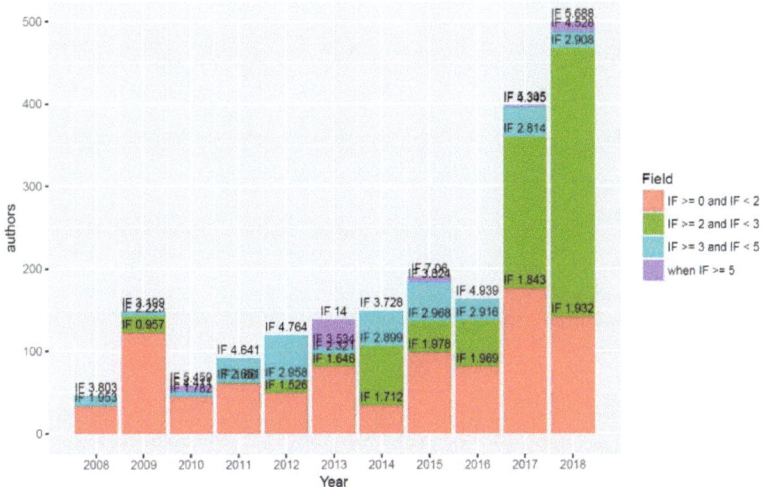

Figure 3.5. The total number of articles in Health Care, both categorized by publications' Impact Factor (IF), during the 2008-2018 period. The data labels refer to the highest impact factor recorded for each color-coded category.

Table 3.4 below shows the 20 articles with the highest JIF in the period 2008-2018. The most striking fact is that all of the 20 articles are led by Vietnamese authors. There are 3 solo papers, and 6 papers are authored by only Vietnamese, suggesting a full integration of Vietnamese healthcare research with the rest of the world. In addition, the majority of the top articles are the product of collaboration (17/20), in which, the highest number of co-authors is 14, and the lowest is 2. More than half of these top 20 articles in terms of JIF are co-authored by a medium range of the number of collaborators: 4-8 people. Regarding international collaboration, 14 papers in the top 20 are the result of international collaborative efforts.

	Article Name	No. Authors/ Foreign authors	Vietnamese lead author	Year	Journal	JIF
1	Effect of Facilitation of Local Maternal-and-Newborn Stakeholder Groups on Neonatal Mortality: Cluster-Randomized Controlled Trial	12/6	Yes	2013	PLOS Medicine	14
2	The Effect of Intermittent Antenatal Iron Supplementation on Maternal and Infant Outcomes in Rural Viet Nam: A Cluster Randomised Trial	13/7	Yes	2013	PLOS Medicine	14
3	Postpartum change in common mental disorders among rural Vietnamese women: Incidence, recovery and risk and protective factors	6/1	Yes	2015	British Journal of Psychiatry	7.06

	Article Name	No. Authors/ Foreign authors	Vietnamese lead author	Year	Journal	JIF
4	The Dark Side of Female HIV Patient Care: Sexual and Reproductive Health Risks in Pre- and Post- Clinical Treatments	12/0	Yes	2018	Journal of Clinical Medicine	5.688
5	Common perinatal mental disorders in northern Viet Nam: community prevalence and health care use	6/3	Yes	2010	Bulletin of the World Health Organization	5.459
6	Survey data on Vietnamese propensity to attend periodic general health examinations	1/0	Yes	2017	Scientific Data	5.305
7	Interventions for common perinatal mental disorders in women in low- and middle-income countries: A systematic review and meta-analysis	8/7	Yes	2013	Bulletin of the World Health Organization	5.112

	Article Name	No. Authors/ Foreign authors	Vietnamese lead author	Year	Journal	JIF
8	Willingness to pay for methadone maintenance treatment in Vietnamese epicentres of injection-drug-driven HIV infection	1/0	Yes	2013	*Bulletin of the World Health Organization*	5.112
9	Access to iodized salt in 11 low- and lower-middle-income countries: 2000 and 2010	3/1	Yes	2016	*Bulletin of the World Health Organization*	4.939
10	Impact of health insurance on health care treatment and cost in Vietnam: a health capability approach to financial protection	5/0	Yes	2012	*American Journal of Public Health*	4.764
11	Human papillomavirus vaccine delivery strategies that achieved high coverage in low- and middle-income countries	14/3	Yes	2011	*Bulletin of the World Health Organization*	4.641

	Article Name	No. Authors/ Foreign authors	Vietnamese lead author	Year	Journal	JIF
12	Iodine status in late pregnancy and psychosocial determinants of iodized salt use in rural northern Viet Nam	8/3	Yes	2011	*Bulletin of the World Health Organization*	4.641
13	Effect of health expenses on household capabilities and resource allocation in a rural commune in Vietnam	6/4	Yes	2012	*PLOS ONE*	4.537
14	Quality of Life Outcomes of Antiretroviral Treatment for HIV/AIDS Patients in Vietnam	1/0	Yes	2012	*PLOS ONE*	4.537
15	Patient Satisfaction with HIV/AIDS Care and Treatment in the Decentralization of Services Delivery in Vietnam	2/0	Yes	2012	*PLOS ONE*	4.537

	Article Name	No. Authors/ Foreign authors	Vietnamese lead author	Year	Journal	JIF
16	Multilevel Predictors of Concurrent Opioid Use during Methadone Maintenance Treatment among Drug Users with HIV/AIDS	7/3	Yes	2012	PLOS ONE	4.537
17	Health-related work productivity loss is low for patients in a methadone maintenance program in Vietnam	4/3	Yes	2018	International Journal of Drug Policy	4.528
18	Long-Term Weekly Iron-Folic Acid and De-Worming Is Associated with Stabilised Haemoglobin and Increasing Iron Stores in Non-Pregnant Women in Vietnam	7/3	Yes	2010	PLOS ONE	4.411

	Article Name	No. Authors/ Foreign authors	Vietnamese lead author	Year	Journal	JIF
19	Application of the Consolidated Framework for Implementation Research to assess factors that may influence implementation of tobacco use treatment guidelines in the Viet Nam public health care delivery system	8/3	Yes	2017	Implementation Science	4.345
20	What drives young Vietnamese to use mobile-health innovations? Implications for health communication and behavioral interventions	9/6	Yes	2018	JMIR mHealth and uHealth	4.3

Table 3.2. The 20 articles in the field of Health Care published by Vietnamese authors in journals with the highest impact factors (JIF) in 2008-2018.

In sum, four major trends can be from extracted: (i) the leadership of Vietnamese authors; (ii) the prevalence of co-authorship (see Figure 3.6), which is understandable in a large social medicine project; (iii) the involvement of foreign co-authors, with certain exceptions; and (iv) the common use of randomized controlled trial, convenient sampling method, in-depth interviews and focus group discussion.

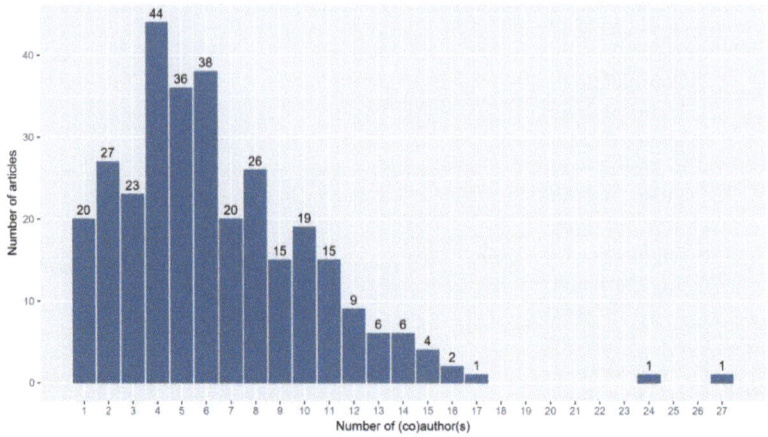

Figure 3.6. The trend in co-authorship within the field of Health Care in 2008-2018.

Figure 3.6 illustrates the common practice of collaborating with two or more authors in doing Health Care research in Vietnam. Of the 313 articles published in the field in the ten years, 44 articles (14%) were published in a team of four authors, 38 articles (12%) in a team of six authors; one article even had 24 authors, and the highest one had 27 authors. By comparison, there were 20 articles (6.38%) written and published by one author.

Lastly, it is worth highlighting the fact that five of the nine journals in Table 3.2, namely *PLOS Medicine, PLOS ONE, Scientific Data, Journal of Clinical Medicine,* and *Bulletin of the World Health Organization,* are peer-reviewed and fully open-access journals while *British Journal of Psychiatry,* and *International Journal of Drug Policy* are partially open-access. For public health results to be widely read, understood, and applied in reality, it is important that health and medicine-related journals become open access. Not only would public sharing of health data increase collaboration across disciplines and countries, it could even foster better control of disease outbreaks as well as more effective and timely discoveries, which would, in turn, enable effective diagnostics, vaccines, and treatments (Yozwiak, Schaffner, & Sabeti, 2015). The open access movement in scientific publishing is gaining momentum and acceptance of the wider research community (Ho & Vuong, 2019; Vuong, 2017), a point that we will visit in-depth in Chapter 6.

Educational research: internationalization and single authorship dominance

As a country steeped in Confucian traditions (Nguyen & Ho, 2019; Vuong, Bui, et al., 2018; Vuong, Vuong, Ho, & Nguyen, 2019), it is no surprise that interests in education research in Vietnam have always been high, fueling the international publications in the field. In the 2008-2018 period, our database records a total of 338 articles published in Education, equivalent to 12.38% of the total output (Table 3.1.). The number puts Education at second behind Economics in terms of publication output.

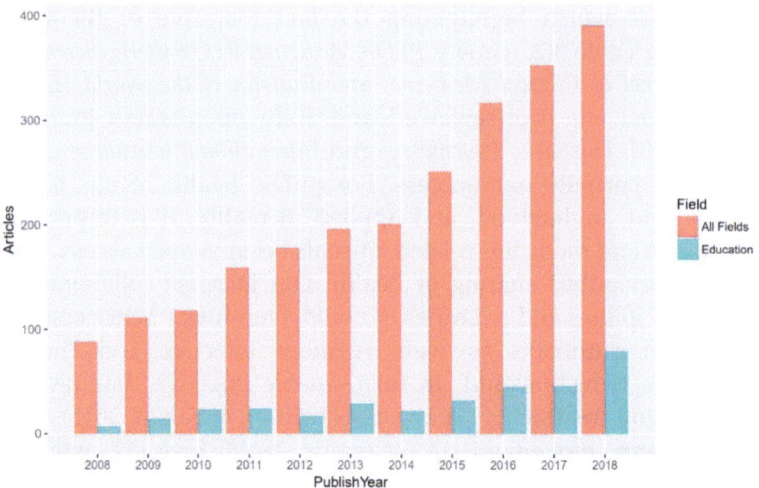

Figure 3.7. A visual comparison of total articles published in Education versus all fields in 2008-2018.

In terms of longitudinal data, the number of published articles in Education jumped from just 7 in 2008 to 79 in 2018 (Figure 3.7.). The first output hike was seen in 2010 when 23 articles were published, the second in 2016 with 45 articles published, and the third and most recent one in 2018. In terms of content, our data from 2018 show that topics such as the internationalization of higher education, private higher education, and overseas and international students' experience accounted for a large part of the research topics.

Table 3.3 shows the top 20 articles in terms of JIF in the field of Education. Similar to the trend in Healthcare, it appears that all education articles in high impact factor journals are led by Vietnamese researchers. However, even when publishing in top JIF journals, researchers in the field of education seem to prefer single-authorship and small group cooperation, compared to healthcare. There are 7 single-author articles, and 12 articles co-authored by groups of up to four people.

	Article Name	No. Authors/ Foreign authors	Vietnamese lead author	Year	Journal	JIF
1	An open database of productivity in Vietnam's social sciences and humanities for public use	8/0	Yes	2018	*Scientific Data*	5.929
2	Interactional Practices across Settings: From Classroom Role-plays to Workplace Patient Consultations	1/0	Yes	2016	*Applied Linguistics*	3.593
3	Has Management Accounting Research been critical?	2/1	Yes	2018	*Virtual Reality*	2.906
4	Behavioural intentions of using virtual reality in learning: perspectives of acceptance of information technology and learning style	4/3	Yes	2018	*Virtual Reality*	2.906
4	Effects of work environment and collaboration on research productivity in Vietnamese social sciences: evidence from 2008 to 2017 Scopus data	7/1	Yes	2018	*Studies in Higher Education*	2.854

	Article Name	No. Authors/ Foreign authors	Vietnamese lead author	Year	Journal	JIF
6	Student Engagement in Internationalization of the Curriculum: Vietnamese Domestic Students' Perspectives	2/1	Yes	2018	Journal of Studies in International Education	2.547
7	Internationalization, Student Engagement, and Global Graduates: A Comparative Study of Vietnamese and Australian Students' Experience	3/1	Yes	2018	Journal of Studies in International Education	2.547
8	Hospitality higher education in Vietnam: Voices from stakeholders	3/2	Yes	2018	Tourism Management Perspectives	2.485
9	What hinders teachers from translating their beliefs into teaching behaviors: The case of teaching generic skills in Vietnamese universities	1/0	Yes	2017	Teaching and Teacher Education	2.473

	Article Name	No. Authors/ Foreign authors	Vietnamese lead author	Year	Journal	JIF
10	Exploring contextual factors shaping teacher collaborative learning in a paired-placement	1/0	Yes	2017	*Teaching and Teacher Education*	2.473
11	Autonomy in teaching practice: Insights from Vietnamese English language teachers trained in Inner-Circle countries	2/1	Yes	2018	*Teaching and Teacher Education*	2.411
12	University strategic research planning: a key to reforming university research in Vietnam?	2/1	Yes	2017	*Studies in Higher Education*	2.321
13	Hybridity in Vietnamese universities: an analysis of the interactions between Vietnamese traditions and foreign influences	4/0	Yes	2017	*Studies in Higher Education*	2.321

	Article Name	No. Authors/ Foreign authors	Vietnamese lead author	Year	Journal	JIF
14	A New Application of Raymond Padilla's Unfolding Matrix in Framing Qualitative Data and the Follow-Up Activities for Educational Research	1/0	Yes	2018	*International Journal of Qualitative Methods*	2.257
15	Integration of Work Experience and Learning for International Students: From Harmony to Inequality	2/1	Yes	2017	*Journal of Studies in International Education*	2.255
16	Team learning: The missing construct from a cross-cultural examination of higher education	4/3	Yes	2016	*Asia Pacific Journal of Management*	2.024
17	Health-related work productivity loss is low for patients in a methadone maintenance program in Vietnam	4/3	Yes	2018	*International Journal of Drug Policy*	4.528

	Article Name	No. Authors/ Foreign authors	Vietnamese lead author	Year	Journal	JIF
18	The career paths of social marketing doctoral graduates	1/0	Yes	2017	Journal of Social Marketing	2
19	BAAL/CUP Seminar 2014: The Multilingual University: Linguistic diversity in higher education in English-dominant settings and English-medium instructional contexts	2/1	Yes	2016	Language Teaching	1.913
20	Analysis of Social Media Influencers and Trends on Online and Mobile Learning	3/1	Yes	2017	International Review of Research in Open and Distributed Learning	1.826

Table 3.3. The 20 articles in the field of Education published by Vietnamese authors in journals with the highest impact factors (JIF) in 2008-2018.

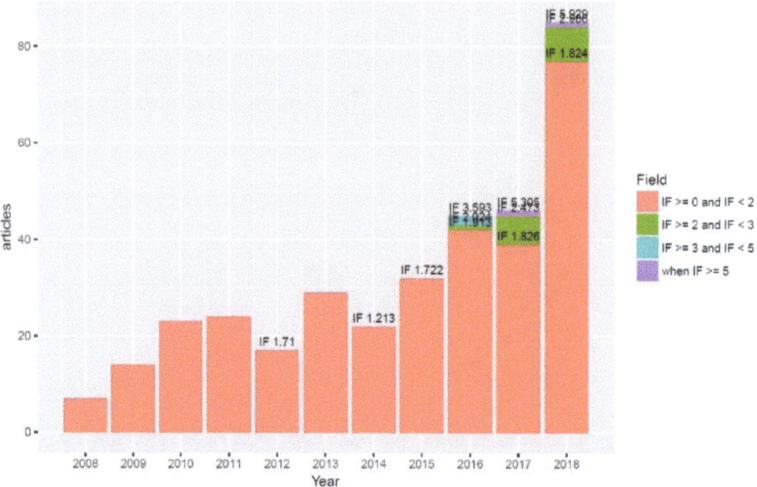

Figure 3.8. The total number of articles in Education, both categorized by publications' Impact Factor (IF), during the 2008-2018 period. The data labels refer to the highest impact factor recorded for each color-coded category.

With regard to the publication quality, as examined through the lens of a journal's impact factor (JIF), Figure 3.8 shows that the majority of authors and articles in the field of Education belong to journals with IF between 0 and 2. All publications from 2008 to 2015 are in the low JIF group. The number of articles in journals of higher IF only appears from 2016 onward, with the highest JIF recorded at 5.929 for *Scientific Data* of Nature Publishing Group. Table 3.5 gives more details into the articles published in journals with high IF.

Unlike researchers in the fields of Health Care, their peers in Education are largely writing and publishing papers solo or in a small group. This is most evident in the trend of co-authorship over the 2008-2018 period (Figure 3.9) – during which 132 articles (39%) were the results of single authorship. The number of articles with two authors followed closely at 125 or about 37% of the total.

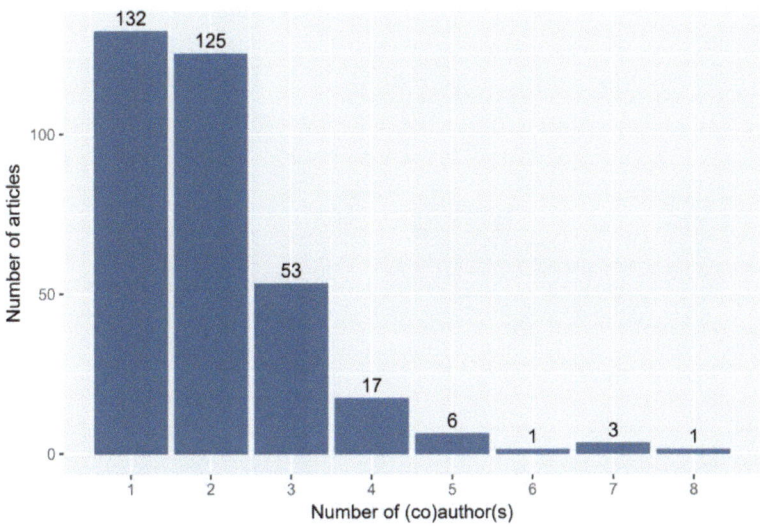

Figure 3.9. The trend in co-authorship within the field of Education in 2008-2018.

Besides the co-authorship trend, looking at the number of new authors entering a field can also offer great insights. A comparison of the number of new authors by year across the three fields of Economics, Health Care, and Education shows that what these three fields share in common is not just the prevalent co-authorship or foreign author involvement but also a dramatic surge in the number of new authors in 2016-2018. This observation is confirmed in Figure 3.10. In terms of the proportion to the total number of new authors per year, in 2017, Economics accounted for 32.8%, Health Care 29.2%, Education 12.3%; in 2018, the figures were respectively 24.1%, 29.9%, and 15.5%. Meanwhile, the compound annual growth rates of new authors were 9.75% in Economics, 22.87% in Health Care, and 24.46% in Education. These numbers clearly help explain the consistent rise in the publication of these fields.

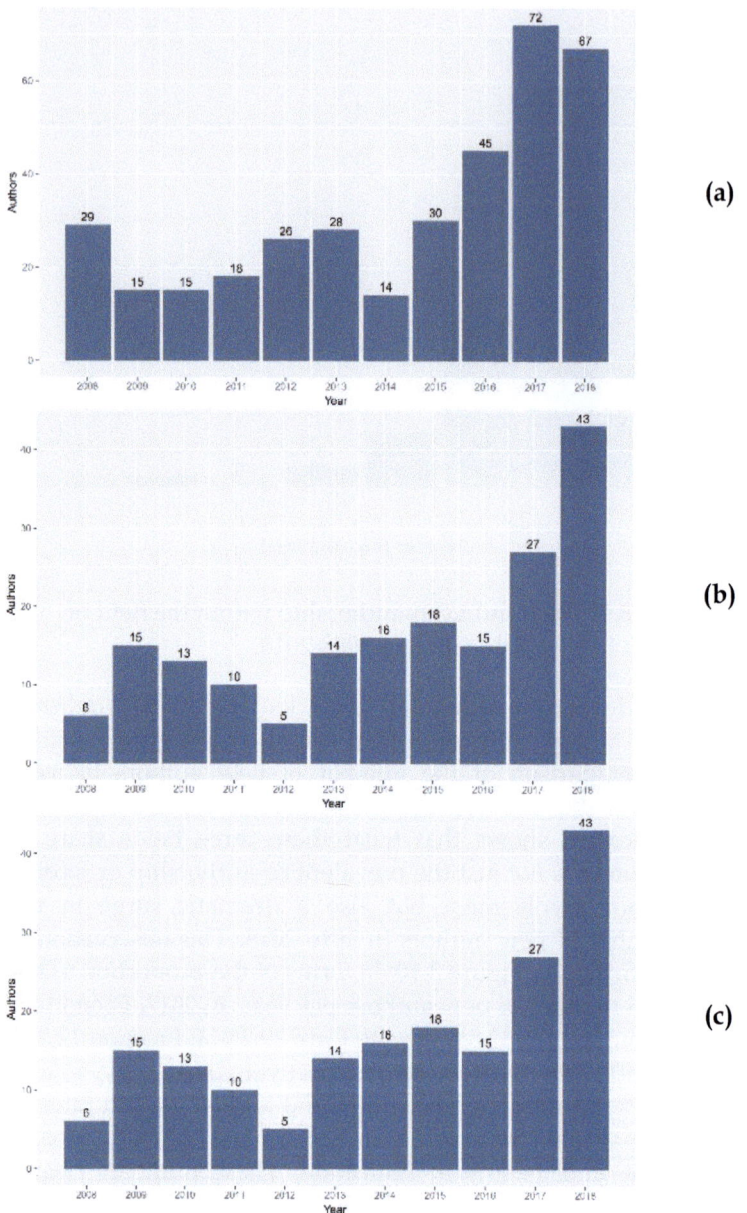

Figure 3.10. A comparison of the number of new authors each year in (a) Economics, (b) Health Care, and (c) Education in 2008-2018.

To sum up some noteworthy observations from the three most prolific fields analyzed above, for a research field to take off, reach and maintain high productivity levels, the research content notwithstanding, there have to be: (i) stable co-authorship network, (ii) support from foreign colleagues in the field, (iii) outstanding research leaders, and (iv) a sustainable inflow of new researchers (Figure 3.10). Next, we will turn to the most productive field in the past 10 years, the field of Economics.

References

Dang, H. A. H., & Glewwe, P. W. (2018). Well begun, but aiming higher: A review of Vietnam's education trends in the past 20 years and emerging challenges. *Journal of Development Studies, 54*(7), 1171-1195.

Ho, M.-T., & Vuong, Q.-H. (2019). The values and challenges of 'openness' in addressing the reproducibility crisis and regaining public trust in social sciences and humanities. *European Science Editing, 45*(1), 14-17. doi:10.20316/ESE.2019.45.17021

Le, A. H., McDonald, C. V., & Klieve, H. (2018). Hospitality higher education in Vietnam: Voices from stakeholders. *Tourism Management Perspectives, 27*, 68-82.

Le Ha, P. (2018). Higher education, English, and the idea of 'the West': globalizing and encountering a global south regional university. *Discourse: Studies in the Cultural Politics of Education, 39*(5), 782-797. doi:10.1080/01596306.2018.1448704

Nguyen, T.-D., & Ho, M.-T. (2019). People as the roots (of the State): Democratic elements in the politics of traditional Vietnamese Confucianism. *Journal of Nationalism, Memory and Language Politics, 13*(1), 90. doi:10.2478/jnmlp-2019-0001

Nguyen, X. N. C. M., & Walkinshaw, I. (2018). Autonomy in teaching practice: Insights from Vietnamese English language teachers trained in Inner-Circle countries. *Teaching and Teacher Education, 69*, 21-32. doi:https://doi.org/10.1016/j.tate.2017.08.015

Noorden, R. V. (2015). Interdisciplinary research by the numbers. *Nature*. Retrieved from https://www.nature.com/news/interdisciplinary-research-by-the-numbers-1.18349

Phan, H. L. T., Tran, L. T., & Blackmore, J. (2018). Internationalization, student engagement, and global graduates: A comparative study of Vietnamese and Australian students' experience. *Journal of Studies in International Education, 23*(1), 171-189. doi:10.1177/1028315318803717

Tran, L. T., & Vu, T. T. P. (2018). 'Agency in mobility': towards a conceptualisation of international student agency in transnational mobility. *Educational Review, 70*(2), 167-187.

Trinh, A. N., & Conner, L. (2019). Student engagement in internationalization of the curriculum: Vietnamese domestic students' perspectives. *Journal of Studies in International Education, 23*(1), 154-170.

Truong, V. D., & Dietrich, T. (2018). Master's thesis research in social marketing (1971-2015). *Journal of Social Marketing, 8*(1), 58-98.

Vuong, Q.-H. (2017). Author's corner: Open data, open review and open dialogue in making social sciences plausible. *Nature: Scientific Data Updates*. Retrieved from http://blogs.nature.com/scientificdata/2017/12/12/authors-corner-open-data-open-review-and-open-dialogue-in-making-social-sciences-plausible/

Vuong, Q.-H., Bui, Q.-K., La, V.-P., Vuong, T.-T., Nguyen, V.-H. T., Ho, M.-T., . . . Ho, M.-T. (2018). Cultural additivity: behavioural insights from the interaction of Confucianism, Buddhism and Taoism in folktales. *Palgrave Communications, 4*(1), 143. doi:10.1057/s41599-018-0189-2

Vuong, Q.-H., La, V.-P., Vuong, T.-T., Ho, M.-T., Nguyen, H.-K. T., Nguyen, V.-H., . . . Ho, M.-T. (2018). An open database of productivity in Vietnam's social sciences and humanities for public use. *Scientific Data, 5*, 180188. doi:10.1038/sdata.2018.188

Vuong, Q.-H., Napier, N. K., Ho, M.-T., Nguyen, V.-H. T., Vuong, T.-T., Pham, H. H., & Nguyen, H.-K. T. (2018). Effects of work environment and collaboration on research productivity in Vietnamese social sciences: evidence from 2008 to 2017 scopus data. *Studies in Higher Education*, 1-16. doi:10.1080/03075079.2018.1479845

Vuong, Q.-H., Vuong, T.-T., Ho, M.-T., & Nguyen, H. K. T. (2019). The 'same bed, different dreams' of Vietnam and China. *European Journal of East Asian Studies*, *18*(1), 93. doi:https://doi.org/10.1163/15700615-01801007

Yozwiak, N. L., Schaffner, S. F., & Sabeti, P. C. (2015). Data sharing: Make outbreak research open access. *Nature*. Retrieved from https://www.nature.com/news/data-sharing-make-outbreak-research-open-access-1.16966

Chapter 4
Economics: The trend-setting field
Thi-Hanh Vu, Trung Tran,
Phuong-Hanh Hoang, Minh-Hoang Nguyen

This chapter is dedicated to the most prolific field in Vietnam's social sciences and humanities (SSH): Economics. The field, also known as the queen of social sciences, is the front runner not only with the highest productivity, but as shown by the data, it is also a trend-setter in terms of interdisciplinary collaboration and timely integration of foreign publishing practices. Nonetheless, some signs within the field do raise alarm over the urgency of appropriate research investment and incentives – a lesson that is no doubt replicable across the whole domain of SSH.

A leader in social scientific productivity

If Table 3.1 (in Chapter 3) shows the total number of publications throughout the ten years from 2008-2018, then Table 4.1 offers a more condensed look at the top ten fields in international publications in three recent years, from 2016 to 2018. One trend is confirmed over and again: Economics related research consistently leads in publication output, and even surpasses other fields by a considerable distance. For instance, in 2018, the number of articles published in Economics was 1.69-times and 4.45-times as high as that in Business and Management, respectively. The output within Economics was stable, averaging at 91 articles per year during the 2016-2018 period. Publications in the two Economics-related fields of Business and Management also help consolidate the position of Economics as the leader in SSH research.

2018		
Rank	Field	Article
1	Economics	98
2	Education	79
3	Health Care	61
4	Business	58
5	Sociology	28
6	Environment/Sustainability Science	27
7	Tourism	23

8	Management	22
9	Agriculture	16
10	Law	13
2017		
1	Economics	97
2	Health Care	59
3	Business	56
4	Education	46
5	Environment/Sustainability Science	29
6	Management	22
7	Sociology	17
8	Political Science	13
9	Agriculture	12
10	Law	20
2016		
1	Economics	79
2	Education	45
3	Business	38
4	Health Care	33
5	Law	24
6	Sociology	22
7	Management	20
8	Agriculture	17
9	Environment/Sustainability Science	16
10	Political Science	14

Table 4.1. The leading fields in international publication within Vietnamese SSH in three recent years, 2016-2018.

From a more holistic view, Figure 4.1 presents a comparison between the number of articles published in Economics and the total number of articles. For a decade, the publication output in Economics was constantly rising to account for a significant portion of the entire production. The number of publications in 2008-2010 hovered from 24 to 34, followed by an upsurge to 50 in 2011, attributable to a resurgent interest in the economic crisis. The number of published articles stayed relatively stable at about 45 in 2012-2014 before rising consistently and doubling by 2015-2018. The boom in the empirical analysis of economic issues is thanks to advances in computing technology and statistical analysis of micro datasets.

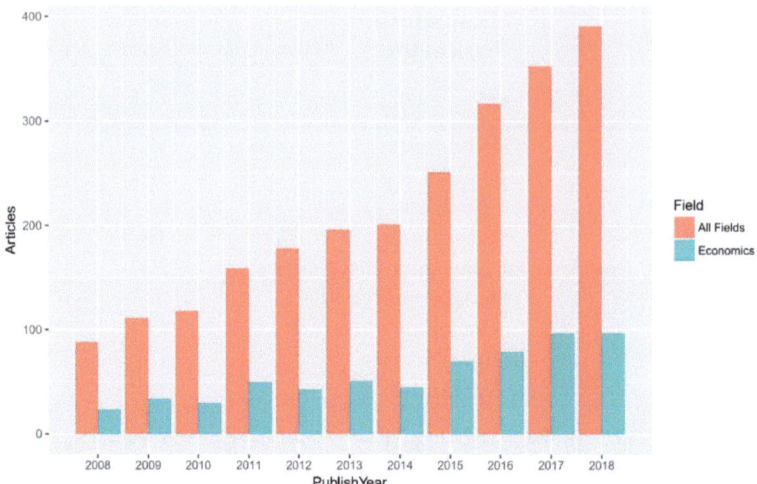

Figure 4.1. A visual comparison of total articles published in Economics versus all fields in 2008-2018.

To gauge the quality of the publications, we suggest looking at the impact factor (IF) of the journals in which these articles were published during the period. Similar to the JIF landscape captured in Figure 4.1, for the field of Economics, Figure 3.5 shows that a significant proportion of publications were in journals with IF between 0 and 2, although the shares of higher IF journals appeared to be rising.

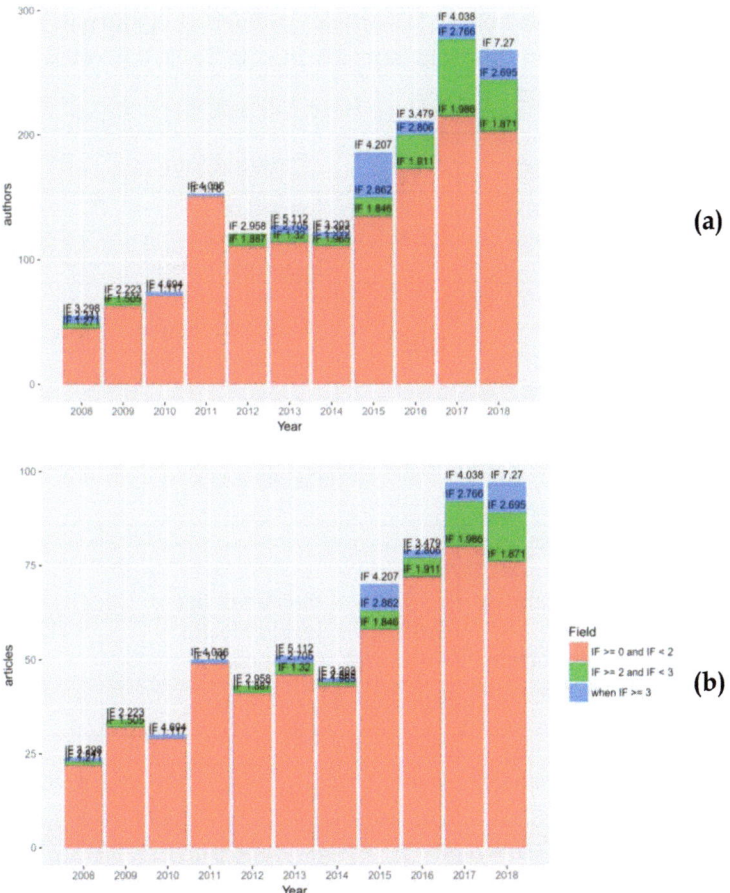

Figure 4.2. (a) The total number of authors in Economics and **(b)** The total number of articles in Economics, both categorized by publications' Impact Factor (IF), during the 2008-2018 period. The data labels refer to the highest impact factor recorded for each color-coded category.

A closer look at the list of the ten articles published in journals with the highest IF in this field, summarized in Table 4.2, reveals some interesting observations.

	Article Name	Publish Year	Journal Name	JIF
1	Policy uncertainty, derivative use, and firm-level FDI	2018	Journal of International Business Studies	7.724
2	Natural resource extraction and household welfare in rural Laos	2018	Land Degradation and Development	7.27
3	Eco-efficiency analysis of sustainability-certified coffee production in Vietnam	2018	Journal of Cleaner Production	5.651
4	Willingness to pay for methadone maintenance treatment in Vietnamese epicentres of injection-drug-driven HIV infection	2013	Bulletin of the World Health Organization	5.112
5	Bioeconomic Losses from Overharvesting Tuna	2010	Conservation Letters	4.694
6	Impulse controls and uncertainty in economics: Method and application	2015	Environmental Modelling and Software	4.207
7	One Mandarin Benefits the Whole Clan: Hometown Favoritism in an Authoritarian Regime	2017	American Economic Journal: Applied Economics	4.038
8	Striped catfish farming in the Mekong Delta, Vietnam: a tumultuous path to a global success	2011	Reviews in Aquaculture	4.036
9	Energy demand convergence in APEC: An empirical analysis	2017	Energy Economics	3.91

10	Are Ecosystem Services Complementary or Competitive? An Econometric Analysis of Cost Functions of Private Forests in Vietnam	2018	Ecological Economics	3.895

Table 4.2. The top ten articles in the field of Economics published by Vietnamese authors in journals with the highest impact factors (JIF) in 2008-2018.

According to Table 4.2, the highest IF for an Economics publication was recorded in 2018, at 7.724 — which was of the *Journal of International Business Studies* published by Palgrave MacMillan Ltd. The article titled "Policy uncertainty, derivative use, and firm-level FDI" was co-written by three authors, two of whom are Vietnamese: Nguyen Quang (affiliated with Middlesex University Longdon, UK) and Kim Huong Trang (affiliated with Foreign Trade University, Vietnam) and the third author is a professor of international business also affiliated with Middlesex University London, UK (Nguyen, Kim, & Papanastassiou, 2018). A closer follower was published in *Land Degradation and Development* journal with the IF of 7.27 put in print by John Wiley & Sons Ltd. The article, titled "Natural resource extraction and household welfare in rural Laos," was also co-written by three authors, two of whom are Vietnamese: Nguyen Trung Thanh (affiliated with the Institute for Environmental Economics and World Trade, Leibniz University Hannover, Germany) and Do Truong Lam (affiliated with both Leibniz University Hannover, Germany and the Faculty of Economics and Rural Development, Vietnam National University of Agriculture, Hanoi, Vietnam) (Nguyen, Do, & Grote, 2018).

With the exception of one single-authored article by Tran Xuan Bach (affiliated with the Institute for Preventive Medicine and Public Health, Hanoi Medical University, Hanoi, Vietnam) in 2013 in the *Bulletin of the World Health Organization* (Tran, 2013), the remaining nine articles share these four characteristics: (i) the prevalence of co-authorship, especially in group of two and three authors (confirmed in Figure 3.6 for the whole ten-year period); (ii) the participation of foreign authors; (iii) the affiliation of a Vietnamese author with a foreign institution; and (iv) the interdisciplinary nature of these research projects (see Figure 3.14.), such as health economics, environmental economics (Lambini, Nguyen, Abildtrup, Tenhunen, & Garcia, 2018; Le, Chang, & Park, 2017; Parvathi & Nguyen, 2018), agricultural economics (Ho, Hoang, Wilson, & Nguyen, 2018; Kompas, Grafton, & Che, 2010), and political economics (Do, Nguyen, & Tran, 2017). In particular, many of the articles in the top ten list (Table 4.2.) are concerned with ecological sustainability through the lens of economic analysis (Lambini et al., 2018; Le et al., 2017; Parvathi & Nguyen, 2018), which hints at the growing importance of cross-disciplinary research methodologies and perspectives.

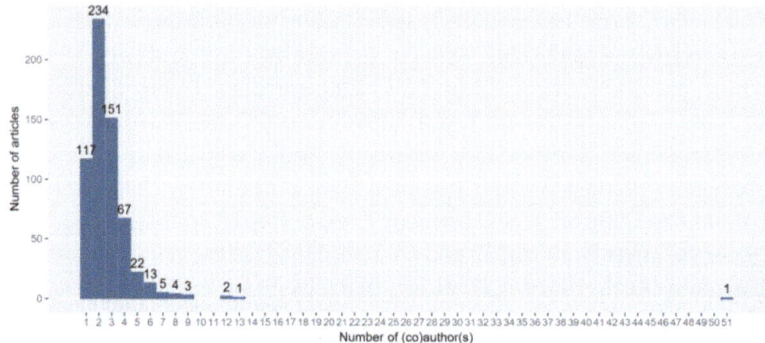

Figure 4.3. The trend in co-authorship within the field of Economics in 2008-2018.

The positive relationship between the number of Vietnamese authors and the number of economics-related articles which are published in various journals shows that the strong collaboration of authors helps increase their research output. In comparison with the other research fields such as "Health" and "Education", there is a diversification of publications of Vietnamese authors in different IF journals mainly ranging from IF 0.1 to IF 5.

Moving toward interdisciplinary research

As shown in the previous chapter and in the current chapter, there are three important characteristics of high-performing fields in Vietnam's SSH: (i) stable co-authorship networks, (ii) collaboration with foreign colleagues in the field, (iii) outstanding research leaders, and (iv) a sustainable inflow of new researchers. However, potential fields of research are areas that should exhibit these characteristics as well as have room for cross-field collaboration. The field of Economics offers a vivid example of how interdisciplinary research could boost both the quality and quantity of research publications at the international level.

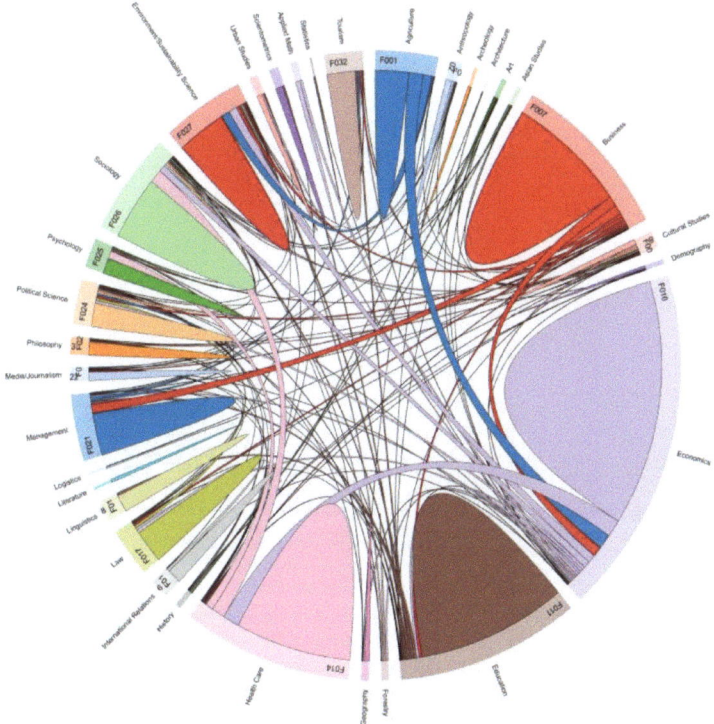

Figure 4.4. The interdisciplinary network of all 32 fields in Vietnam's SSH, 2008-2018.

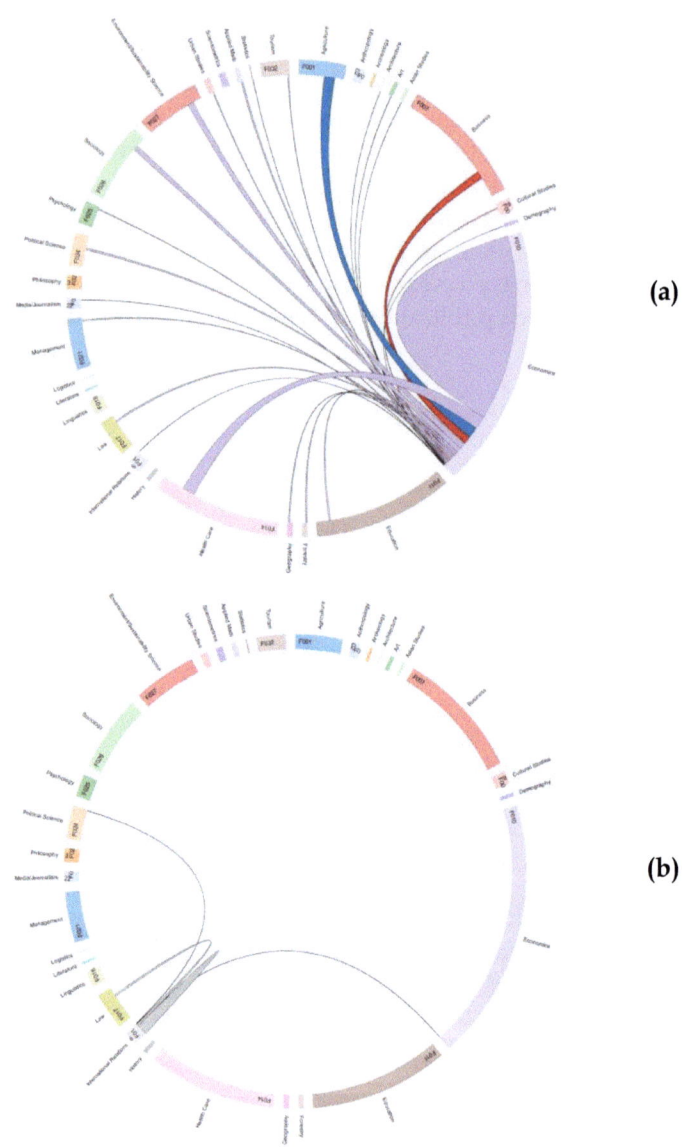

Figure 4.5. A comparison between the interdisciplinary networks of **(a)** Economics and **(b)** International Relations, 2008-2018.

Figure 4.4 provides an excellent visualization of the interdisciplinary network of all 32 SSH fields from 2008 to 2018. The figure highlights once again the highly interdisciplinary nature of Economics, Education, Health Care, and Business. Figure 4.5 offers a comparative perspective into the interdisciplinary networks of Economics and International Relations, the latter showing very little connection to other fields.

The interdisciplinary trends are new to Vietnam but are increasingly seen as the new norm in academic research worldwide. According to a Nature analysis that tracked the citation of research articles outside their own disciplines in the Web of Science, the proportion of paper references that direct to other disciplines in both the natural and social sciences have been rising steadily since the mid-1980s (Noorden, 2015). Notably, the 21st century saw the fraction of papers with the word "interdisciplinary" in their titles at an all-time high. The study also points out that Health is a very disciplinary field, thanks to its ability to incorporate a wide array of topics such as public health and social studies of medicine (Noorden, 2015).

"I think interdisciplinary research is very important and it is the inevitable trend in scientific research. Personally, I really enjoy collaborating with researchers from other fields. For example, I have been working with a biochemist and a *Hán-Nôm* researcher." Dr. Ho Huu Loc, *Ho Chi Minh City University of Science, Ho Chi Minh City, Vietnam*

Reaching out to and bringing home international publishers

As a field that records a high number of publications within Vietnam's social sciences, Economics also stands out for marking the presence of a wide range number of world renowned publishers such as Elsevier, Taylor & Francis, Wiley, and Springer, etc. These names have almost become household names for Vietnamese economists over the past decade. Based on SSHPA's data from 2008 to 2018, the number of economics-related articles published by these publishers accounted for nearly 80% of the total. These publishers have been mentioned in the list of international and national journals in social sciences and humanities which was approved by the government-run National Foundation for Science and Technology Development (hereafter NAFOSTED) (Vuong, 2019). Accordingly, having publications in these journals would entitle Vietnamese authors to research grants provided by the national science funding agency. This decision, on the one hand, intensifies the competition among Vietnamese authors, and on the other hand, stimulates the co-authorship, and thus, enhancing research networks in Vietnam.

> "I think for international collaboration to be effective, we must focus on the substance, rather than the appearance. Some universities spend a fortune to organize international conferences, but the central theme of the conference has nothing to do with the university; we should keep practice like this from happening. I also think international collaboration should focus on specific individuals, research projects, or organizations." *Dr. Huynh The Du, Fulbright University Vietnam, Ho Chi Minh City, Vietnam*

As can be seen in Figure 4.6, Elsevier secured the top position with 183 Economics-related articles by Vietnamese authors in the 2008-2018 period. It was followed by other old guards such as Taylor & Francis, Wiley, Springer, and Emerald Publishing. Other long-established publishers not named in Figure 4.6 include De Gruyter, and Brill, among others. The review speed of these publishers is comparatively slow and the acceptance rate is quite low that challenge the perseverance of most researchers.

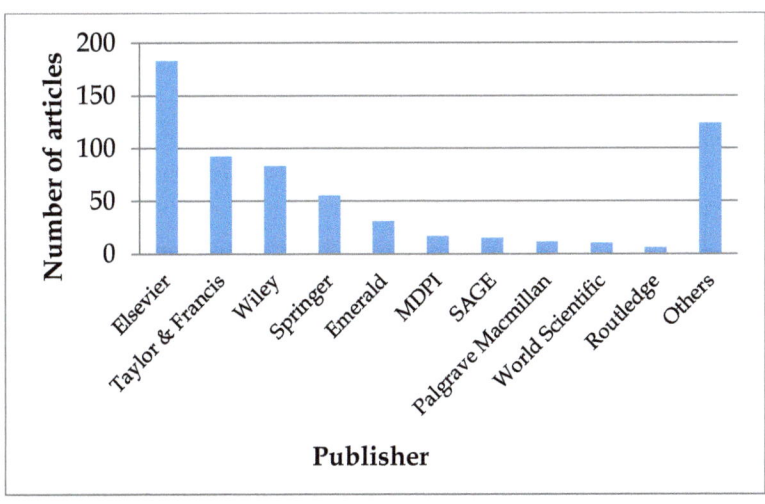

Figure 4.6. Publishers present in Vietnam's international publications in Economics during 2008-2018.

However, it is also noticeable that a newly-established publisher like MDPI (founded in 1996) is quickly attracting publications from Vietnam, as it enjoys the 6th place. Perhaps, the reason is that MDPI journals offer a very rapid decision, quick publication process, and open access, as opposed to the slow process of journals from older publishers. The entrance of new publishers such as MDPI, Hindawi (established in 1997), Inderscience (1979), and Dove Press (founded in 2003 and acquired by Taylor & Francis in 2017) has generated more intense competition and created a lively academic publishing market.

In addition to setting Vietnamese footprints in prestigious foreign-published journals, there is also a recent movement toward improving domestic journals via partnership with an international publishing house. The advantages are clear: foreign publishers have advanced submission and publishing systems as well as professional quality proofing. More importantly, having a journal managed by a well-established academic publisher could increase the chance of it being indexed in Scopus or Web of Science as the publishers themselves are incentivized properly to have all of its journals indexed in quality databases. This trend, as previously pointed out in Chapter 1, has largely been pursued by Vietnamese academics in the natural sciences. In Vietnam's social sciences, Economics is the only field to date that has marked the joint publishing partnership. In particular, from 2018, the Journal of Asian Business and Economic Studies (JABES) has been published by Emerald Publishing on behalf of the University of Economics Ho Chi Minh City. What is most notable here are: (i) JABES is owned by the Vietnamese university and runs under an open access agreement, and (ii) authors submitting articles to JABES do not have to pay the article processing charge for it is covered by the university (Emerald Publishing, 2019a). The other Vietnamese journal that is slated to published by Emerald from 2019 is the Journal of Economics and Development (JED), owned by the National Economics University in Hanoi (Emerald Publishing, 2019b). At the moment, given their new international status, the two journals are only indexed in the ASEAN Citation Index, a regional database for bibliographic and citation records (ACI, 2019).

It becomes clear that, for an academic discipline to truly take off, there require not just time and investment but also coordinated efforts by relevant parties. Here, the field of Economics in Vietnam offers valuable lessons for both researchers as well as education/science policymakers regarding the path of international collaboration.

Achilles' heel

While Economics appears to have been endowed with all the right attributes to be the ruler of the social sciences world, it is not all perfect. There are critical elements still missing for researchers in Economics that those from other disciplines can draw from.

At present, of the 245 universities in Vietnam, 31% provide programs for studying economics. At the same time, driven by a tough competition for student enrolment and better reputation both at home and abroad, universities in Vietnam are also offering increasingly diverse options for multidisciplinary study programs.

This means Economics as an academic discipline has been a fertile crossroad for both those offering and pursuing higher degrees. Yet, one would be mistaken to assume that the number of programs for studying economics at a university is proportional to the number of its publications in economics. Quality cannot be equated with quantity even if it is often preceded by quantity.

When we look at the prolific publication activities of Vietnamese economists over the past ten years solely through the lens of their affiliated institutions, some noteworthy observations emerge. To illustrate this point, we suggest focusing on the data from 2018.

No.	Academic institutions	Number of published articles
1	French-Vietnamese Center for Management Education Ho Chi Minh	13
2	University of Economics Ho Chi Minh City	13
3	National Economics University Hanoi	9
4	University of Economics and Business VNUH	7
5	Mekong Development Research Institute	5
6	RMIT University Vietnam	5
7	Foreign Trade University	4
8	Banking Academy Hanoi	3
9	Hue University of Economics	3
10	Academy of Finance (Vietnam)	2
11	Business and Economics Research Group - OUHCM	2
12	Centre for Interdisciplinary Social Research - Phenikaa Uni	2
13	Faculty of Marketing TMU	2
14	Humanitarian Services for Children of Vietnam	2
15	School of Banking and Finance - NEU	2

Table 4.3. Top 15 academic institutions in Vietnam in terms of the number of publications in Economics in 2018

Zooming in on the data of 2018, Table 4.3 shows that there was a big gap in economics research output even among the most productive universities. Institutions at the top of the table (French-Vietnamese Center for Management Education Ho Chi Minh and University of Economics Ho Chi Minh City) outperformed those at the bottom by nearly seven times.

It is alarming that nearly one-third of the total number of universities offering economics programs across Vietnam have published only one economics-related article in 2018. Two factors could explain this phenomenon. The first is the sub-optimal research performance of lecturers, indicated by the disproportionate rate of lecturers to scientific publications in economics. For example, in 2018, Foreign Trade University and National Economics University recorded four and nine economics-related publications respectively even though the two universities have about 70 and 93 lecturers in economics. The second factor is the limited funding for research by public universities. This calls for nationwide research investment with a comprehensive and sustainable agenda.

As presented in Table 4.3, the French-Vietnamese Center for Management Education Ho Chi Minh and the University of Economics Ho Chi Minh City have the highest number of articles related to economics. Notably, authors from the school of Banking and Finance under the National Economics University also published two articles in the same year. The number of articles of these academic institutions increased steadily in the 2016-2018 period. However, the ratio between the number of lecturers in economics and the number of publications is low, showing research performance of lecturers is still not optimal. For example, in 2018, Foreign Trade University only published four economics-related articles despite having about 70 lecturers in economics.

Through a detailed investigation of economics research activities in Vietnam between 2008 and 2018, we have come to the conclusion that critical factors contributing to the development of economics research involve the collaboration among researchers of both Vietnamese and foreign nationalities, the interdisciplinary nature of the research and the support of academic institutions. Given the problem of large output research gap among universities providing economics program, further support should be given to researchers in the form of funding provided by government and international organizations. In addition, a nationwide network of researchers in Vietnam should be strongly replicated so as to promote the sharing of research ideas and experiences, particularly between reputed authors and inexperienced authors. Last but not least, these prescriptions should be taken to heart across the whole spectrum of Vietnamese social sciences and humanities.

References

Do, Q.-A., Nguyen, K.-T., & Tran, A. N. (2017). One Mandarin Benefits the Whole Clan: Hometown Favoritism in an Authoritarian Regime. *American Economic Journal: Applied Economics, 9*(4), 1-29. doi:10.1257/app.20130472

Emerald Publishing. (2019a). Journal of Asian Business and Economic Studies – Information. *Emerald Publishing Services*. Retrieved August 8, 2019, from http://www.emeraldgrouppublishing.com/services/publishing/jabes/index.htm

Emerald Publishing. (2019b). Journal of Economics and Development – Information. *Emerald Publishing Services*. Retrieved August 8, 2019, from http://www.emeraldgrouppublishing.com/services/publishing/jed/index.htm

Ho, T. Q., Hoang, V.-N., Wilson, C., & Nguyen, T.-T. (2018). Eco-efficiency analysis of sustainability-certified coffee production in Vietnam. *Journal of Cleaner Production, 183*, 251-260.

Kompas, T., Grafton, R. Q., & Che, T. N. (2010). Bioeconomic losses from overharvesting tuna. *Conservation Letters, 3*(3), 177-183. doi:10.1111/j.1755-263X.2010.00103.x

Lambini, C. K., Nguyen, T. T., Abildtrup, J., Tenhunen, J., & Garcia, S. (2018). Are ecosystem services complementary or competitive? An econometric analysis of cost functions of private forests in vietnam. *Ecological Economics, 147*, 343-352.

Le, T.-H., Chang, Y., & Park, D. (2017). Energy demand convergence in APEC: An empirical analysis. *Energy Economics, 65*, 32-41. doi:10.1016/j.eneco.2017.04.013

Nguyen, Q., Kim, H. T., & Papanastassiou, M. (2018). Policy uncertainty, derivative use, and firm-level FDI. *Journal of International Business Studies, 49*(1), 96-126. https://doi.org/10.1057/s41267-017-0124-6.

Nguyen, T. T., Do, T. L., & Grote, U. (2018). Natural resource extraction and household welfare in rural Laos. *Land Degradation & Development, 29*(9), 3029-3038.

Noorden, R. V. (2015). Interdisciplinary research by the numbers. *Nature*. Retrieved from https://www.nature.com/news/interdisciplinary-research-by-the-numbers-1.18349

Parvathi, P., & Nguyen, T. T. (2018). Is environmental income reporting evasive in household surveys? Evidence from rural poor in Laos. *Ecological Economics, 143*, 218-226.

Tran, B. X. (2013). Willingness to pay for methadone maintenance treatment in Vietnamese epicentres of injection-drug-driven HIV infection. *Bulletin of the World Health Organization, 91*, 475-482.

Vuong, Q. H. (2019). The harsh world of publishing in emerging regions and implications for editors and publishers: The case of Vietnam. *Learned Publishing,* doi:10.1002/leap.1255.

Chapter 5
Researchers who lead the trends
Xuan-Hung Doan, Phuong-Tram T. Nguyen,
Viet-Phuong La, Hong-Kong T. Nguyen

Chapter 5 delves deeper into the profiles of the researchers in our database. This chapter makes up the core of this book for its focus on the scholars who have contributed tirelessly to scientific research and international publications and, ultimately, have helped shape a more rigorous and better-quality academic environment for SSH in Vietnam.

We would like to start the chapter with two impressive figures.
- First, the 158 authors with the highest number of published articles in the ten years, or 11.4% all authors, accounted for 64.62% of the total output.
- Second, even more astoundingly, 24.8% of the articles published in Scopus-indexed journals during the period were the works of 10 Vietnamese authors—who we would like to regard as the "most eminent researchers in SSH."

The eminent researchers in SSH

One of our measures for "eminence" is academic productivity, evaluated based on the number of published articles each year of a researcher. To grasp the extent of this productivity, we suggest looking at Figure 5.1 on the highest count of publications by a researcher in a year during the ten-year period, 2008-2018. In Figure 5.1, the y-axis denotes the highest number of articles published by a researcher that year, and the x-axis denotes the year. Accordingly, the all-time high achievement of a Vietnamese SSH author in a year is 34 articles, which has only happened in 2018. The year 2017 came in second with 22 articles. Details about these record-breaking individuals are summarized in Table 5.1.

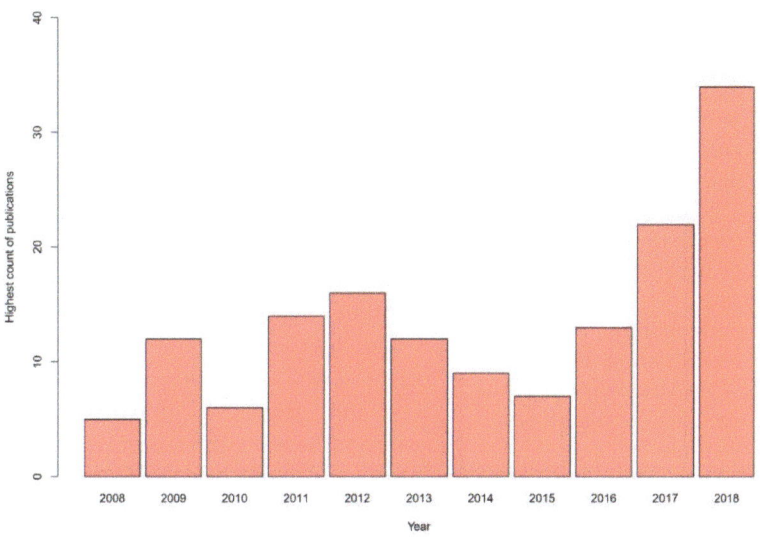

Figure 5.1. The highest count of publications by an individual researcher by year, 2008-2018.

Author Name	Year(s)
(vm.581) Hoang Van Minh	2008, 2009
(vm.16) Luu Trong Tuan	2010, 2011, 2012
(vm.402) Tran Duc Thach	2013, 2014
(vf.146) Nguyen Ngoc Huong	2015
(vm.3) Vuong Quan Hoang	2016
(vm.828) Tran Xuan Bach	2017, 2018

Table 5.1. Researchers with the highest count of publications in a year, 2008-2018.

Among the authors listed in Table 5.1, Luu Trong Tuan (coded vm.16) holds the longest streak of highest publication output—three continuous years 2010-2012—and is also the first to set this kind of record for the 2008-2016 period—with 16 articles/year in 2012. Additionally, the list has only one female author, Nguyen Ngoc Huong (coded vf.146).

> "I think an author, in order to claim credibility, must fulfill the following criteria: publishing in prestigious journals in his/her discipline; authoring articles that are practically and theoretically influential; and actively participating in the assessment and building of research capacity in a specific scientific field or institute."
>
> Dr. Tran Thi Ly, Deakin University, Victoria, Australia.

More noteworthy is the fact that five of the six aforementioned researchers have written and published articles in the field of Health Care and/or Social Medicine. This observation adds to the explanations for why Health Care is among the top three fields in terms of publication output, as pointed out in Chapter 3.

Another sign for an "eminent researcher" is indisputably his or her role as a first or leading author. Here, what the authors in Table 5.1 have in common besides their highly prolific profiles is their role as the first or leading author in their published papers. For instance, Luu Trong Tuan and Nguyen Viet Cuong took the leading role in 96% and 67.7% of their publications, respectively. Meanwhile, the more recent "trailblazers" such as Vuong Quan Hoang and Tran Xuan Bach took the helms in 69% and 55.7% of their publications, respectively. See Figure 5.7 for our in-depth analysis into the number of lead authors in relation to the number of published articles.

These authors also stand out because of their footprints in a wide array of journals: Luu Trong Tuan has left his mark on 38 journals from 9 publishers; Nguyen Viet Cuong 41 journals from 11 publishers; Vuong Quan Hoang 43 journals from 28 publishers; and Tran Xuan Bach 33 journals from 16 publishers. These numbers indeed bring attention to the need for a pioneering researcher capable of winning over different editorial boards and publishers.

An even closer look at the list of researchers with the highest count of solo publications in a year, summarized in Table 5.2, shows that two of the six authors in Table 4.1, namely Luu Trong Tuan and Vuong Quan Hoang, are also leading as individual researchers in their own solo published articles.

Author Name	Year(s)
(vm.4) Nguyen Viet Cuong	2008, 2009
(vm.16) Luu Trong Tuan	2010, 2011, 2012, 2013, 2014, 2017, 2018
(vm.18) Vo Xuan Vinh	2015
(vm.3) Vuong Quan Hoang	2016

Table 5.2. Researchers with the highest count of solo publications in a year, 2008-2018.

"From my experience, writing a paper solo has the following difficulties. The author needs to possess a very high degree responsibility and self-discipline because a solo author will not face any deadline pressure or receive any cross-checking from co-authors. However, writing a solo paper can, on the other hand, provide the author with the flexibility of time. And, if the article is published, it can prove their ability to work independently." *Dr. Pham Si Cong, Deakin University, Victoria, Australia*

Sole authorship is not rare in Vietnam's SSH publication landscape. Many researchers in our database were found to be writing and publishing papers almost entirely alone, such as Luu Trong Tuan or Pham Quang Minh (coded vm.10). In fact, data from 2008 to 2018 revealed that, when it comes to single authorship, the proportion of authors with only one solo publication accounts for the majority (Figure 4.2), or 59.3%. Meanwhile, 39 authors or 17.4% have published two single-authored articles.

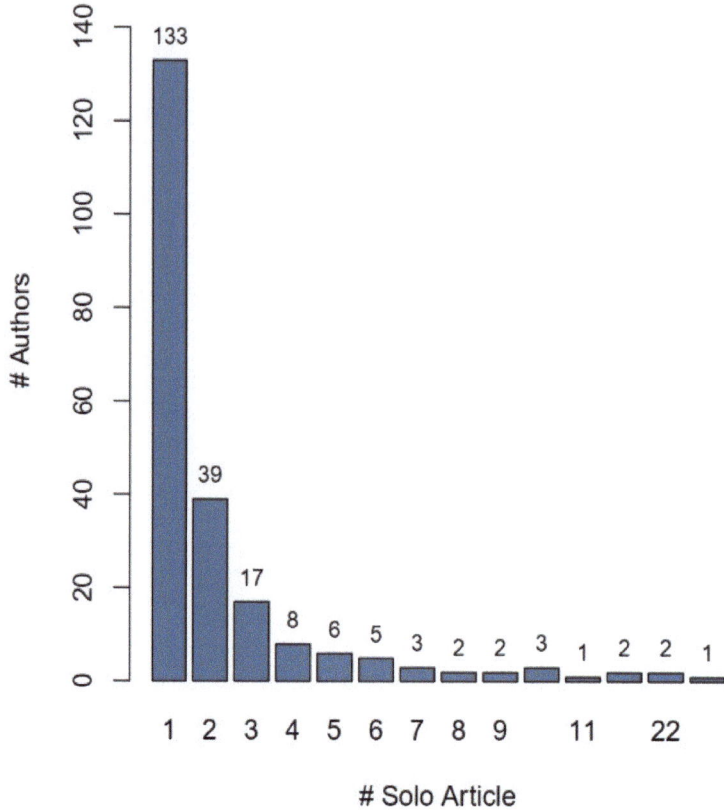

Figure 5.2. The number of authors with solo articles in 2008-2018.

The reasons for single authorship vary depending on a researcher's habit, the nature of certain fields, as well as the benefits for an author. As such, some fields may see more single authorship than others. For instance, our data on co-authorship in the field of Education in 2008-2018, as illustrated in Chapter 3, show that single-authorship is the dominant form of academic production for research on Education. Between 2008 and 2018, there were 132 articles, or 39% of the total, written and published by single authors. Similarly, papers in History during the 2011-2018 period were primarily single-authored, 5 articles or 62.5% of the total. By contrast, the field of Environment/Sustainability Science saw multiple-authorship dominate: the number of articles with two to five authors accounted for nearly 80% of the total 149 published papers on the topic during the ten years. In the following subsection, we will discuss more on the collaborative research patterns.

Gender issues and the rising achievement of female researchers

The list of top prolific authors has revealed one trend: male authors in Vietnam appear to lead over their female colleagues in the international publication landscape in SSH. Figure 5.3 confirms this observation and hints at another trend: male authors consistently accounted for above 60% of the total number of authors from 2008 to 2017, but this fraction dropped below this threshold to 56% for the first time in 2018. An explanation for this change is the sudden hike in the number of 'new' female authors in 2018, as shown in Figure 4.3.b. If this trend continues to hold, it is possible that the gender gap in Vietnamese SSH research will no longer persist.

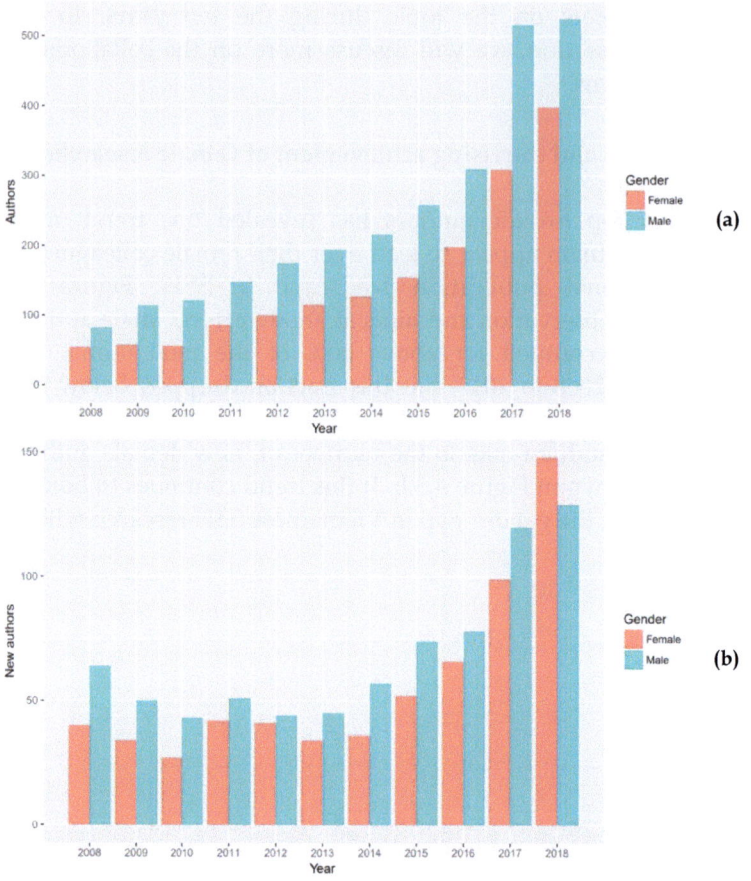

Figure 5.3. (a) The number of authors with published articles in 2008-2018, categorized by gender. **(b)** The number of new authors in SSH by year in 2008-2018, categorized by gender.

In terms of publication output, however, female authors appear to be lagging far behind their male colleagues, as shown in Table 5.3 More interestingly, although author Nguyen Ngoc Huong (coded vf.146) was in Table 5.1 for being the most prolific author in 2015, she did not make the list of the overall output over the ten-year period. Nguyen Ngoc Huong, however, is the sixth most prolific solo female author (with 7 articles) during the decade.

	Female authors	Article	Male authors	Article
1	(vf.294)Tran Thi Ly	45	(vm.828)Tran Xuan Bach	98
2	(vf.842)Le Thi Huong	31	(vm.16)Luu Trong Tuan	75
3	(vf.37)Vuong Thu Trang	25	(vm.4)Nguyen Viet Cuong	62
4	(vf.582)Kim Bao Giang	22	(vm.581)Hoang Van Minh	60
5	(vf.401)Tran Thu Ha	22	(vm.3)Vuong Quan Hoang	59
6	(vf.470)Phan Le Ha	20	(vm.833)Nguyen Hoang Long	51
7	(vf.204)Bui Thanh Huong	18	(vm.402)Tran Duc Thach	50
8	(vf.122)Le Thai Ha	18	(vm.18)Vo Xuan Vinh	48
9	(vf.910)Nguyen Thi Lan Huong	18	(vm.439)Ngo Viet Liem	37
10	(vf.213)Nguyen Thi Thuy Minh	18	(vm.854)Nguyen Trung Thanh	37

Table 5.3. The publication output of the top ten female and male authors, 2008-2018.

Recall Figure 3.3. in Chapter 3 on the publication differences across research fields by gender between 2008 and 2018: we have noted that the majority of female authors have published articles in the fields of Health Care, Education, Sociology, and Economics. The list of top female authors in Table 4.3 confirms the heavy concentration of leading female authors in the aforementioned four disciplines.

Moving forward, it is important to note that, upon running a categorical data analysis on an old version of this dataset, we have not found any statistically significant gender differences in modern Vietnamese social sciences (Vuong et al., 2017). The conclusion carries an encouraging implication: women with marital status and parental responsibilities are no longer held back in their academic career as they used to be. In other words, the conditions are becoming more favorable for female researchers to become more productive.

Collaborative research

Scientific research, especially in the race for international publications, has long been known as a challenging and tumultuous task. For this task to be completed in a sustainable manner over a long period of time, rarely do scientific researchers work alone.

Our examination into the profiles of high-productivity authors has indeed pointed out the commonality of multiple authorships. During the documented ten years, there were 1,766 articles published by more than two authors, equivalent to 74.7% of the total published articles. Of the multiple-authored articles, those published by two authors took up 38%. Figure 5.4 illustrates the distribution of articles by the number of co-authors over the 2008-2018 period. The figure sheds light on the collaborative trend between two and four authors in a published article. One can conclude that social scientists in Vietnam have mostly collaborated in small groups during the ten years.

> "Doing research on your own is laborious because you have to do everything it takes to complete a study, including planning your ideas, constructing the theoretical framework, collecting and analyzing data, examining the results, drafting and writing up the manuscript. Such well-rounded and capable scientists are not everywhere. Therefore, scientists are better off working together to accentuate each one's strength. Particularly for Vietnamese SSH scientists who are not fluent in English and quantitative methodology, doing research in groups helps address the problem more effectively." *Dr. Le Quan, Vietnam National University Hanoi, Hanoi, Vietnam*

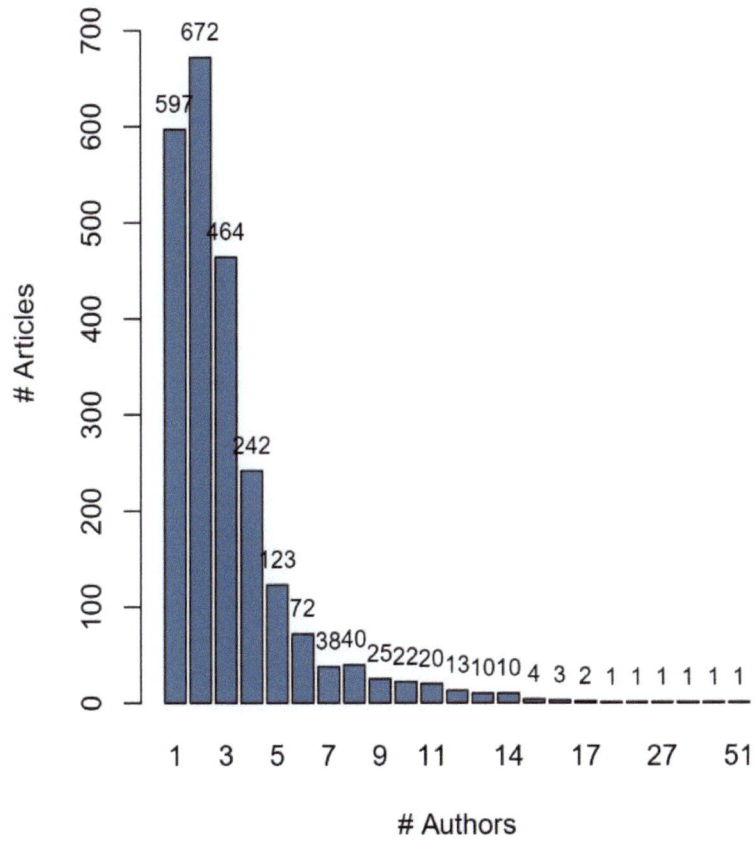

Figure 5.4. The number of articles in relation to the number of authors, 2008-2018.

At the same time, one cannot overlook the fact that there exists, albeit a very small number of, published articles that were authored by more than 14 researchers. In particular, 10 papers mark the presence of 14 authors/each, and the highest number of authors in one publication is 51.

Our data also allow an in-depth look into the transformation of the co-authorship patterns over time. Figure 5.5. shows that from 2008 to 2018, the number of single-authored articles rose 3.2-fold from 27 to 87 while that of multiple-authored jumped 4.9-fold from 58 to 286. Within multiple authorship, the number of articles with two and three authors account for a significant share: 67.2% in 2008 and 63.3% in 2018.

In Chapters 3 and 4, as part of our evaluation into the faster-growing fields in Vietnamese SSH, we have touched on the co-authorship trends in the fields of Economics (Figure 3.9.), Health Care (Figure 3.6.), and Education (Figure 4.3). In Economics and Education, we have observed the prevalence of published articles with two and three authors while in Health Care, the number of co-authors in published articles is higher by comparison. As we have noted in this chapter, the co-authorship patterns vary by field depending on the nature of each research project and the interest of the researchers involved.

> "A solo researcher will face many difficulties when entering into a new field, especially one that is different and difficult to access. If the author lacks skills and experiences, it would not be an easy task to write and publish in a good journal. When an author's skills are limited, without collaboration, he or she will not be able to learn from other deep experience or new knowledge. Therefore, collaboration in doing research and publishing is an advantage that solo authorship does not bring: specialization by parts will yield higher productivity when the group members are compatible, complementing each other in learning and exchanging techniques and ideas." *Dr. Tran Quang Tuyen, Hanoi National University, Vietnam*

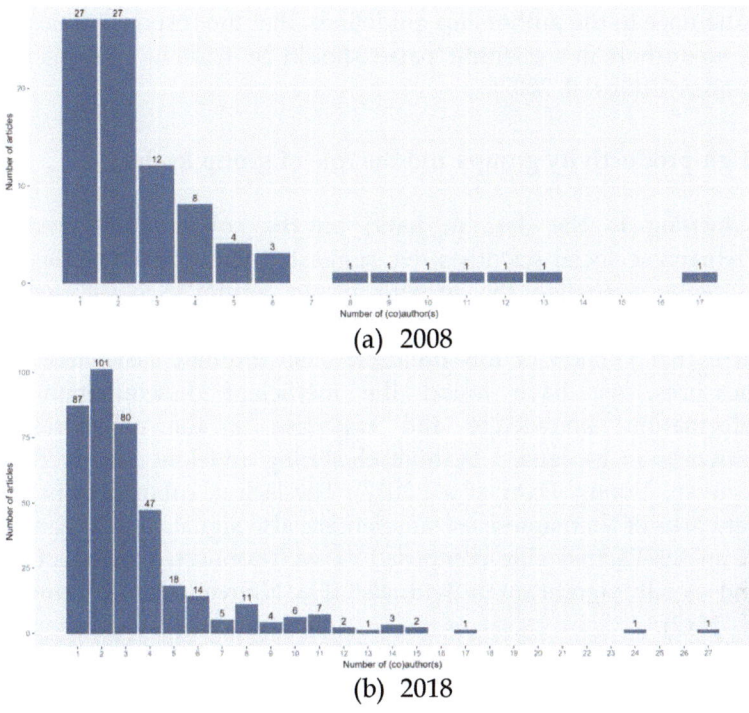

Figure 5.5. The number of articles with co-authorship by count of authors in **(a)** 2008 and **(b)** 2018.

The uptrend in multiple authorship in academic production is happening not just in Vietnam but also throughout the world (Nabout et al., 2015; Rath & Wohlrabe, 2016). For example, in the field of biology, decreases in the relative number of single-authored papers have been observed globally and attributed to the increase in the number of authors and number of citations, which suggests "the greater scientific impact of interdisciplinary research" (Nabout et al., 2015). Multiple authorship is indeed increasingly common across a wide array of disciplines due to the specialized skills required to complete more complex multidisciplinary research projects (Teixeira da Silva & Dobránszki, 2016). Given the rise of interdisciplinary research, collaboration in academic publication is likely to be even more prevalent, with different research teams growing more connected, and consequently, boosting the productivity overall. What is important to keep in mind is the constant call for ethical adherence to the authorship guidelines, that the responsibilities of all co-authors in a scientific paper should be made more explicitly (Nature Editorial, 2007).

High-productivity groups and the role of group leaders

Returning to the data at hand on the collaboration among Vietnamese social scientists, we suggested using network theory to better visualize the growth of an author's co-authorship network over the years. In one of our published works that used an earlier version of this database, also through basic network measures, we have found the inefficient dissemination of information, knowledge and expertise in the collaborative networks to be caused by high clustering and low density (Ho, Nguyen, Vuong, Dam, et al., 2017). The lack of robustness in the networks of Vietnamese social scientists also signals the "potential of an intellectual elite composed of well-connected, productive, and socially significant individuals" (Ho, Nguyen, Vuong, Dam, et al., 2017).

In the following images, we show an example of an author's network growing from 2008 to 2018. In Figure 5.6., the ratios are kept unchanged to reflect the changes in the network as well as its constituents, the size of each data point represents the number of published articles by that author. Figure 5.6. depicts the network structure at the end of 2010, 2014, and 2018, respectively. While the network did not look as dense in 2010, we could already see the collaborative links and possible group formation. Over the next few years, the shape of the network became increasingly complex: in end-2010, there were few data points, with limited linkages, and even the size of the data points is relatively small; by end-2014, this all changed. In Figure 5.6.b., the number of authors in vm.4's network has increased by more than three times, the number of linkages also surged and became clearer, with more arrows being bi-directional, i.e., the researchers got more opportunities to lead in their publications. The size of vm.4 also grew substantially, evidenced in the higher number of published articles over the four years. The 2010-2014 period is arguably the time for accumulation and development.

Thanks to the unchanged ratios in these images, the complexity of the evolving networks has retained their integrity. By end-2018, the size of the vm.4 data point has expanded significantly thanks to increases in publication output and strengthening leading role in his research network. The diversity of the network and the involvement of more foreign authors over the years have both contributed to the development of a strong collaborative team, such as in the case of (vm.4) Nguyen Viet Cuong. These factors are also crucial to the successful integration of Vietnamese SSH into the international publication world.

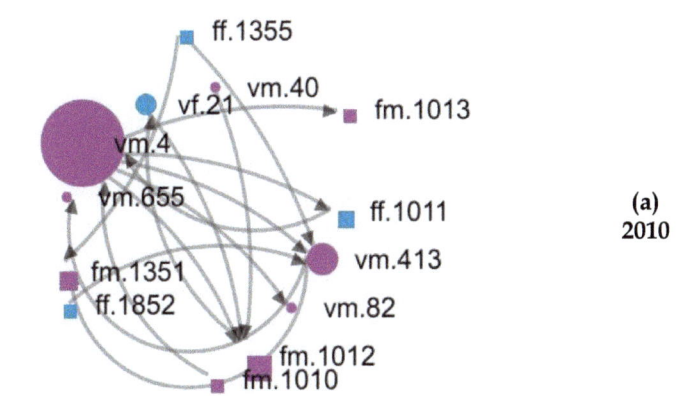

(a) 2010

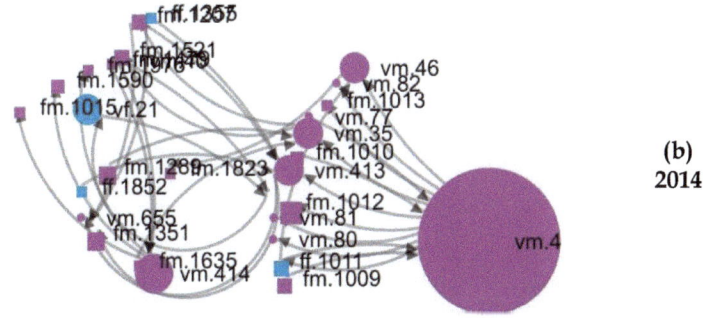

(b) 2014

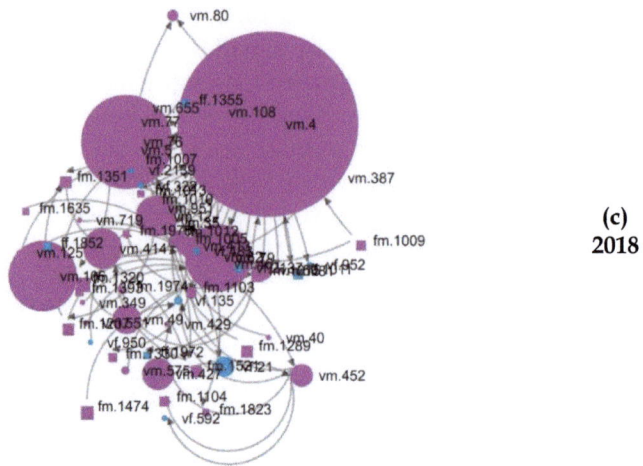

Figure 5.6. The network of (vm.4) Nguyen Viet Cuong in three years, 2010, 2014, and 2018.

The expansion of the network in Figure 5.6. suggests the importance of a leader in a research team. Based on our database, we were able to create Figure 5.7. below on the number of articles in relation to the number of lead authors. First, in terms of the total number, there were 618 authors who have led at least one article. Figure 5.7. shows clearly that the majority of authors have led between one and three articles. This finding is consistent with our previous observation that a large proportion of published articles were written in a team of two to three people. In particular, 347 authors have led one article, which fell to 107 authors for two articles and just 48 authors for 3 articles.

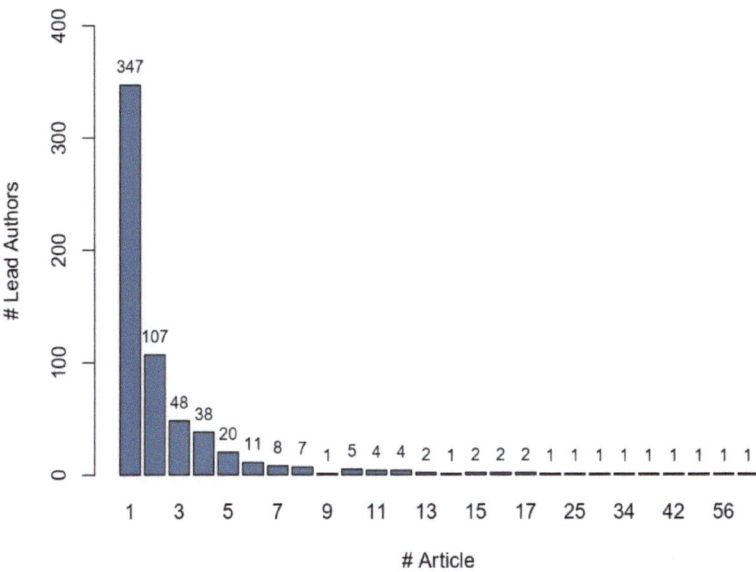

Figure 5.7. The number of lead authors in relation to the number of articles published, 2008-2018.

The rapid drop in the number of people leading as the number of articles rises is easy to understand. To be a lead author in many papers, one first needs to have written and published just as many papers. But as we have shown throughout this chapter, as the number of published articles increases, the number of authors involved would fall. Moreover, to take the leading position in a research project involves many challenging tasks, from preparation, implementation to project conclusion. Authors also seek to publish in more competitive journals, which have higher impact factors and CiteScore metrics – an ambition that poses even more challenges. Table 5.4. provides details into the authors who have published at least five articles in the lead author position, not counting their solo publications. Of the 50 authors on the list, 36 authors are male and 14 are female. Additionally, 16 authors have led above 10 articles while 21 authors, have led above 5 but under 10 articles, equivalent to respectively 2.58% and 3.39% of the total number of authors who have published as lead authors.

Author	Article	Author	Article
(vm.828) Tran Xuan Bach	54	(vf.146) Nguyen Ngoc Huong	7
(vm.581) Hoang Van Minh	26	(vm.459) Nham Phong Tuan	7
(vf.294) Tran Thi Ly	26	(vm.116) Tran Huu Tuan	7
(vm.3) Vuong Quan Hoang	26	(vm.2149) Vu Duy Kien	7
(vm.4.) Nguyen Viet Cuong	20	(vm.49) Do Quy Toan	6
(vm.5) Giang Thanh Long	15	(vf.275) Hoang Lan Anh	6
(vm.18) Vo Xuan Vinh	15	(vm.853) Hoang Viet Ngu	6
(vm.694) Truong Van Dao	14	(vm.427) Nguyen Le Hau	6
(vf.122) Le Thai Ha	13	(vf.2233) Nguyen Minh Ha	6
(vf.204) Bui Thanh Huong	12	(vf.213) Nguyen Thi Thuy Minh	6
(vm.106) Nguyen Dinh Tho	12	(vm.469) Phan Chi Anh	6
(vm.854) Nguyen Trung Thanh	12	(vf.27) Tran Thi Bich	6
(vm.402) Nguyen Duc Thach	12	(vf.214) Bui Thi Hong Minh	5
(vm.76) Tran Quang Tuyen	12	(vm.548) Ho Huu Loc	5
(vm.697) Nguyen The Ninh	11	(vm.432) Le Van Cuong	5
(vm.12) Nguyen Van Thang	11	(vm.16) Luu Trong Tuan	5
(vm.691) Huynh Viet Khai	9	(vm.438) Ngo Vi Dung	5
(vm.414) Dang Hoang Hai Anh	8	(vm.318) Nguyen Dang Lam	5
(vm.108) Doan Thanh Tinh	8	(vm.393) Nguyen Dong Phong	5
(vm.787) Ho Huy Tuu	8	(vf.238) Nguyen Le Mai	5
(vm.219)	8	(vf.240)	5

Le Trinh Hai (vm.439)	8	Nguyen Quynh Trang (vf.256)	5
Ngo Viet Liem (vf.904)	7	Nguyen Thi Hanh (vf.103)	5
Bui Thanh Binh		Nguyen Thi Minh Trang	
(vf.2081) Mai Thi Thanh Thai	7	(vm.134) Nguyen Tien Thong	5
(vm.833) Nguyen Hoang Long	7	(vm.452) Nguyen Van Tuan	5

Table 5.4. Top 50 authors who have led at least five articles (excluding solo publications), 2008-2018.

Social scientist network over time

The network of all social scientists in SSH, including their international collaborators, in the period 2008-2011 and 2008-2014, is presented in Figure 4.10. This figure is created using the open-source library 'd3.js' (Bostock, 2019). Figure 5.8 presents a force-directed network, with the underlying layout algorithm inspired by Tim Dwyer and Thomas Jakobsen (Dwyer, 2009). This algorithm allows users to arrange the position of the nodes (authors) in a network, without changing the underlying relationship among the nodes. Plotting the co-authorship network of Vietnamese researchers in SSH and their international colleagues using these techniques enable a macro-perspective of the growth of Vietnam's SSH in the last decade. In both earlier periods, the edges are still sparse, which allows both figures to be presented together. However, by 2018, the network has grown substantially, the density of the nodes and edges requires the period 2008-2018 to be presented alone in Figure 5.9. It is worth noting that, although the networks were generated based on different time frames, the scale is the same. Thus, one can compare and contrast the growth of the network of Vietnamese social scientists over time.

With regards to the spearheading of eminent researchers, when we compare all three figures, it is easy to recognize there are several clusters of authors with certain authors reside in the middle. The arrow in the figures represent the first-authorship, meaning when an author is the first author of a co-authoring paper, the arrow will go from he or she to other authors. In Figures 5.8a and 5.8b, there are noticeably fewer clusters of authors, compared to Figure 5.9.

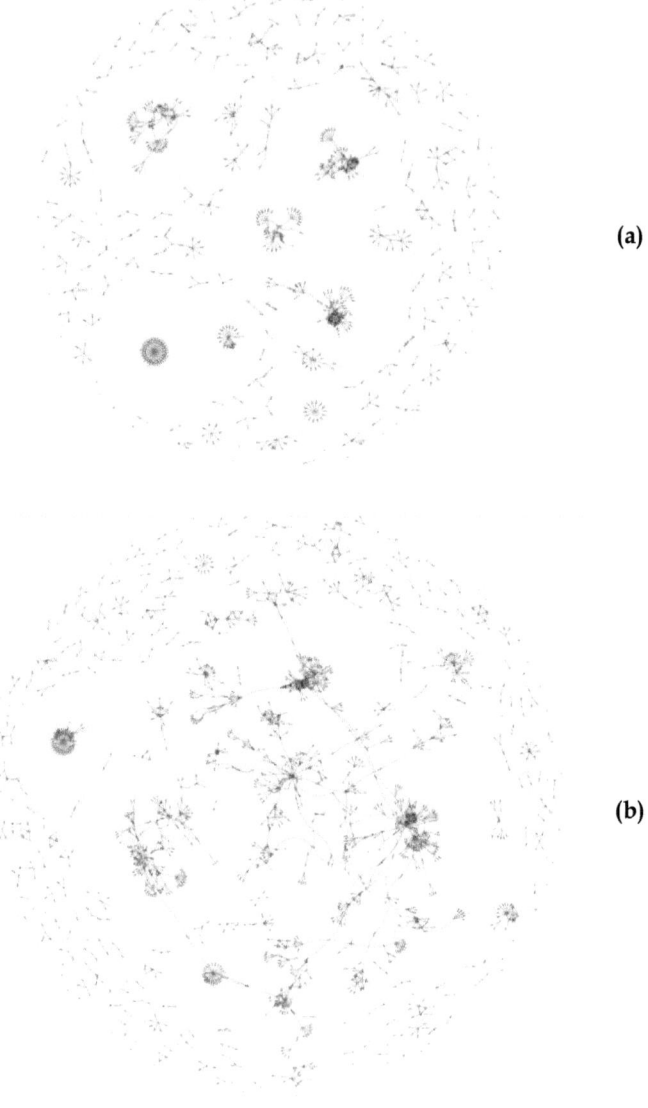

(a)

(b)

Figure 5.8. (a) A co-authorship network of all Vietnamese social scientists and their international collaborators in the period 2008-2011. (b) A co-authorship network of all Vietnamese social scientists and their international collaborators in the period 2008-2015.

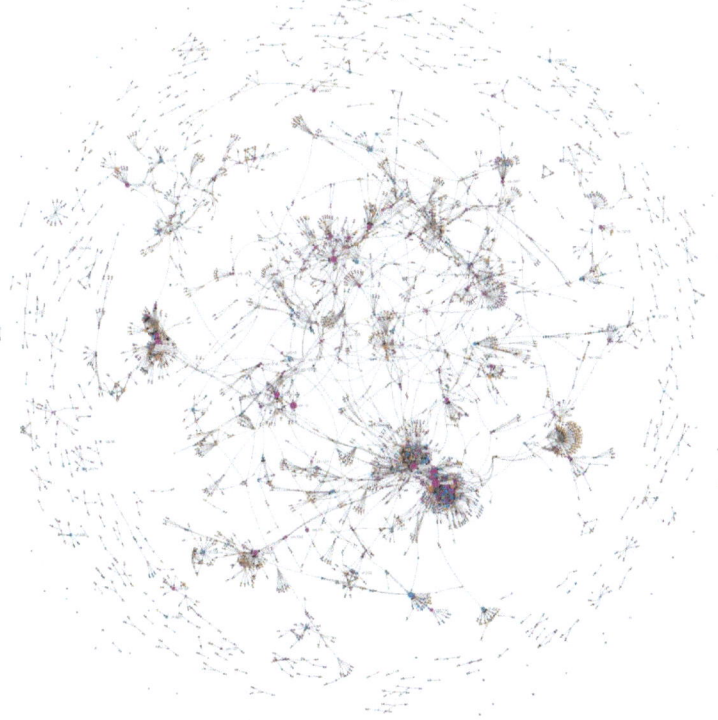

Figure 5.9. A co-authorship network of all Vietnamese social scientists from 2008-2018.

Another important point in observing the growth of Vietnamese network of social scientist in Figure 5.9 is that there are many noticeable purple nodes compared to blue or orange nodes. Purple is the color code for male Vietnamese researchers, blue is the color code for female researchers and orange is the code for international authors. As such, Figure 5.9 reveals visually the influence of eminent male researchers presented in table 5.1.

The network analysis technique used in this section has previously been used in two publications: Ho, Nguyen, Vuong, Dam, et al. (2017) presents the preliminary results of analyzing the co-authorship networks of Vietnamese researchers in SSH, while Ho, Nguyen, Vuong, and Vuong (2017) explores the concept of sustainable co-authorship network by calculating the distance from the members with highest productivity to other members for 20 groups of Vietnamese co-authors. The research studies point out the important role of those researchers with leadership and connections to form sustainable collaborating groups. Moreover, they raise a warning on the overreliance on these high-performing researchers, suggesting it is important for each co-authoring group to make the productivity of any member more compatible with the leader(s) in the group.

Social network analysis has been widely applied all over the world due to the dramatic improvement of computing power. In Vietnam, this field has only begun to thrive, which leaves much more valuable findings for future studies. One is intrigued to test the well-known "small world" property in social network of scientists (Newman, 2001), or whether scientists doing qualitative research are prone to collaborate with quantitative researchers (Moody, 2004), or whether highly-cited scientists would be more likely to collaborate with people in the same field (Ding, 2011). Further studies in these directions would reveal much more about the extent to which the high-productivity researchers are shaping the academic community in Vietnam, which will be especially helpful to prevent failures of policy-making and policy-implementation in such a transitioning environment (Vuong, 2018a, 2018b). It would also be beneficial to utilize various statistical approaches that would further tap into the potential of network data, such as Bayesian techniques. A suggestion would be to manipulate our SSHPA database using Bayesian tools in R (La & Vuong 2019; Vuong et al. 2019).

References

Bostock, M. (2019). Data-driven documents. *D3js.* Retrieved from https://d3js.org/

Ding, Y. (2011). Scientific collaboration and endorsement: Network analysis of coauthorship and citation networks. *Journal of Informetrics, 5*(1), 187-203.

Dwyer, T. (2009). Scalable, Versatile and Simple Constrained Graph Layout. *Computer Graphics Forum, 28*(3), 991-998. doi:10.1111/j.1467-8659.2009.01449.x

Ho, M.-T., Nguyen, H.-K. T., Vuong, T.-T., & Vuong, Q.-H. (2017). On the Sustainability of Co-Authoring Behaviors in Vietnamese Social Sciences: A Preliminary Analysis of Network Data. *Sustainability, 9*(11). doi:10.3390/su9112142

Ho, M.-T., Nguyen, V.-H. T., Vuong, T.-T., Dam, Q.-M., Pham, H.-H., & Vuong, Q.-H. (2017). Exploring Vietnamese co-authorship patterns in social sciences with basic network measures of 2008-2017 Scopus data. *F1000Research, 6*, 1559.

La, V.P, & Vuong, Q.H. (2019). bayesvl: Visually Learning the Graphical Structure of Bayesian Networks and Performing MCMC with 'Stan'. *The Comprehensive R Archive Network (CRAN)*: <https://cran.r-project.org/web/packages/bayesvl/index.html>; version 0.8.5 (August 16, 2019).

Moody, J. (2004). The structure of a social science collaboration network: Disciplinary cohesion from 1963 to 1999. *American Sociological Review, 69*(2), 213-238.

Nabout, J. C., Parreira, M. R., Teresa, F. B., Carneiro, F. M., da Cunha, H. F., de Souza Ondei, L., . . . Soares, T. N. (2015). Publish (in a group) or perish (alone): the trend from single- to multi-authorship in biological papers. *Scientometrics, 102*(1), 357-364. doi:10.1007/s11192-014-1385-5

Nature Editorial. (2007). Who is accountable? *Nature, 450*, 1. doi:10.1038/450001a

Newman, M. E. (2001). Scientific collaboration networks. I. Network construction and fundamental results. *Physical Review E, 64*(1), 016131.

Rath, K., & Wohlrabe, K. (2016). Recent trends in co-authorship in economics: evidence from RePEc. *Applied Economics Letters, 23*(12), 897-902. doi:10.1080/13504851.2015.1119783

Teixeira da Silva, J. A., & Dobránszki, J. (2016). Multiple authorship in scientific manuscripts: Ethical challenges, ghost and guest/gift authorship, and the cultural/disciplinary perspective. *Science and Engineering Ethics, 22*(5), 1457-1472. doi:10.1007/s11948-015-9716-3

Vuong, Q.-H. (2018a). "How did researchers get it so wrong?" The acute problem of plagiarism in Vietnamese social sciences and humanities. *European Science Editing, 44*(3), 56-58.

Vuong, Q.-H. (2018b). The (ir)rational consideration of the cost of science in transition economies. *Nature Human Behaviour, 2*(1), 5-5. doi:10.1038/s41562-017-0281-4

Vuong, Q.-H., Ho, M.-T., Vuong, T.-T., Napier, N. K., Pham, H.-H., & Nguyen, V.-H. T. (2017). Gender, age, research experience, leading role and academic productivity of Vietnamese researchers in the social sciences and humanities: exploring a 2008-2017 Scopus dataset. *European Science Editing, 43*(3), 51-55.

Vuong, Q.H. & La V.P. (2019). BayesVL package for Bayesian statistical analyses in R. *Github*: <https://github.com/sshpa/bayesvl>; V0.8.4.

Chapter 6
The question of quality
*Phuong-Thao T. Trinh, Thu-Hien T. Le,
Thu-Trang Vuong, Phuong-Hanh Hoang*

Previous chapters in this book have discussed the quantity aspect of research on social sciences and humanities (SSH) in Vietnam. We have touched on the national productivity, the rise of scientific publications, and the ways Vietnamese researchers adapt to the changes. This chapter now turns to the quality aspect of research publications. In order to achieve the outcome of high-quality publications, there has to be a synthesis of at least three elements: (i) an institutional push, whether that be professional or financial incentives, state or non-state resources, (ii) the application of international standards, such as indexed peer-reviewed journals, replicable and reproducible data and research projects, and openly accessible, and (iii) adherence to research ethics. The framework in Figure 6.1 is used to examine the issue of quality in Vietnam's SSH research.

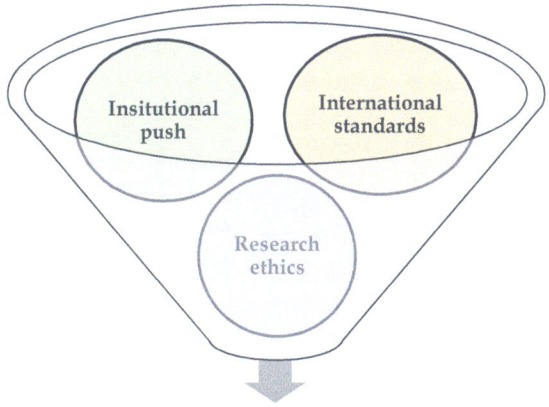

Quality publications

Figure 6.1. Three fundamental elements for producing quality publications

The institutional factor

In popular culture, scientists are often portrayed as eccentric and working days and nights in the basement. It is a stereotypical and largely inaccurate portrayal. One thing is true, though, that scientists do spend a lot of time working. A 2016 survey from Nature shows that 38% of surveyed early-career researchers work more than 60 hours/week, while 9% of all researchers work more than 80 hours (Woolston, 2016). Why do scientists need to work that hard? David Labaree compares academics with Easter egg hunters, whose career is purposely aimed for achievements: fellowship, editorship, managerial roles, member of committee, awards, and publications in prestige journals (Labaree, 2018). Yet, scientists, especially social scientists, do not conduct research in a vacuum—not only are the subjects of their research concerned with the society, their relationships with society also determine many aspects of their works. Throughout this book, we have noted the expansion of collaborative research networks within and beyond Vietnam. These networks are sustained thanks to the tireless efforts of researchers at home and overseas as well as to the institutional support. Three types of institution play an important role in this process.

> "High-level scientific research certainly does not come cheap. Under the current economic condition in Vietnam, it is probably not possible to invest in all fields. There should be a national independent committee that specializes in identifying scientific fields that are worthy of ambitious investment. For example, Taiwan's semiconductor technology provides a valuable lesson. If we have one or two fields that reach the "top," it is better than having all fields being mediocre. Moreover, when the budget is limited, the efficiency of funding is critical. Unfair competition in accessing research funding is the factor we should be worried the most about at the present." *Dr. Tran Dinh Phong, University of Science and Technology of Hanoi, Vietnam*

First, the state has to initiate the promotion of science and scientific value through concrete actions, such as measurable policies and transparent investment. There are even state-led movements to commercialize academic advances derived from highly-successful research projects. In developed countries such as the United States or the United Kingdom, state-funded research projects have yielded a stable output of such products (Williams, 2005).

Second, non-state actors should also be encouraged to take on more responsibilities toward the national research and development (R&D) scene. Cases from developed countries once again highlight how the private sector can make meaningful contributions to science through various means. Notable examples include the gigantic sponsorship from the Bill & Melinda Gates Foundation or the initiatives of Ernest Solvay to pull together the top-notch experts for discussions about the most critical topics of all times. Aside from financial support, contributions could also be the devotion of time and efforts such as the case of Elon Musk leading numerous crucial projects by Tesla, Hyperloop, and SpaceX. Similarly, in Japan, there is a proliferation of academic start-ups and huge investment into this area (Ichiko, 2006). According to research by Nikkei Inc., in the fiscal year of 2017, approximately 40% of major Japanese corporations had spent a combined amount of USD107 billion on R&D, which marks a record-breaking surge of 5.7% year-on-year (Nikkei, 2017). Non-state investments in R&D, even if they are driven by profitability concerns, in this sense can still create a ripple effect across society—scientists are motivated to work, quality products are created, and society members get to reap the benefits.

Third, higher education institutions themselves have to create the right environment and incentives to facilitate the work of researchers. An example that best illustrates this point is the case of China where a large amount of state and non-state money has been poured into basic science. It is estimated that investment for scientific research in China can jump by three-fold from 2010 to reach USD34.5 billion in 2020 (Xin, 2016). On average, co-authoring in a *Nature* or *Science* paper could bring Chinese scientists a prize of USD44,000 each in cash (Ball, 2018). Non-financial investment and support for science development in China are offered in the form of tenure tracks and/or overseas training opportunities to lift labor productivity in research. It is clear, however, that the superstars from prestigious institutions would have more chances, and indeed, researchers from big economies will have more opportunities than their colleagues in the smaller economies.

Using the above lens to look at Vietnam, we can see the growing presence of all three types of institution. Here, the private business sector and the educational establishments are grouped together as non-state actors for the purpose of examination.

State actors
Among the baby steps taken by the Vietnamese government to boost scientific productivity was the reform made by the National Foundation for Science and Technology Development of Vietnam (NAFOSTED). Accordingly, projects that seek NAFOSTED grants must meet the minimum requirement of two to three articles published in international indexed journals. More recently, in April 2017, Circular 08/2017/TT-BGDDT issued by the Ministry of Education and Training set a higher standard for PhD candidates in terms of academic publishing. As such, a PhD candidate can defend his/her thesis only when the research result is published internationally in peer-reviewed or ISI/Scopus-indexed journals or conferences.

The conditions have pushed the academic sphere in Vietnam toward an inevitable change, particularly for SSH, where standards were already outdated. These requirements are not only indispensable for research fellows and mentors; scholars are also required to fulfill the same criteria of publication count to be eligible for project applications and research grants. While the new standards sparked controversy regarding its legitimacy, especially the pertinence of the criteria, one could not deny that the regulation has brought forth awareness for scientific credentials and international qualifications. As a more concrete result, the reform, though initially thought of as only of administrative order, has offered a set of criteria for academics and institutions alike to gauge their own merits, productivity and competitiveness, not only among themselves but also in an international context.

The criteria, in fact, have started to raise the bar for the quality of scientific production in Vietnam by creating competition between Vietnamese universities. Universities are now ranked based on scientific production – namely, the number of publications affiliated with them. They in turn wanted to improve productivity to climb the ranking table. To do this, there are various possible strategies. One of those is to set standards: for example, a university in Hanoi only considers scholars with over 40 publications in ISI/Scopus for tenure tracks. Another strategy is to offer monetary recompense for each publication that a researcher affiliated to them authored (Vuong, 2019).

This has truly had an effect on scientists, encouraging them to produce more all while making them aware of the – both global and local – race in quality.

Non-state actors
Just as universities in China, a growing number of Vietnamese universities have begun to offer monetary rewards for international publications, only far lower in value. On average, compensations given out by universities to affiliated scientists for international publication range from USD1,000 to USD2,000 per article/book. Notably, as of 2017, an ISI/Scopus indexed article, stated as the highest tier of award, could earn the author a bonus of USD10,000 if said author was affiliated to the University of Social Sciences and Humanities, Vietnam National University Hanoi (Vuong, 2019). Besides universities, state organizations also issue policies to promote international research publication, mainly supporting young scientists who are not affiliated with public academic institutions. For example, research conducted in Vietnam could be filed for grants covering the incurred implementation and labor costs as well as article processing charge (APC) by NAFOSTED (NAFOSTED, 2019).

Increased support and investment have resulted in significant growth of publications from Vietnam (Manh, 2015; T. V. Nguyen, Ho-Le, & Le, 2017), but in comparison with ASEAN member states, Vietnam remains far behind (T. V. Nguyen & Pham, 2011). However, within the field of SSH, which previous chapters in this book have thoroughly discussed, the overview picture offers a significant development and change.

International standards
Getting indexed in reputable databases

Along with the aforementioned regulation on qualifications for research fellows and doctorate mentors, NAFOSTED has published a list of reputable international journals for reference. Basically, if an author had published articles, but these works do not figure in journals on this list, then those articles would not count. In order to dress up this official list, the databases of ISI Web of Science and Scopus – the two big names in scientific indexing – have been used.

The Web of Science (formerly Web of Knowledge) database is a product of the Institute for Scientific Information (ISI), founded by Eugene Garfield. Besides the Web of Science, ISI also owns other highly influential tools in scientific productivity assessment, such as the Journal Citation Reports – which tracks the Journal Impact Factor (JIF) of all indexed journals and updates yearly in the last week of June. In 1992, ISI was bought and developed by Thompson Reuters and, in 2016, transferred to Clarivate Analytics.

In the academic community, referring to ISI is equal to referring to the Web of Science (WoS). ISI has so far indexed about 15,000 journals, 50,000 academic book titles and about 160,000 conference proceedings in various fields. The ISI Web of Science system also provides other indexing services, the most important being the Core Collection of the most important sub-databases, as follows:

- Science Citation Index (SCI);
- Expanded (SCIE);
- Conference Proceedings Citation Index (CPCI);
- Social Science Citation Index (SSCI);
- Arts & Humanities Citation Index (AHCI);
- Book Citation Index (BCI);
- Emerging Sources Citation Index (ESCI).

ISI WoS held the monopoly of leading scientific databases until 2004, when Scopus was born under Elsevier's wing and became a proper counterweight. Scopus indexes approximately 21,500 journals, 131,000 book titles, over 7.5 million conference proceedings. The Scopus database also has its own measure of impact based on citations called CiteScore, in competition with the JIF. It should be noted that Elsevier is a large publishing house, which means that the potentials of Scopus lie in the fact that its database is much more sensitive to new developments in academic publishing than WoS, which only specializes in indexing and data recording. As Scopus builds up its footprint as a true giant in the realm of scientific indexing, it has become a reliable source of reference on scientific investment in the official reports by many world powers such as the United States, Russia, China, Spain, France, the United Kingdom, and Belgium, etc. Renowned rankings such as Times Higher Education or QS World University Ranking also uses Scopus and SciVal algorithms to calculate the most important scores: productivity, effectivity and academic reputation.

Striving for higher JIF, CiteScore

The two largest scientific publication databases in the world, WoS and Scopus, have each developed their own indicator of academic reach: Journal Impact Factor and CiteScore, respectively. The Journal Impact Factor was created, along with the Web of Science, by Eugene Garfield. Since then, indexing systems and impact factors have grown to become one of the most important criteria in expert assessments of the influence of journals.

The Journal Impact Factor of a scientific journal is calculated as follows: total number of citations in a year (denoted year t) of all articles published from two years back (year t-1 and year t-2) divided by the total number of articles published from two years back. Every June, the Impact Factor is published in Journal Citation Reports (JCR), which has for a long time garnered attention from the entire academic world. A particular point to note is that JCR contain a list of all journals publishing their JIF for the first time. It often happens that journals often receive large influx of manuscripts after their first publication of JIF. Similarly, journals that have a boost in JIF according to JCR would also see the number as well as quality of manuscripts skyrocket. Though few may dare to admit, the truth is that most journals would pride on a slim acceptance rate, which could only be enhanced with a high number of manuscripts sent to them. In fact, the more manuscripts they receive, the more they get to pick and choose for solid papers. Given the effect of JIF on the number of received manuscripts as detailed above, it is no wonder that publishers would prefer their journals to grow in JIF. This growth would create a positive feedback loop, a virtuous circle of: a considerable number of manuscripts would lead to stronger publications, therefore higher impact and subsequently JIF. This, in turn, would bring in even more, higher quality manuscripts.

Scopus released CiteScore in December 2016, which quickly gained attention due to Scopus' existing influence. The method of calculation for CiteScore is similar to that of JIF; except that the data used for computing stretch back 3 years rather than 2. Scopus also produces reports the CiteScore points of journals every May. One may even speculate that Scopus has done this on purpose, in order for their annual reports to be released before the traditional JCR of Web of Science every year. A feature unique to CiteScore is that one can observe monthly fluctuations of the indication using CiteScore Tracker, without having to wait until May.

CiteScore is used freely among journals indexed by Scopus as long as there are sufficient data, whereas the Journal Impact Factor is only available for journals under SCIE and SSCI. Other Web of Science indexes, such as AHCI or ESCI, despite being just as prestigious, do not provide their journals with a JIF. Consultation of the CiteScore indicator is also free of charge (at a basic level), in contrast to the paid services of Web of Science.

In addition to JIF and CiteScore, there exists a multitude of other indicators that are country- or region-specific, such as C-SSCI of China, T-SSCI of Taiwan, or ACI of ASEAN, etc. They typically don't "count" as much as the classifications made by the giants ISI and Scopus. It should also be mentioned that highly prestigious publishers or systems of journals might become their own type of indexing. *Nature* and *Science*, for example, consider being published in their journals as a type of "indexing" in itself. *Nature* also has its own Nature Index and publishes its own reports, equally as looked forward to as those of the JIF and CiteScore. The only difference: Nature Index has a very restricted coverage and is considered by academics to be a sort of Pantheon.

The reference of impact factors as a means to measure quality of research is much controversial. Most of the opposers argue that quality assessment of research based on JIF/CiteScore of where it comes out is indeed invalid since this index is an average. The way this figure is computed means that it could be lifted by some exceptionally highly cited papers and does not represent the citation count of most other articles in that journal. It is, therefore, unreasonable to deem a research good quality solely on the basis of its journal statistics.

Likewise, impact factors are relative and thus are not adequate for use as a general reference framework of comparison. For example, in the discipline of philosophy, the highest CiteScore that could be found is 2.59 (*Journal of Political Philosophy*); however, in the field of human resource management and organizational behavior, the indicator could go up to 11.96 (*Academy of Management Annals*). This may in fact be explained by the varying degrees of openness across disciplines. Concretely speaking, fields such as philosophy or culture studies would have a harder time getting citations compared to "hot" subjects such as economics or finances.

> "To select a suitable journal to submit one's article is an important task but is equally difficult for those who lack experience. [...] The average rejection rate in social sciences is 70%, i.e. only three articles are accepted out of ten submissions, with the rejection rate in some journals as high as 90%. If an author wants to submit their work to a journal with a high impact factor (JIF), they must modestly and seriously evaluate the research work to see if it would meet the requirements of the journal. Otherwise, it could be a waste of time." Dr. Le Van Canh, Vietnam National University Hanoi, Hanoi, Vietnam

Entering the 1% of the academic world

The hunt for Easter egg requires a perpetual journey of raising the standard. As a PhD candidate, two peer-reviewed articles are enough, but growing in academia will always ask for more publications with better quality. Thus, the big names, such as *Nature, Science,* or *PNAS*, become the ultimate Easter eggs. These over 100-year-old journals, which are homes of the biggest scientific break-throughs in the history of mankind, make up the top 1% of the academic publishing world for their superb indices of impact level.

Having their research published in top-tier journals, whose acceptance rates are often below 5%, could be a career boost opportunity to most scientists. In fact, a *Nature* or *Science* paper is considered equivalent to membership grant of an elite club with privileges of speech invitations, research funds, tenure positions or cash rewards. It is even more so in developing countries such as China or India where getting a paper into the leading titles means straight salary increase and bonus since it is the ranking of the journal, not necessarily the quality of the work itself, that concerns most people (Reich, 2013).

Meanwhile, in Vietnam, the progress is somewhat behind when the standards are limited at minimum level of ISI/Scopus indexed journals for eligibility to research funding or academic titles. This could be in part attributed to the various hardships that emergent countries such as Vietnam have to face as they catch up to the international academic sphere (Vuong 2019a). However, it can be seen that the quality race in this emerging market has kicked off with the rise of pioneer academics having research of JIF ≥ 5 in the second half of the 10-year period (Table 1). It will not be long until JIF/CiteScore and top-tier titles become widely known or even the new legitimate standards, as it is unlikely for Vietnam to stay out of the global game.

Articles	Authors	Journals
The (ir)rational consideration of the cost of science in transition economies	(Vuong, 2018b)	*Nature Human Behaviour*
Policy uncertainty, derivatives use, and firm-level FDI	(Q. Nguyen, Kim, & Papanastassiou, 2018)	*Journal of International Business Studies*
Eco-efficiency analysis of sustainability-certified coffee production in Vietnam	(T. Q. Ho, Hoang, Wilson, & Nguyen, 2018)	*Journal of Cleaner Production*
Regional research priorities in brain and nervous system disorders	(Ravindranath et al., 2015)	*Nature*
Postpartum change in common mental disorders among rural Vietnamese women: Incidence, recovery and risk and protective factors	(T. T. Nguyen et al., 2015)	*British Journal of Psychiatry*
Effect of Facilitation of Local Maternal-and-Newborn Stakeholder Groups on Neonatal Mortality: Cluster-Randomized Controlled Trial	(Persson et al., 2013)	*PLOS Medicine*

The Effect of Intermittent Antenatal Iron Supplementation on Maternal and Infant Outcomes in Rural Viet Nam: A Cluster Randomised Trial	(Hanieh et al., 2013)	*PLOS Medicine*
Cohort Profile: The Young Lives Study	(Barnett et al., 2013)	*International Journal of Epidemiology*
Trends, drivers and impacts of changes in swidden cultivation in tropical forest-agriculture frontiers: A global assessment	(van Vliet et al., 2012)	*Global Environmental Change*
B_{MEY} as a Fisheries Management Target	(Grafton, Kompas, Che, Chu, & Hilborn, 2012)	*Fish and Fisheries*

Table 6.1. Top ten SSH publications with highest JIF in Vietnam from 2008 to 2018

Research practices and ethics

It is foreseeable that without established regulations and measures to improve the assessment of research quality, Vietnam would undoubtedly fall into the same trap of brand name chasing as mentioned earlier. As a latecomer to the market with mostly inexperienced researchers, Vietnam needs to find ways to stimulate academic development in a professional manner, and keep an appropriate attitude in these aspirations (Vuong 2019b). While too much focus on top-notch journals might discourage young researchers from pursuing the academic pathway, successful publication in some less competitive outlets with more positive peer-review experience would definitely be a pleasant start for their later, more ambitious goals (Arvan, 2016).

Even though JIF/CiteScores and journal acceptance rates can provide a quick capture of the significance of the research at some point (Tregoning, 2018), they are by no means sufficient and comprehensive criteria for quality evaluation of academic works (Wouters et al., 2019). It is the validity of research methods and reliability of produced results that are fundamental when examining the soundness of a study. In fact, for sustainable and realistic advancement of research quality, the country needs to develop mechanisms that support and stimulate quality-wise inspection of publication through transparency of data collection and analysis as well as replication of research findings. Here, we discuss two topics that could improve the quality of research publications: (i) the adoption of the Open Access movement, and (ii) the promotion of science communications.

> "In the current social conditions of Vietnam, I think that the difficulty of ensuring the reliability of data might result from the negligence of Vietnamese scientists in organizing data as well as making the data accessible for peer-review and public replication after being published. Providing open access to data is now a common practice in leading Economics journals, so I believe it will be a scientific trend in the future." *Dr. Pham Si Cong, Deakin University, Victoria, Australia*

> "I think that it is necessary to invest in data-generating activities, for example, the access to databases of the General Statistics Office, original databases of state-level and ministry-level projects, and international databases." *Dr. Tran Van Kham, University of Social Sciences and Humanities, Hanoi, Vietnam.*

To be replicable, reproducible, and accessible

While debates surrounding impact factor have not yet resolved, SSH research worldwide has to face the 'replication crisis' (Loken & Gelman, 2017). Due to a high rate of replication failures, the scientific community has raised concerns about the validity and reliability of results in SSH studies. As reproducibility has emerged as a core quality issue, the demand for transparency and open access of data is growing and gradually transforming the publication industry. The drive behind the open access movement, and more general, Open Science, is to facilitate replication and triangulation of findings from different places all over the world, which helps save researchers from time, efforts and costs of doing the same works all over due to lack of access to similar datasets and study projects.

In September 2018, Robert-Jan Smits proposed a radical change for science: Everything has to be open (Else, 2018). Plan S immediately receives supports in Europe, and later the United States, China, and influential funders. Even though Open Access movement is slow in gaining attention, Plan S is definitely the game changer. With the support and joining of national, international and private funding agencies such as Welcome Trust and the Bill & Melinda Gates Foundation into the Open Access Coalition, all scientific publications subsidized by 13 National Funding Agencies and 4 non-profit funding organizations will have to become freely accessible since January 1, 2020.

Publishers have also made movements to adhere to core principles of Plan S that seek to retain authors' copyrights and secure their ability to publish openly regardless of financial capacity. However, there needs to be ample time for changes to take place comprehensively. Some journals have switched to the hybrid model of open access which offers a mix of openly accessible articles whose APC is paid by authors or funding agencies and restricted publications that requires subscription fees. Despite its signaling a step forward to the OA movement, the model faces harsh criticisms for making authors and readers shoulder the financial burden. In general, even though arguments regarding hybrid open access journals, fair APC and timing have not been settled, many of the journals have agreed on a possible renovation of mechanism in order to better serve the public and stimulate the dissemination of research results.

Compared to the hotly debated situation worldwide, the publication scenario in Vietnam is rather isolated and outdated. Except for a very limited number of journals (all in the field of natural sciences) indexed in the Directory of Open Access

Journals, almost all Vietnamese academic journals resemble the Western model in the old days, which can be characterized by the prevalence of paper-based, restricted access and an anonymous peer-review process. The key words Open Access and Open Science are rarely discussed or even heard of by most researchers in Vietnam. In the absence of established criteria for quality control, it is critical for the mechanism of publication in such an emerging context as Vietnam to stay as open and responsive to supervision and feedback from expert scientists as possible. It is only through open discussions and peer-to-peer challenging that awareness of and concerns for authentic quality are raised, conditioning for a clearly defined system of criteria and standards to measure and optimize the quality threshold of Vietnamese research. Vietnam could see its future in the case of China where the Government is proactive in constructing clear definitions and criteria for the supervision of scientific research and publication, based on which low-quality journals are blacklisted when applying for funding and grants (Jia, 2018).

Besides the OA movement, Open Science also initiates changes addressing other aspects of the publication industry. For example, transparent peer-review processes that makes reviewers take responsibility for their feedbacks and arguments by revelation of identity helps improve the quality of peer review and publication in general. In addition, the development of pre-registration platforms facilitates the transfer of research findings, data, computer codes, as well as experiment procedures and protocols. The preprint culture also helps address ethical issues such as plagiarism by easing and shortening the process of registering ownership over academic outputs.

In developing countries where scientific practices are not as established as in Western societies, integrity is an alarming issue topped up by the lack of clear regulations of quality inspection and intellectual property. Recently, China has pioneered to approve penalties of scientific misconduct cases. Under the controversial social credit system, Chinese scientists who violate the codes of conduct in scientific research will be restricted from bank loan access, job application and business foundation and operation (Cyranoski, 2018).

Intellectual ownership and codes of conduct in scientific research are rather novel concepts to most Vietnamese people. The prevalence of misconduct incidents in Vietnam could be attributed to the lack of social awareness and the vagueness and incoherence of legal regulation concerning this issue (Vuong, 2018a). The consequence is often violators easily getting away unpunished while victims appeal in vain. Together with measures to improve knowledge and awareness of research ethics and integrity, promoting the use of open online resources and platforms is expected to help improve transparency of system and liberate the research industry in Vietnam from mistreats and misconducts.

To be understandable: the role of science communications
What is the ultimate goal of scientific development in Vietnam? As a member of the public, and also as a researcher, we cannot content ourselves with simply running after high numbers without pondering over what we truly hope to achieve beyond academic credentials. Much of the above discussion in this chapter has inferred a need for renovation of the inefficient organization and mechanisms currently in place in Vietnam. In fact, the much-needed revolution in the Vietnamese culture of debate and discourse faces a big obstacle among others: the lack of awareness of the general public about the standards of formal knowledge and scientific evidence, which necessitates an understanding of significance of high-quality scientific research.

To many Vietnamese people, science stays distant from their daily life. First, this is because the practice of science (i.e. investigating matters using the scientific method; looking for evidence in academic literature to back up claims; etc.) is not deeply rooted in Vietnam. This is reflected in the Vietnamese language with more than half of the abstract vocabulary that whose semantic fields concern cognition, social and political relations are Sino-Vietnamese loan words (Alves, 2009). Therefore, scientific-related texts are generally difficult to understand to most Vietnamese audience. Moreover, as a result of a prolonged period of battles and war, the country was isolated and has fallen behind from the rest of the world in terms of information and scientific updates (Nature, 1978). In addition, superstitions and religion practices make up a large account of cultural behaviors of Vietnamese people (Vuong et al., 2018); the direct implication is that laypeople would find religious practitioners more reliable than scientists, while as more subtle cultural undertone, this means that most Vietnamese people prefer to find comfort and reassurance rather than challenge themselves and seek truth. Thus, in order to promote high-quality science in Vietnam, it is important to cultivate a strongly founded research ecosystem that stimulates the conveyance of accurate scientific information to the general public.

The biggest problem when it comes to communicating scientific findings is the gap existing between expert and lay viewpoint. Attempts to reach out to the public of Vietnamese researchers mainly follow the Knowledge Deficit Model (Kearnes, Macnaghten, & Wilsdon, 2006) which emphasizes the provision of accurate, objective and emotionless information to improve understanding. However, research into science communication has pointed out that scientific facts can only be welcomed by the general public if the topics can connect to audiences from a more appealing and laypeople-friendly approach that highlights their significance in everyday matters. One of the attempts to generalize scientific updates to a more human level is "Total SciComm" (Total Science Communication) or all-out science communication which exploits every channel of the media to convey scientific ideas to society. Examples of this include the production of scientific novels, films, videos, games and art works (M.-T. Ho & Ho, 2018). These Total SciComm techniques surely need to be adapted according to the contextual conditions of specific communities. In Vietnam in particular where television ownership and internet users rates are relatively high (Statista, 2019), TV live shows and social networking sites appear to be viral channels to disseminate scientific knowledge. In addition, D. Jones & Anderson Crow (2017) suggested the use of narrative structure by science communicators to effectively present truthful scientific knowledge. The ultimate goal is to help audiences recognize and form personal connections to the academic world, from which to appreciate the role of science in their own daily life.

In this chapter, we have discussed criteria for quality control in research regarding impact factor, the big names, and the global movements that improve the transparency and reliability of science. The question remains: what would be qualified as quality science? At the moment, Web of Science, Scopus and their scores are being used as first-hand measures of the excellence of research. An WoS/Scopus-indexed journal is supposedly better than a non-indexed one, and within the indexed journals, the higher the scores, the better the quality. Then there are the big names in academia, which constitute various characteristics considered as gold standards. However, sole reliance on the name of a journal and its impact factor or CiteScore is not the ultimate way to define the quality of science. Publications in good journals, great journals, even big-name journals, are not exempted from retraction, nor from failing to have the reported results replicated. Thus, the scientific community is pushing towards a new age of transparency with open science. Preregistration, data repository, open access and open peer review all share the same goal: secure the finest quality of scientific research. In Vietnam, WoS/Scopus standards are widely used to set the bar for scientists, and slowly, the standards are becoming the norms. However, in order to foster a vibrant and sustainable academic ecosystem that yields authentically high-quality outputs, measures for quality control must be developed on the basis of good understanding and knowledge of science from all stakeholders, including the general public and policy makers. Effective communication of science is, therefore, fundamental to the future prospect of the Vietnamese science community.

References

Alves, M. (2009). Loanwords in Vietnamese. In *Loanwords in the world's languages: A comparative handbook* (pp. 617–637). Berlin: Walter de Gruyter.

Arvan, M. (2016, August 15). Potential risks & benefits of publishing in lower-ranked journals. *The Philosophers' Cocoon.* Retrieved July 16, 2019: https://philosopherscocoon.typepad.com/blog/2016/08/risks-a.html

Ball, P. (2018, February 18). China's great leap forward in science. *The Guardian.* Retrieved from https://www.theguardian.com/science/2018/feb/18/china-great-leap-forward-science-research-innovation-investment-5g-genetics-quantum-internet

Barnett, I., Ariana, P., Petrou, S., Penny, M. E., Duc, L. T., Galab, S., ... Boyden, J. (2013). Cohort Profile: The Young Lives Study. *International Journal of Epidemiology*, 42(3), 701–708. https://doi.org/10.1093/ije/dys082

Cyranoski, D. (2018). China introduces 'social' punishments for scientific misconduct. *Nature*, 564, 312. https://doi.org/10.1038/d41586-018-07740-z

D. Jones, M., & Anderson Crow, D. (2017). How can we use the 'science of stories' to produce persuasive scientific stories? *Palgrave Communications*, 3(1), 53. https://doi.org/10.1057/s41599-017-0047-7

Else, H. (2018). Radical open-access plan could spell end to journal subscriptions. *Nature*, 561, 17. https://doi.org/10.1038/d41586-018-06178-7

Grafton, Q. R., Kompas, T., Che, T. N., Chu, L., & Hilborn, R. (2012). BMEY as a fisheries management target. *Fish and Fisheries*, 13(3), 303–312. https://doi.org/10.1111/j.1467-2979.2011.00444.x

Hanieh, S., Ha, T. T., Simpson, J. A., Casey, G. J., Khuong, N. C., Thoang, D. D., ... Biggs, B.-A. (2013). The Effect of Intermittent Antenatal Iron Supplementation on Maternal and Infant Outcomes in Rural Viet Nam: A Cluster Randomised Trial. *PLOS Medicine*, 10(6), e1001470. https://doi.org/10.1371/journal.pmed.1001470

Ho, M.-T., & Ho, M.-T. (2018). Total SciComm — All out science communication. *OSF Preprints*. https://doi.org/10.31219/osf.io/r5fxp

Ho, T. Q., Hoang, V.-N., Wilson, C., & Nguyen, T.-T. (2018). Eco-efficiency analysis of sustainability-certified coffee production in Vietnam. *Journal of Cleaner Production*, 183, 251–260. https://doi.org/10.1016/j.jclepro.2018.02.147

Ichiko, F. (2006). Japanese spin-offs face struggle for survival. *Nature*, 441, 280–281. https://doi.org/10.1038/441280a

Nikkei. (2017, July 27). R&D budgets in Japan soaring to record-breaking levels. *Nikkei Asian Review*. Retrieved August 9, 2019: https://asia.nikkei.com/Business/R-D-budgets-in-Japan-soaring-to-record-breaking-levels

Jia, H. (2018, June 2). China gets serious about research integrity. *Nature Index*. Retrieved July 16, 2019: https://www.natureindex.com/news-blog/china-gets-serious-about-research-integrity

Kearnes, M. B., Macnaghten, P. M., & Wilsdon, J. (2006). *Governing at the Nanoscale: People, Policies and Emerging Technologies*. London: Demos.

Labaree, D. (2018, December 18). Gold among the dross. *Aeon*. Retrieved July 15, 2019: https://aeon.co/essays/higher-education-in-the-us-is-driven-by-a-lust-for-glory

Loken, E., & Gelman, A. (2017). Measurement error and the replication crisis. *Science, 355*(6325), 584. https://doi.org/10.1126/science.aal3618

Manh, H. D. (2015). Scientific publications in Vietnam as seen from Scopus during 1996–2013. *Scientometrics, 105*(1), 83–95. https://doi.org/10.1007/s11192-015-1655-x

NAFOSTED. (2019). Chương trình hỗ trợ nâng cao năng lực khoa học và công nghệ quốc gia [Programs to promote national science and technology capability]. *NAFOSTED*. Retrieved July 15, 2019: https://nafosted.gov.vn/chuong-trinh-tai-tro/chuong-trinh-ho-tro-nang-cao-nang-luc-khoa-hoc-va-cong-nghe-quoc-gia/

Nature. (1978). Vietnam—an inexpensive form of help. *Nature*. https://doi.org/10.1038/271099a0

Nguyen, Q., Kim, T., & Papanastassiou, M. (2018). Policy uncertainty, derivatives use, and firm-level FDI. *Journal of International Business Studies, 49*(1), 96–126. https://doi.org/10.1057/s41267-017-0090-z

Nguyen, T. T., Tran, T. D., Tran, T., La, B., Nguyen, H., & Fisher, J. (2015). Postpartum change in common mental disorders among rural Vietnamese women: Incidence, recovery and risk and protective factors. *British Journal of Psychiatry, 206*(2), 110–115. https://doi.org/10.1192/bjp.bp.114.149138

Nguyen, T. V., Ho-Le, T. P., & Le, U. V. (2017). International collaboration in scientific research in Vietnam: An analysis of patterns and impact. *Scientometrics, 110*(2), 1035–1051. https://doi.org/10.1007/s11192-016-2201-1

Nguyen, T. V., & Pham, L. T. (2011). Scientific output and its relationship to knowledge economy: An analysis of ASEAN countries. *Scientometrics*, *89*(1), 107–117. https://doi.org/10.1007/s11192-011-0446-2

Persson, L. Å., Nga, N. T., Målqvist, M., Thi Phuong Hoa, D., Eriksson, L., Wallin, L., ... Ewald, U. (2013). Effect of facilitation of local maternal-and-newborn stakeholder groups on neonatal mortality: Cluster-randomized controlled trial. *PLOS Medicine*, *10*(5), e1001445. https://doi.org/10.1371/journal.pmed.1001445

Ravindranath, V., Dang, H.-M., Goya, R. G., Mansour, H., Nimgaonkar, V. L., Russell, V. A., & Xin, Y. (2015). Regional research priorities in brain and nervous system disorders. *Nature*, *527*, S198.

Reich, E. S. (2013). Science publishing: The golden club. *Nature*, *502*, 291–293. https://doi.org/10.1038/502291a

Statista. (2019). Number of televisions owned in Vietnam from 2011 to 2018 (per 1,000 population). *Statista*. Retrieved July 16, 2019: https://www.statista.com/statistics/618400/amount-of-televisions-in-vietnam/

Tregoning, J. (2018). How will you judge me if not by impact factor? *Nature*, *558*, 345. https://doi.org/10.1038/d41586-018-05467-5

van Vliet, N., Mertz, O., Heinimann, A., Langanke, T., Pascual, U., Schmook, B., ... Ziegler, A. D. (2012). Trends, drivers and impacts of changes in swidden cultivation in tropical forest-agriculture frontiers: A global assessment. *Global Environmental Change*, *22*(2), 418–429. https://doi.org/10.1016/j.gloenvcha.2011.10.009

Vuong, Q.-H. (2018a). "How did researchers get it so wrong?" The acute problem of plagiarism in Vietnamese social sciences and humanities. *European Science Editing*, *44*(3), 56–58. https://doi.org/10.20316/ESE.2018.44.18003

Vuong, Q.-H. (2018b). The (ir)rational consideration of the cost of science in transition economies. *Nature Human Behaviour*, *2*(1), 5–5. https://doi.org/10.1038/s41562-017-0281-4

Vuong, Q.-H. (2019a). The harsh world of publishing in emerging regions and implications for editors and publishers: The case of Vietnam. *Learned Publishing*, DOI: 10.1002/LEAP.1255

Vuong Q. -H. (2019b). Breaking barriers in publishing demands a proactive attitude. *Nature Human Behaviour 3*; doi: 10.1038/s41562-019-0667-6.

Vuong, Q.-H., Bui, Q.-K., La, V.-P., Vuong, T.-T., Nguyen, V.-H. T., Ho, M.-T., … Ho, M.-T. (2018). Cultural additivity: Behavioural insights from the interaction of Confucianism, Buddhism and Taoism in folktales. *Palgrave Communications*, 4(1), 143, DOI: 10.1057/s41599-018-0189-2

Williams, E. (2005). Too few university spin-out companies?. *Warwick University*. Retrieved July 15, 2019: https://warwick.ac.uk/services/ventures/spin-outs.pdf

Woolston, C. (2016). Salaries: Reality check. *Nature, 537*(7621), 573–576. https://doi.org/10.1038/nj7621-573a

Wouters, P., Sugimoto, C. R., Larivière, V., McVeigh, M. E., Pulverer, B., Rijcke, S. de, & Waltman, L. (2019). Rethinking impact factors: Better ways to judge a journal. *Nature, 569*(7758), 621, DOI: 10.1038/d41586-019-01643-3

Xin, H. (2016). Five-year plan boosts basic research funding. *Science, 351*(6280), 1382–1382, DOI: science.351.6280.1382

Chapter 7
Scientific publishing: the point of no return
Hong-Kong T. Nguyen, Thu-Hang T. Nguyen,
Manh-Toan Ho, Manh-Tung Ho, Quan-Hoang Vuong

Circular 08: Publish or perish

On April 4, 2017, the Ministry of Education and Training issued Circular 08/2017/TT-BGDDT that outlines the regulations on doctoral enrolment and training (Vietnam MOET, 2017). The Circular, effective from May 20, 2017, requires a doctoral candidate to have a publication of (i) at least two articles on ISI/Scopus-indexed journals or (ii) two peer-reviewed reports or articles at international conferences. For a research adviser, the requirements include (i) at least one peer-reviewed articles in ISI/Scopus-indexed journals, or (ii) an article published in a reference manual with the standard ISBN, which could be substituted by two peer-reviewed journal articles related to the content of the mentee's research.

The Circular itself is met with mixed public opinions. Some argued that it is essentially "new bottle, old wine" — some of the requirements have been masked with convenient substitutions for the more difficult publications on ISI/Scopus journals (Ngo, 2017). For instance, doctoral candidates who were not able to publish in ISI/Scopus-indexed journals have the option of publishing at least two articles in peer-reviewed conference proceedings, including in Vietnam. The standards of this latter option are arguably less stringent than those of quality indexed journals (Ngo, 2017). Along the same vein, doctoral research advisers can also substitute peer-reviewed journal articles with peer-reviewed conference articles. The arguments go on.

Empirical evidence

From a scientific point of view, however, only after the Circular took effect could one truly evaluate its impact, all comments *a prior* reek of assumptions and biases. Two years have passed since this legal regulation was enforced, during which one cannot dispute the increasingly robust scientific publishing landscape in

Vietnam. Using our database, we attempt to show the vivid changes Circular 08 has brought about. Our main argument is Circular 08 is inevitable and effective to a certain extent in pushing for improvements in scientific research and publishing in Vietnam.

More new and young authors joining the picture

The first evidence lies in the sudden surge in the total number of authors in 2017-2018, as shown in Figure 2.2 in Chapter 2. At the end of 2016, there were 508 published authors in our database, but by the end of 2017, this figure has jumped 1.6-fold to 825 authors. As of late 2018, the database recorded a total of 923 authors, an 81.6% hike from the figure in 2016 before the Circular was issued. When looking at a long period of time, from 2008 to 2014, each year, just around or fewer than 100 new authors joined the international publishing world, and the number did not really skyrocket until after 2016-2017. In 2018, the number of new authors reached its all-time high at 277.

Based on the available data on the age of new authors by year (not all of whom we were able to obtain their year-of-birth), we were able to construct Figure 7.1 on the number of young authors by year, defined as those aged 20 to 35. The reason for narrowing to this age group is based on the understanding that this demographic is the main target subject—the potential doctoral candidates—of Circular 08.

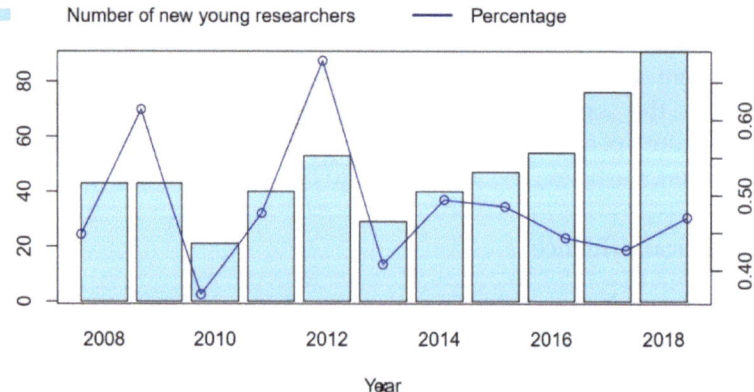

Figure 7.1. The number of new authors aged 20-35 by year and its percentage to the total number of new authors by year, 2008-2018.

Figure 7.1 highlights a definitive upward trend in the number of published authors aged 20-35 after the year 2016. In fact, this number jumped by 40.7% to 76 in 2017, followed by another 19.7% hike to peak at 91 in 2018. In terms of the proportion to the total number of new authors by year, the rates stay relatively stable at approximately 44% a year in the 2016-2018 period. For the whole ten years, only in 2010 and 2013 did the proportion of new young researchers fall from the previous years, attributable to the drop in the total numbers of new authors in the two years.

The statistics clearly show that the rate of researchers seeking to meet the new doctoral training requirements is rising faster than the rate of publication output. Figure 7.2 recapitulates the year-on-year increases in both the numbers of authors and articles over decade. If the total number of authors recorded in our database as of end-2018 has jumped by 81.6% from that in 2016, then the rate of publications during this period pales in comparison. The number of published articles in 2017 rose by 11.35% on year to 353, which also increased by 10.76% to reach 391 by the end of 2018. Meanwhile, the faster-growing period in terms of output actually happened in 2014-2016 when the rate of published papers jumped by over 20% each year. The higher productivity back then was not attributable to a surge in new authors but likely to increased collaboration with international colleagues.

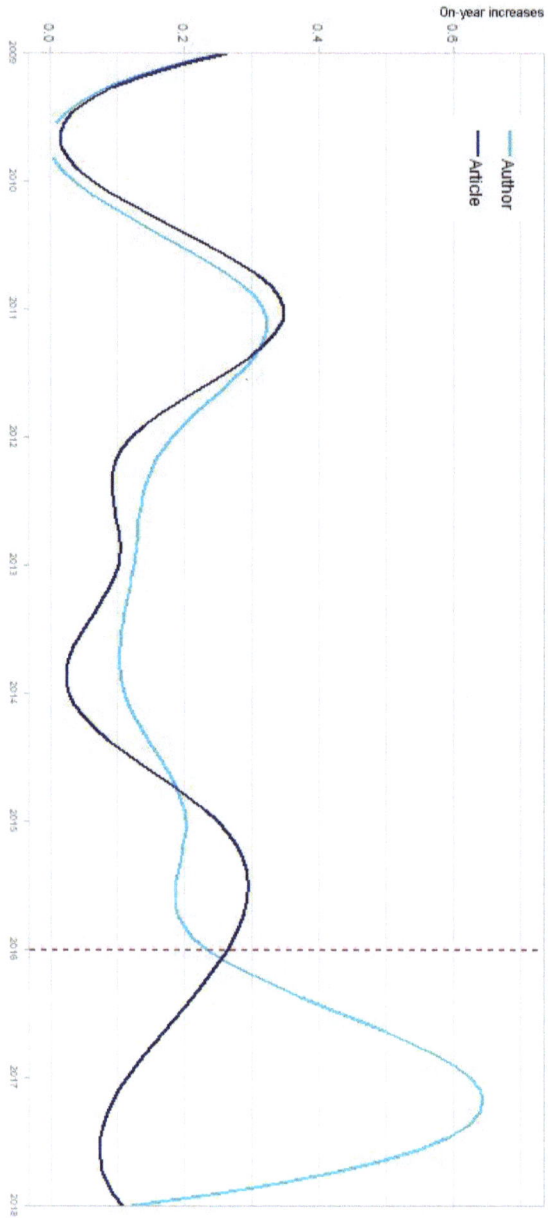

Figure 7.2. The year-on-year increases (percent) of the total numbers of authors and articles, 2008-2018.

To further support this point, we suggest reviewing Figure 2.7 in Chapter 2 on the ratio of Vietnamese-authored articles to those involving foreign co-authors. Between 2014 and 2015, the total number of published papers rose by 24.87%, yet the fraction of articles published fully by Vietnamese authors over those having foreign co-authorship stayed relatively unchanged at around 35%. This hints at an increase in international collaboration during the period.

As previously pointed out, this proportion suddenly climbed to above 40% after nearly 8 years of little development. In 2016 when the draft version of Circular 08 was publicized for comments, perhaps people with stake in the doctoral training programs had felt threatened enough to move ahead with their own international publications. This move is reflected in our data: in 2016, while the total number of publications rose by 26.2% year-on-year, the number of papers published completely by Vietnamese authors jumped by a whopping 62% year-on-year to 149. This momentum was carried through the next two years. In 2017 and 2018, there were 171 and 176 articles published fully by Vietnamese authors, accounting for respectively 48.4% and 45% of the total published articles in the two years. Figure 7.3 recaptures this uptrend.

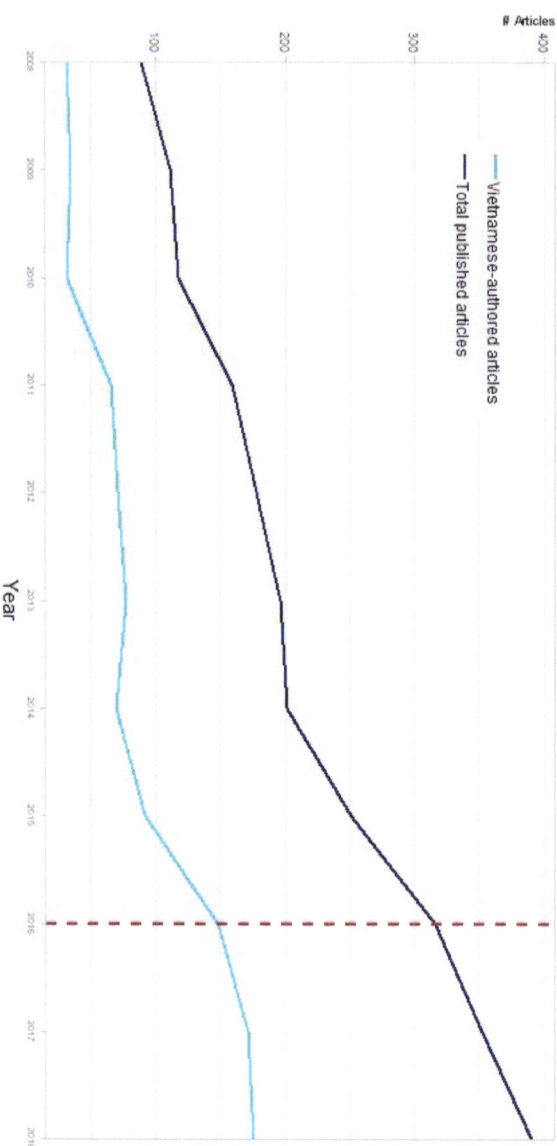

Figure 7.3. The number of articles published fully by Vietnamese authors versus the total number of published articles, 2008-2018. The dashed red line marks 2016 as 'the point of no return'.

More Vietnamese authors leading

Another important aspect to look for post-2016 is the increased involvement of Vietnamese authors in the higher volume of published works. As previously noted, the ratio of Vietnamese to foreign authors in publish papers was consistently around the 0.65 mark between 2011 and 2015. A breakthrough was seen in the 2016-2018 period when the ratio surpasses 0.7 and even peaks at 0.74 in 2017 (See Figure 2.8.).

Along with this change, we also paid attention to the number of publications fully authored by Vietnamese researchers: the ratio of fully Vietnamese authored articles to partially foreign-authored articles only surpasses 0.45 in 2016 onward, having ranged mostly below or near 0.4 from 2008 to 2015 (Figure 7.4.).

More importantly, when looking at the number of articles led by Vietnamese authors, we saw a remarkable surge after 2016. While the proportion of Vietnamese authors in a published article has consistently been larger than that of foreign authors during the whole ten years, this ratio was below 3 from 2008 to 2015. After 2016, this all changed: the number articles led by Vietnamese authors rose by 37% from 243 in 2016 to 333 in 2018. Figure 7.4 illustrates this uptrend in Vietnamese-led articles.

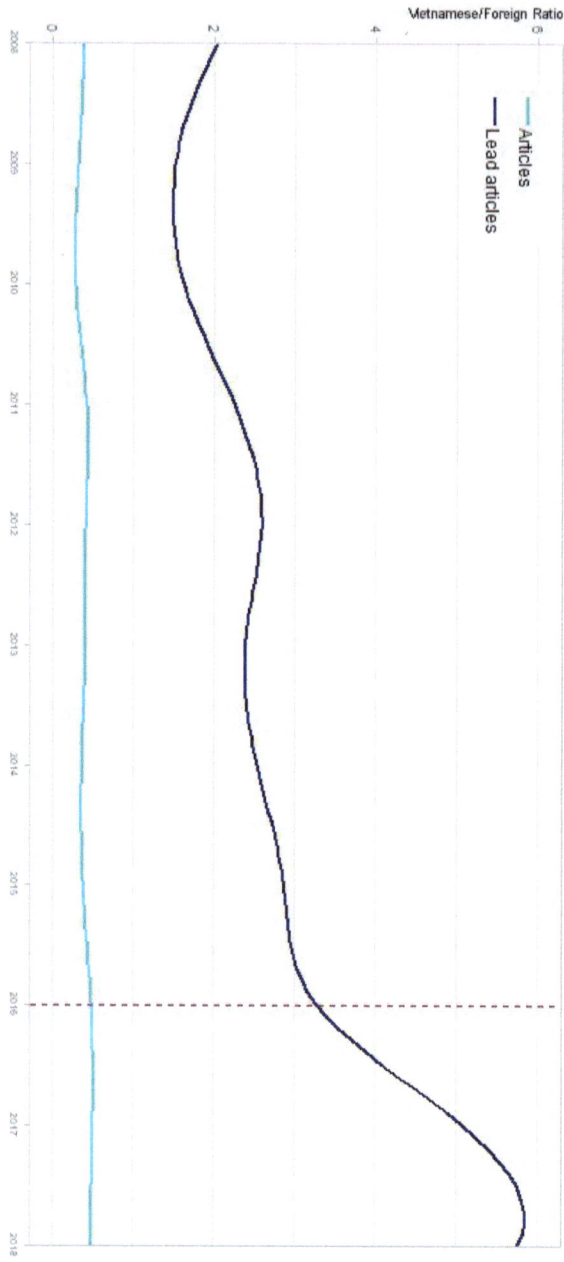

Figure 7.4. The ratio of Vietnamese to foreign in terms of total articles and lead articles, 2008-2018.

More institutions competing for higher output
In addition to the number of new authors in general and new authors who are young in particular, our database also allows us to extract data on the number of published articles claimed by higher education institutions in Vietnam. By 'higher education institutions', we refer to all universities, colleges, schools, departments, faculty, and academies within the formal schooling system, including both private and public establishments. Figure 7.5 depicts a clear uptrend in the number of articles claimed by higher education institutions over the ten years, with a drastic surge recorded in 2016 onward. In fact, from 2008 to 2015, the average annual growth rate of this number is 30%, while just between 2016 and 2018, the rate amounts to already 33%. These numbers suggest an increasingly heated race among universities and colleges across Vietnam in getting more research published under their names.

The main reasons why we did not draw comparisons to the total number of published papers in Figure 7.5. are: (i) an author may be affiliated with more than one institution, which means the count of articles by institutions could be duplicate, (ii) authors from different institutions may co-publish one article, which results in one count of article for each institution even though technically the output is one. However, counting the number of published articles claimed by Vietnamese higher education institutions is meaningful in the sense that it gives empirical confirmation for the increased pressure to publish in international journals after 2016, per the requirements of Circular 08.

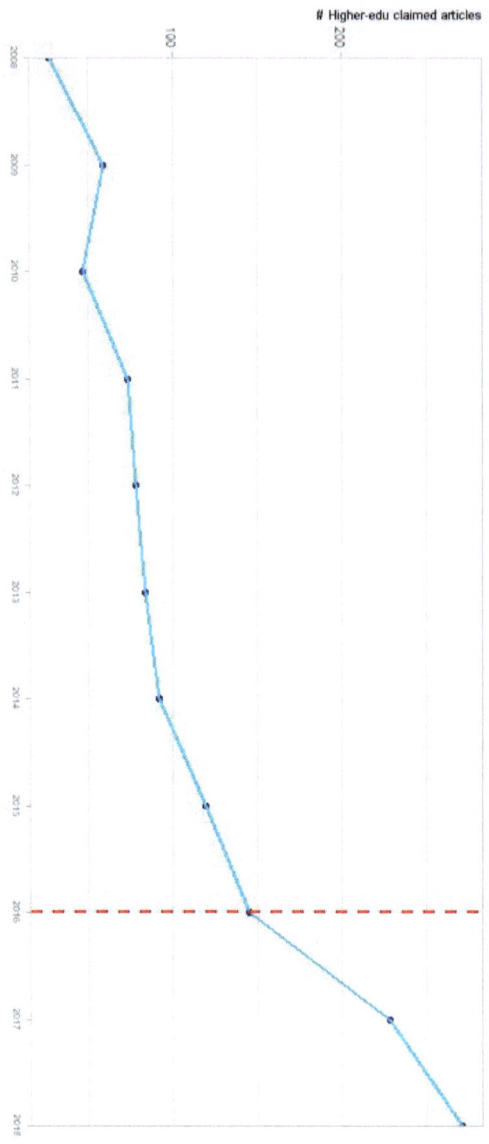

Figure 7.5. The number of articles claimed by higher education institutions in Vietnam, 2008-2018.

More research groups emerging
Another unique aspect of our database is its ability to generate network visualization of different research teams based on their published articles and co-authoring patterns. In Figure 7.6a, it is clear that in 2008, not only there were few research teams, but the linkages and size of the teams were also small. Researchers appeared to work mainly in groups of two, back then. By 2015 (Figure 7.6b), this has changed: more groups have formed, with their networks extending slightly longer with more members. The complexity of the networks heightened in 2008, as shown in Figure 7.6c, with one network dominating the picture with its thick collaboration linkages. The number of research teams has also increased significantly and few published authors appeared to work alone.

(a) As of 2008

(b) As of 2015

(c) As of 2018

Figure 7.6. The transformation of author group networks over the years, (a) 2008, (b) 2008-2015, and (c) 2008-2018.

The emergence of more research groups is in line with our observations on the increase in published authors and collaboration with both domestic and international colleagues.

The race out there

The numbers provided by our database have provided an empirical basis for evaluating the effect of Circular 08. They are, however, insufficient to conclude that international publications may be the new norms in scientific research in Vietnam. While one cannot definitively conclude the changes were brought about solely by Circular 08, one cannot dispute there exists an association between the new policy and the increased pressure to publish research articles in international journals. Here, we suggest looking at the data from our society, including the investment in scientific research, the financial rewards for international publications, the number of conferences as well as online articles on the topic.

At the national level, there is more attention paid to investment to boost scientific research and publications. From its establishment in 2008 to end-2017, the National Foundation for Science and Technology (NAFOSTED) – the first

> "In my opinion, it is necessary to give investment priority to strong research teams in order to increase the productivity and quality of science and technology activities, as well as to promote international publishing. However, such a policy must be implemented in a very organized and flexible manner...If the policy is not implemented correctly, it will be taken advantage of by interest groups (rent-seeking groups).
>
> To ensure the effectiveness of the investment policy, I think NAFOSTED also needs to leverage market mechanism by encouraging fair competition through open research calls. In that way, the mechanism will oblige researchers to form research teams strong enough to propose valuable research ideas that can compete against other proposals. Besides, it is necessary to continue to set higher criteria for principal investigators and co-authors involved with projects funded by NAFOSTED (qualified by publication in SCI, SSCI, Scopus, etc.)" *Dr. Tran Huu Tuan, Hue University, Hue, Vietnam.*

national scientific funding agency of Vietnam – had disbursed VND2.3 trillion, equivalent to approximately US$100 million, for nearly 2,800 science and technology research projects. According to NAFOSTED Director Do Tien Dung, in the near future, the fund is expected to have a running budget of VND500 billion a year, up nearly 70% from the current figure (Tia Sang, 2017). In 2017, NAFOSTED allocated VND400 billion for funding scientific research, which increased 30% from that in 2016 (Tia Sang, 2017). The role of NAFOSTED, thus, is important in easing financial concerns for researchers as well as in fostering better research skills and output nationwide (VnExpress, 2018). However, this is not the only role that NAFOSTED is playing. With a recent experiment with setting investment priority for strong research teams, the foundation is actively trying to intensify the competition for accessing grants (Thanh-Nhan, 2017).

At the institutional level, an increasing number of higher educational establishments are reportedly giving extra financial support and incentives to encourage and promote their faculty to boost scientific publishing. For instance, regarding public institutions, the University of Social Sciences and Humanities under the Vietnam National University Hanoi is willing to fund up to VND250 million (US$10,780) for a research article published in a journal indexed in ISI/Scopus (Dan Tri, 2018). Even the University of Dong Thap in the Mekong Delta province of Dong Thap said it is ready to fund faculty with international publications up to VND41 million in article processing charges (GDTD, 2019). In some cases, such as at the University of Economics Ho Chi Minh City, graduate students who have published a scientific article on the university's English-language Journal of Asian Business and Economic Studies (JABES) or on any indexed international journals (Tuoi Tre, 2018) are compensated. While it might be new for public institutions to provide economic incentives for scientists to publish in international journals, non-public universities and institutions are no strangers to the idea. Non-public universities such as Duy Tan University or Ton Duc Thang University are arguably among the firsts in Vietnam to follow this strategy, and with success. They are known in the media for their high number of ISI-indexed journal articles, especially in natural sciences. Recently, major private brands and wealthy individuals have also shown a higher willingness to increase their contribution to science. VinGroup has invested in a publication-focused artificial intelligence lab, called VinAI Research; Mr. Ho Xuan Nang of Ho Xuan Nang Science Foundation, the chairman of Phenikaa Corporation, has committed to invest in eight research groups, each at least VND 4billion for three consecutive years (Nhan-Dan, 2019).These are some of the notable incentive programs being publicized in the media in the past two years. Given the increase in publications claimed by higher education institutions since 2016, there are undoubtedly similar types of financial support at various institutions that are not being reported.

In terms of media reporting on the issue, using Google News to track the number of Vietnamese articles with the exact key words *"công bố quốc tế"* (international publications) in two periods, 2008-2015 and 2016-2018, we noted a clear rise in public interest on the topic. For the seven years from 2008 to 2015, cleaning the pool of items from Google News in R version 3.4.4 (package *rvest*), we compiled a list of 66 unique articles having the key words either in their titles or content. This all changed after 2016, as depicted in Figure 7.7.

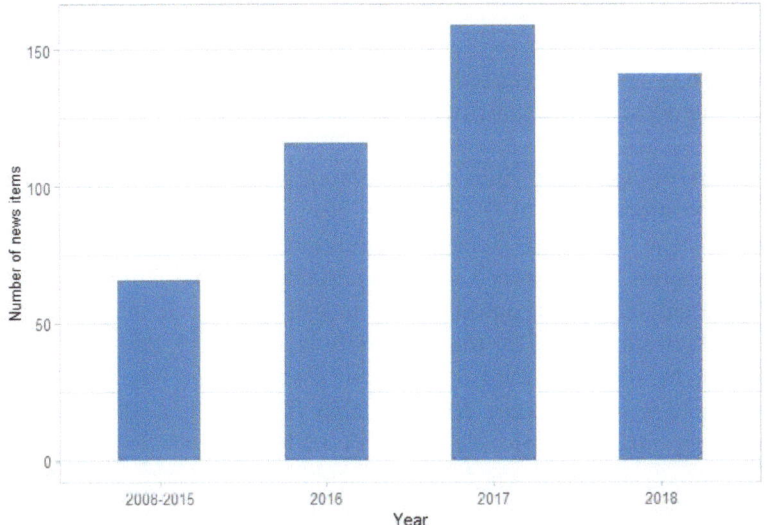

Figure 7.7. A count of news items in Vietnamese fetched by Google News on the key words *"công bố quốc tế"* (international publications), 2008-2018.

For each of the year from 2016 to 2018, the number of news articles having the key words we looked for was above 110, with the peak of 159 items in 2017 alone. For the three years, the news reports on the topic averaged at one article a month. This surge in media reporting reflects the increased public curiosity into the world of international publishing in general, and the growing public demand for better transparency in scientific funding and research publishing. Data provided by Nature Research's Nature Index 2018 also confirm the impact of the new policy: from the beginning of 2017 to June 2018, the top 30 universities in Vietnam published a total of 10,515 articles, equivalent to the national output in the 2011-2015 period (SGGP, 2018; Tien Phong, 2018).

Our projection

The extensive review of the empirical data and social observations on the new trends of scientific publishing in Vietnam all points to one direction: we have passed "the point of no return" in 2016. With the official issuance of Circular 08 and its effective implementation in 2017, the standards for doctoral training now include a more demanding set of rules, one that is necessary to improve research capacity at the national level as well as Vietnam's scientific standing in the world.

The more stringent rules mean that graduate school admission will be more difficult than before. News reports in 2018 already noted the drop in doctoral candidate recruitment at many universities. For instance, at the Vietnam National University Ho Chi Minh City, compared to the height of over 10,000 doctoral candidates applying for the university in 2012-2013, this figure has fallen by half in 2014 and even dwindled to merely 2,912 candidates in 2017 and 1,139 in 2018 (Thanh Nien, 2018b). The final acceptance pool only met 85% of the recruitment target in 2017-2018. Similarly, the National Economics University in Hanoi used to admit 150-160 graduate students a year, but is now getting only one third of the usual pool (Thanh Nien, 2018b). This situation is also being reported in the higher education institutions in the natural sciences (Thanh Nien, 2018a). Here lies a big implication: universities will be forced to improve their doctoral training programs, in the short run at least to meet Circular 08's requirements. In the long run, this will likely result in an increasing number of "high-quality doctoral programs" across the nation. The foreseeable result is a larger number of well-equipped researchers at higher education establishments nationwide, as opposed to the excess pool of PhD graduates who lack skills and publications in the previous years.

What we expect to see in Vietnam in the near future is clearly a strong demand for better quality in scientific research and training as well as scientific publications. Such demand will translate into a rising need for evidence-based policies on science development. More importantly, discourses on research quality in Vietnam will hopefully take on the ethical, legal and social aspects in order to increase public engagement with scientific publishing. For instance, while policy discourse in Europe and other developed nations has touched on 'responsible research and innovation' for a decade (Owen, Macnaghten, & Stilgoe, 2012), this has yet to happen in Vietnam.

To meet the growing demand for quality research, improving research capacity is a must-do, one that requires significant investment in science. In Vietnam, as the three Great Religions or Teachings of Confucianism, Buddhism, and Taoism are known to exert certain influences on the local behaviors (Vuong et al., 2018), it is important to not overlook the close linkage between the investment *modus operandi* and the socio-cultural system of values. By understanding the socio-cultural drivers of science investment in Vietnam, one could better hold the financing of scientific research and publications to be accountable.

Circular 08 as *Khoán 10* of scientific publishing

In wrapping up this chapter, we would like to draw a parallel between Circular 08 and the milestone implementation of a quota-threshold contractual system for purchasing agriculture produce from farmers during Vietnam's 1980s economic reform era. The innovative agricultural policy, well-known as *Khoán*, was one of the first market-oriented contractual systems in the country for recognizing the rights of farming households to keep some share of their output (Vuong, Dam, Daniel, & Tran, 2011). It was in fact initiated back in 1966-1967 by a medium-ranked official named Kim Ngoc in the northern province of Vinh Phuc with the purpose of ensuring farmers' livelihood and meeting the required state budget contribution (Vuong et al., 2011). Being given the right to keep of their agricultural products after contributing to the state the required portion, farmers were then motivated to constantly innovate, such as how to best use their land or water. When this policy was institutionalized in Resolution 10 of the Communist Party of Vietnam's Politburo in 1988, it transformed Vietnam from a country that had faced food insecurity problems for decades to one that exported rice just one year later (Vuong et al., 2011). The Southeast Asian country is now among the five biggest rice exporters in the world (FAO, 2018).

What is clear from the rice export story is the cause of the decades-long food insecurity problem in Vietnam was not low farming productivity or experience. It was a combination of inappropriate agricultural production policy and non-existent trading-distribution market system, as dictated by the collective management modality at the time. Similarly, the cause of low scientific output in Vietnam for a long period was neither low productivity nor lack of experience and skills on the part of the researchers. Vietnamese social scientists have not been motivated enough to do and publish quality research due to the absence of support policies, as well as research investment. Our empirical data on the sudden increase in the number of new authors and published articles since 2016 back up our projection that Circular 08 is indeed a game-changing policy in scientific publishing in Vietnam. It is highly possible that Vietnam's scientific research productivity will improve leaps and bounds in the near future.

References

Hanh, H. (2018). Hỗ trợ 250 triệu đồng cho một xuất bản khoa học trên ISI/Scopuss [250 million VND for a publication in ISI/Scopus journal]. *Dan Tri*. Retrieved from https://dantri.com.vn/giao-duc-khuyen-hoc/ho-tro-250-

trieu-dong-cho-mot-xuat-ban-khoa-hoc-tren-isi-scopuss-20180426154740385.htm

FAO. (2018). Round up. Retrieved from http://www.fao.org/3/I9243EN/i9243en.pdf

GDTD. (2019). Trường ĐH Đồng Tháp công bố 216 bài báo quốc tế [Dong Thap University published 216 international publications]. *Giáo Dục và Thời Đại*. Retrieved from https://giaoducthoidai.vn/giao-duc/truong-dh-dong-thap-cong-bo-216-bai-bao-quoc-te-3990333-v.html

Nhan-Dan. (2019). Trường Đại học Phenikaa công bố tám nhóm nghiên cứu mạnh [Phenikaa University announced eight strong research teams]. *Nhân Dân*. Retrieved from https://nhandan.com.vn/khoahoc-congnghe/khoa-hoc/item/40194002-truong-dai-hoc-phenikaa-cong-bo-tam-nhom-nghien-cuu-manh.html

Ngo, T. T. (2017). Đào tạo tiến sĩ sau năm 2017 - càng lên cao tiêu chuẩn càng… thấp [Doctoral training after 2017 - the higher training level, … the lower the standards]. Retrieved from http://giaoduc.net.vn/Giao-duc-24h/Dao-tao-tien-si-sau-nam-2017--cang-len-cao-tieu-chuan-cang-thap-post175997.gd

Owen, R., Macnaghten, P., & Stilgoe, J. (2012). Responsible research and innovation: From science in society to science for society, with society. *Science and Public Policy, 39*(6), 751-760. doi:10.1093/scipol/scs093

SGGP. (2018). Công bố quốc tế của Việt Nam tăng mạnh [Rise in Vietnamese international publications]. Retrieved from http://www.sggp.org.vn/cong-bo-quoc-te-cua-viet-nam-tang-manh-564688.html

Thanh-Nhan. (2017). NAFOSTED đầu tư cho nhóm nghiên cứu mạnh [NAFOSTED invests in strong research teams]. Retrieved on August 12, 2019 from http://tiasang.com.vn/-quan-ly-khoa-hoc/NAFOSTED-dau-tu-cho-nhom-nghien-cuu-manh--10876

Thanh Nien. (2018a). Học tiến sĩ được trả lương [PhD has salary]. Retrieved from https://thanhnien.vn/giao-duc/hoc-tien-si-duoc-tra-luong-1064247.html

Thanh Nien. (2018b). Vì sao không còn nhiều người làm tiến sĩ? [Why nobody is taking PhD program]. Retrieved from https://thanhnien.vn/giao-duc/vi-sao-khong-con-nhieu-nguoi-lam-tien-si-1020445.html

Tia Sang. (2017). Nafosted sẽ tăng 70% đầu tư cho khoa học [Nafosted will raise scientific funding up to 70%]. Retrieved from http://tiasang.com.vn/-tin-tuc/Nafosted-se-tang-70-dau-tu-cho-khoa-hoc-10352

Tien Phong. (2018). Đột phá trong công bố bài báo khoa học quốc tế của ĐH Việt Nam [Breakthrough in scientific publication fom Vietnamese unniversity]. Retrieved from https://www.tienphong.vn/giao-duc/dot-pha-trong-cong-bo-bai-bao-khoa-hoc-quoc-te-cua-dh-viet-nam-1333074.tpo

Tuoi Tre. (2018). Học viên cao học có bài báo quốc tế được miễn học phí [Graduate students who have international publications will be waved from tuition fee]. *Tuoi Tre*. Retrieved from https://tuoitre.vn/hoc-vien-cao-hoc-co-bai-bao-quoc-te-duoc-mien-hoc-phi-20181213112816703.htm

Vietnam MOET. (2017). Circular 08/2017/TT-BGDDT: Introducing regulations on doctoral enrolment and training. *Circular 08*. Retrieved from https://vanbanphapluat.co/circular-08-2017-tt-bgddtdoctoral-enrolment-and-training

VnExpress. (2018). Quỹ Nafosted áp chuẩn bắt buộc, công bố quốc tế Việt Nam tăng mạnh [NAFOSTED increases the pressure, Vietnamese international publications increase rapidly]. *VnExpress*. Retrieved from https://vnexpress.net/khoa-hoc/quy-nafosted-ap-chuan-bat-buoc-cong-bo-quoc-te-viet-nam-tang-manh-3849565.html

Vuong, Q.-H., Bui, Q.-K., La, V.-P., Vuong, T.-T., Nguyen, V.-H. T., Ho, M.-T., . . . Ho, M.-T. (2018). Cultural additivity: behavioural insights from the interaction of Confucianism, Buddhism and Taoism in folktales. *Palgrave Communications, 4*(1), 143. doi:10.1057/s41599-018-0189-2

Vuong, Q.-H., Dam, V.-N., Daniel, V.-H., & Tran, T.-D. (2011). The entrepreneurial facets as precursor to Vietnam's economic renovation in 1986. *The IUP Journal of Entrepreneurship Development, 8*(4), 6-47.

Chapter 8
The emerging business of science in Vietnam
Manh-Tung Ho, Khanh-Linh Hoang,
Minh-Hoang Nguyen, Manh-Toan Ho

This chapter discusses the emerging business of science in Vietnam and how implementing a well-functioning market mechanism in academia can boost scientific productivity and in turn, generate higher quality research in the transition economy. To have a business of science, a well-functioning market for research or research-related activities as products is necessary. Here, one can define a well-functioning market mechanism is a system emerging from the accumulations of individual choices, and entities within the system are subject to competition from one another. In this system, overall economic efficiency is enhanced.

With these concepts in mind, we will first explore several dimensions of how a market-based mechanism has been introduced into the higher education system in Vietnam. Then, we will explore several challenges of for a business of science to capitalize on the gradual wave of internationalization and liberalization of Vietnam's higher education. Examples of successful business of science will be introduced next, and the chapter close with some suggestions moving forward.

Toward a market-based mechanism
In Vietnamese higher education system, the

"In my opinion, sustainable scientific practices need to be built upon the demand of universities, governments, and businesses. In the country where I am currently working, universities are very strong at conducting research. In Vietnam, I feel that universities concentrate more on teaching. A part of this is probably due to financial issues: funding or business revenue from conducting research is not enough to maintain sustainable research activities. In my opinion, NAFOSTED should experiment with supporting university-based research centers. I think it can be done under co-financing format: the funding partly comes from the foundation, partly from the school to make sure all parties are responsible. Likewise, it is feasible to follow the project-based funding mechanism or even set a prize for teams that meet a specific set of goals." *Dr. Pham Van Ha, Australian National University, Australia.*

formal administrative organization in Vietnam was best characterized as highly centralized. The literature around research and research commercialization in Vietnam often points out how the Soviet model in the past still largely influences the current situation. Universities are traditionally teaching-oriented and research is often considered to be the job of specialized institutes and academies only (Nguyen & Meek, 2016; Vuong et al., 2018). However, in recent decades, there is a gradual movement toward decentralization and a more bottom-up system.

In 2005, the Vietnamese government approved the Higher Education Reform Agenda (HERA). The reform agenda has, among its goals, aimed at expanding the private sector substantially and prioritizing the development of research and research culture. The reform aimed at increasing the enrolments from non-public universities and colleges from 13% in 2010 to 40% of all higher education enrolments by 2020, and increasing the revenue from research and development related activities to account for 25% of total revenue by 2020 (Hayden & Thiep, 2007). Indeed, HERA became the foundation for the establishments of well-known private universities later on such as FPT, Nguyen Hoang, Tan Tao, Hoa Sen, Duy Tan. Since the establishment of the first private university in Vietnam in 1994, Duy Tan University (Tran & Thanh-Tam, 2014; Tran, 2018b), non-public universities have risen to popularity due to their success in international publications. According to the 2018 ranking of Nature Index, in the top 10 research institutions in Vietnam, Ton Duc Thang and Duy Tan took the 6th and 8th place, respectively (Nature Index, 2018).

The success of these first private universities has inspired some very wealthy individuals and companies to join the game, either through philanthropic donation or through strategic investment. All of them position research as the central focus. For example, VinGroup invested VND5,000 billion (roughly USD215 million) in the first phase (until 2030) to build VinUniversity, aiming to become a university of "international standards." VinGroup has also launched VinAI Research, a publication-focused research center on artificial intelligence, in 2019. Regarding philanthropy, in 2018, Phenikaa Corporation, the owner of Phenikaa University, has invested VND500 billion (roughly USD21.5 million) in the "Science and Technology Research Fund" to support basic science research in Vietnam. Phenikaa Corporation has also signed an agreement, committed to providing financial support in three consecutive years (2019-2021) for one of the most prestigious science awards in Vietnam, the Ta Quang Buu Prize (NAFOSTED, 2018). Indeed, these developments show that one cannot discount the role of the private sectors and philanthropic actors such as Ho Xuan Nang Science Foundation or VinGroup Innovation Foundation in shaping the path of development for science in Vietnam.

As for the government, realizing that public universities need to improve their efficiency as well as their overall rank in worldwide rankings, the government has been experimenting with increasing their institutional autonomy. By the end of the academic year 2016-2017, 23 pilot public universities have been conferred more freedom in setting their own agenda for training, research, human resource, and budget planning, as well as taking responsibility for it (Resolution No. 77/NQ-CP, 2014). Despite being empowered by the government program, public universities still suffer from the tension between the desire for decentralization and the desire to maintain the socialist orientation in higher education (Tran, 2014). Moreover, common challenges such as the lack of professional staff, the inadequate resources, the institutional rigidity, and a poor understanding of the market have proved to be challenging to overcome (Nguyen & Tran, 2018).

Not only are the government and private organizations pushing forward the market mechanism and research activities, but international donors are also exerting a greater degree of influence. The Asian Development Bank and the World Bank are stated in a government announcement to lend USD400 million to Vietnam to build four "international standard" universities (London, 2011). In addition, Tran (2018a) noted the World Bank stands out as the most massive investor in reforming higher education in Vietnam, having provided a credit of USD140 million until the year 2000 to help to build a higher capacity of education (London, 2011). And from 1998 to 2017, World Bank's policy-based lending programs have amounted to USD450 million (Tran,

2018a). Besides focusing on smaller-scale projects such as curricular reform and teacher training, the World Bank has strongly emphasized on measures to increase cost efficiency and the role of the market. According to Tran (2018a), as the bank has gone beyond the role of a donor, or a policy advisor, to become a policy actor, it is the most influential international organization in Vietnam's higher education reform. The efforts of the World Bank have achieved concrete results: the issuance of a series of legal documents that have kickstarted the current trajectory of Vietnam's higher education system.

Analyzing the current situation, previous studies highlighted the overreliance on policy-borrowing in Vietnam. As Vietnamese culture has possessed certain peculiarities (Vuong, Bui, et al., 2018), too much policies and institutional structures importing from the West would create conflicts. Researchers have urged a balanced reconsideration this trend (Nguyen & Tran, 2018; Tran, 2018a; Tran, 2014). The domestic players in the country, hence, must take a more pro-active role in shaping the higher education system.

We suspect that introducing the concept of business of science can help stimulate the bottom-up responses to generate a more productive, pro-active research culture. The following section discusses the challenges of the emerging business of science in Vietnam.

Challenges of a sustainable business of science in Vietnam
As Vietnam gradually transitions to become a more liberalized and internationally integrated economy, its higher education system also moves forward in this direction. However, for a business of science to capitalize on this wave of internationalization and decentralization, organizations and individual researchers in Vietnam must address the following challenges.

First, there must be a stronger presence of an entrepreneurial spirit among organizations and individual researchers in Vietnam. Nguyen and Meek (2016), when seeking to identify the key problems in organizing and structuring university research in

Vietnam, highlighted the lack of entrepreneurial spirit and vision when it comes to research-related personnel and research office. Through 55 semi-structured interviews in four major universities in Vietnam, the authors found university academics and managers perceived the rectors and vice-rectors of research more effective as "disturbance handler" than as an "entrepreneur." Moreover, the research office was perceived as more effective in "organizing" and "controlling" than on "planning" and "leading" roles. In another related study, Nguyen and Van Gramberg (2018) identified the lack of strategic planning for research among the four universities in Vietnam, although they all aim at being leading research institutions in the country. Rather than planning research activities based on long-term strategies, the universities have chosen a compliance-based planning approach. More specifically, the universities in this study followed grant application procedures prescribed by administrative funding agencies annually rather than proactively creating long-term deliberate strategies to secure government grants. Besides the government grants, researchers in these universities are eligible to apply for funding from a wide range of international and domestic organizations. However, Nguyen and Van Gramberg (2018) showed that at universities level, there had been no serious plan for it. This is perhaps another expression of the absence of entrepreneurial spirit among public universities in Vietnam.

Not only is there a lack of entrepreneurial spirit at the university and institution level, there is also insufficient experience among academic staff in Vietnam when it comes to the commercialization of scientific production. Indeed, the amount of contribution from research to income of the higher education system in Vietnam is minuscule. Tran and Villano (2017) found that the percentage of academic staff with postgraduate degrees was not significantly associated with the efficiency of universities, especially in terms of income from research. It is, therefore, not surprising that, according to a recent study, the revenue from academic activities remained negligible, accounting for only 3% (Hoang, 2018). This number clearly falls short of HERA's target for income from research to account for 25% by 2020. Pham and Hayden (2019) pointed out although most academics in Vietnam feel a personal commitment to engage in research, the institutional pressure for international publications is still low. There appear to be several disincentives to publishing in international journals, including the lack of financial support, the lack of transparency in funding, the interference with academic freedom and the lack of language skills (Pham & Hayden, 2019).

Another challenge that should be addressed is the contradictory legal mandates coming from different ministries. While the Ministry of Science and Technology has issued a number of regulations to induce some changes in the systems of funding and human resource management in public universities and institutions, these regulations meet considerable barriers from the law on tax administration, and the law on public employees, cadres and civil servants (Hao-Linh, 2019). In this regard, one can argue that private universities and institutions, which are not the subject of the law on public employees, cadres and civil servants, enjoy relatively more freedom to create a better incentive system for research activities in Vietnam. However, there are many more researchers working for public universities and institutions than in private ones in Vietnam. In light of this fact, the contradiction in different legal mandates remains an obstacle for the development of the business of science in Vietnam in the near future.

What is a business of science? Examples from successful cases around the world

We propose to define the *business of science* as a business where research and research-based activities and contents are the products. More specifically, this business would offer services such as research, science communication, science journalism, data collection, data analysis, and software developments, to name a few. The obvious examples of science-based business are the commercialization of scientific products, which has been taking place in various fields, from materials science (Editorial, 2006), biomedical marketing (Nelson, 2012), biocontrol products (Droby, Wisniewski, Teixidó, Spadaro, & Jijakli, 2016). Thanks to the permission to patent state-funded research in developed countries such as the United States, United Kingdom, and Japan, an increasing number of researchers have been able to take financial advantages of this practice (Editorial, 2006).

Pisano (2010), using the example of the development of science-based business such as biotech start-ups in the U.S., argued that science and business are two very different fields and that the convergence of the two will necessarily create frictions. This would call for organizational innovations to solve problems on three fronts: risk, integration, and learning. In terms of risk, the iterative research and development (R&D) process of science-based business usually takes a long time to solve the fundamental uncertainty problem. In terms of integration, a successful business of science must be able to integrate and combine relevant existing bodies of knowledge. As a business of science must find a way to integrate existing disciplines and solve the problem of uncertainty, first and foremost, for their survival and thriving, it is important for them to implement a learning culture in all levels of the organization: learning how to take risks, how to learn from failures, how to make decisions under immense uncertainty. Pisano (2010) indicated the limits of the "visible hands of the hierarchies" and the "invisible hand of the markets" in solving these three problems. He suggested when designing a business of science, the goal would be to design it to be good at "managing and rewarding long-term risky investments, integrating varieties of bodies of knowledge, and learning cumulatively over time."

However, as he only grounded this account on high-tech areas such as biotech, nanotech, and energy, he had overlooked the possibility of entrepreneurial firms that take other fields such as social sciences and humanities as the foundation of their business. Moreover, as Pisano (2010) published his article when there is little understanding of a new economy powered by the abundance of data and the advancement in computing technology, he might have missed the important implications of these factors for science-based business.

In recent years, the frenzied development of advanced computational platforms, social networks and high-speed Internet connectivity has generated business opportunities in velocity and volume the world has never seen. Business and technology researchers have called this trend by different names: "computational entrepreneurship" (Vuong, 2019), "the digital economy," "the gig economy," "the sharing economy," "the platform economy" (Bodie, 2017). Entrepreneurs in the business world are seizing these opportunities and turn them into enormous economic successes; the same trends can also be observed among their academic counterparts. One of most successful examples of academic entrepreneurship in the age of social networks is the Intellectual Dark Web, a group of public intellectuals who started their own podcasts/YouTube channels, regularly publishing long-form conversations, discussing all kinds of subjects covering religions, politics, science, philosophy. To get a sense of how each of them is an Internet sensation, Sam Harris, a neuroscientist, told the New York Times that his "Making Sense" podcast is estimated to reach a million listeners each episode; Dave Rubin, a conservative commentator and comedian, said his YouTube channel has more than 700,000 subscribers. All of their works are funded by their fans; for example, Jordan Peterson, a psychology professor in the University of Toronto, shared that he made USD80,000 in fan donations. Their online success has translated offline as they are found talking to one another in packed auditoriums around the world and their books are found in the best-seller sections (Weiss, 2018).

We can also list other examples of successful academic start-ups such as Publons. Publons is a start-up firm that creates a platform for scientists to share their peer review history on the Internet to get credit for doing the peer review, a pillar of scientific process. By June 2017, there were more than 150,000 researchers who registered with Publons, and together, they have shared 800,000 review records on the website (Van Noorden, 2017). On 2017, Publons were bought by Clarivate Analytics, the owner of

> "The role of funding depends on the type of research. For instance, the research that is based on freely available, open access information would only need financial support for the working hours of the researchers, which is the salary. On the other hand, finance will be a major concern for a research project that requires a large-scale survey. In my opinion, researchers can still perform with a limited budget, they only need to be clear about what they can and cannot do in that situation. Therefore, it is perhaps an overstatement to say that the lack of budget is restraining the development of SSH."
>
> Dr. Giang Thanh Long, National Economics University, Hanoi, Vietnam.

the giant science-citation database Web of Science. The data provided by Publons have clearly enabled a wide range of valuable insights into the global state of peer review. For example, we now know peer reviewers for high-quality journals write on average 300 more words than they do for other journals; or reviewers for psychology, humanities, earth sciences tend to write longer review (Conroy, 2018); or the peer review community is not diverse enough (Publons, 2018). Clearly, Publons is a shining example of a business of science that takes advantages of advancement of technological platforms and generates both social and financial profits.

The emerging business of science in Vietnam: the role of academic entrepreneurship

As noted above, there are numerous challenges to build a sustainable business of science in Vietnam. The challenges range from the influence of the Soviet model of higher education in the past, the lack of entrepreneurship spirit among research institutions, the lack of a robust research culture, the passive attitude of researchers in finding ways to commercialize their research products. In this section, we focus on the important mindset and skills necessary for the owner of the business of science, the researchers themselves.

The different examples of successful science-based business strongly indicate the importance of a pro-active mindset among researchers to seek and seize opportunities to commercialize their research products. Here, the general principle of academic entrepreneurship can be useful. Built on the generic definition of entrepreneurship by the notion of Stevenson, Roberts, and Grousbeck (1989), Glassman et al. (2003) argued that academic entrepreneurship is essentially about the creation and pursuit of opportunities in the university setting, regardless of available resources. The ability to scrounge for or scavenge scarce resources, which has been highlighted in the literature on public entrepreneurship, becomes a skill that academic entrepreneurs cannot do without in the process of creating values (Glassman et al., 2003). Glassman et al. (2003) identified four dimensions that influence the degree of success for academic entrepreneurs: (i) opportunities, both actual and potential; (b) people who can identify and seize opportunities; (c) the ability to generate as well as optimally use resources; and (d) an entrepreneurship culture.

For the first three dimensions, arguably, one cannot dispense with the role of judgment and intuition; Pisano (2010) has claimed, "Judgment and intuition must suffice where "hard" data and good predictive models are lacking," as a formula of success in the emerging business of science. Adding to this discussion, one can also list serendipity, defined as the ability to recognize and leverage value from unexpected information that comes from all areas of life, among one of the critical strategic advantages (Napier & Vuong, 2013). Indeed, not only the science-based business owners must have a strong entrepreneurial spirit, but they also need to rely on sharp intuition and judgment to successfully capture and deliver value in this market.

More importantly, as a business of science is supposed to offer research and research-related contents and activities as products, the gold standards of scientific conducts must be upheld: oversight committees, a mechanism to maintain research integrity, a mechanism to evaluate research quality, developing professionalism in research. Nguyen and Meek (2016) have listed such elements as lacking in the situation of Vietnam, creating a tremendous barrier for developing research capacity in the country. However, in the paradigm of building a business of science, entrepreneurial researchers must actively find ways to establish such standard practices. One suggestion is that researchers can work together to create these integrity-safeguarding practices to ensure that the self-correcting mechanism of science is at work. The Institute of Social Development Studies, Hanoi, Vietnam, an NGO and NPO that focuses on solving social problems by applying knowledge gained from research, is an example in this regard. The research institute regularly trains its members when conducting research with human subjects and establishes an internal review board to make sure the research process complied with the international standard (Khuat et al., 2018).

With regards to social sciences and humanities, especially in a transition economy such as Vietnam, the opportunities to commercialize research products based on patent might be rare. However, as shown by the example of the Intellectual Dark Web (Weiss, 2018), their work on social and cultural phenomenon, with a right kind of packaging, can reach out to a public through the deployment of science communication. Websites such as sc.sshpa.com or Tiasang.com are currently the front players in the nascent science communication sector in Vietnam. They work to educate the public about important issues in science such as new scientific discoveries, movements in science as well as science policies. Another area that social science researchers can find opportunities is social data and its construction and management. Without a strong technical and computer background, this prospect of going into data/database management can be daunting. However, the availability of computing resources and talented collaborators can compensate for these shortcomings, as shown in the case of Publons (Van Noorden, 2017). This book and the database, on which it is based, can also be considered an attempt on business of science, which takes advantage of available resources online to create social database and software that have potential business values (Vuong, La, et al., 2018).

As a business of science is centered around research, a research project should be a unit for management. Here, it is important for science-based business owners to define success in managing a life cycle of a research project. As for any business activities, the ultimate measure of business success is profitability. However, in the beginning of a business of science, especially, when the business is focusing on building its brand, success should be measured by the number of articles published, the number of articles published in highly prestigious journals, the number of clean and tidy datasets produced for science and society, the number of data management procedures and data treatment procedures invented. All of these metrics should all be tied down to the most important one: peer-reviewed publication. This is also a training phase for the members of the start-ups, to learn necessary research skills and critical thinking skills to be successful as researchers. Once the brand for the business is established, the business owners could move on to the "business phase." In this phase, the business can take on products and services that are derived from their research: speaking engagement, science communication, consultancy services, etc.

Vietnamese researchers, many of whom have experience international environment, can look outward and learn from their colleagues overseas how they could commercialize scientific knowledge. However, in the end, for that commercialization to succeed in Vietnam, the researchers must do more than mere copy-paste: they must look inward and design their products according to cultural expectations and local demands, all of which are critical for their success.

References

Bodie, M. T. (2017). Lessons from the dramatists guild for the platform economy. *University of Chicago Legal Forum*. Retrieved from https://chicagounbound.uchicago.edu/uclf/vol2017/iss1/2/

Conroy, G. (2018). Scientists go to great lengths in reviewing high-quality research. *Nature Index*. Retrieved from https://www.natureindex.com/news-blog/scientists-go-to-great-lengths-in-reviewing-high-quality-research

Droby, S., Wisniewski, M., Teixidó, N., Spadaro, D., & Jijakli, M. H. (2016). The science, development, and commercialization of postharvest biocontrol products. *Postharvest Biology and Technology, 122*, 22-29. doi:https://doi.org/10.1016/j.postharvbio.2016.04.006

Editorial. (2006). The business of science. *Nature Materials, 5*(12), 921-921. doi:10.1038/nmat1796

Glassman, A. M., Moore, R. W., Rossy, G. L., Neupert, K., Napier, N. K., Jones, D. E., & Harvey, M. (2003). Academic entrepreneurship: Views on balancing the Acropolis and the Agora. *Journal of Management Inquiry, 12*(4), 353-374. doi:10.1177/1056492603258979

Hao-Linh. (2019). Tư nhân đầu tư vào giáo dục đại học và nghiên cứu: Bây giờ chính là thời cơ [Private investment into university education and research: now is the time]. *Khoa hoc va Phat trien*. Retrieved from http://khoahocphattrien.vn/chinh-sach/tu-nhan-dau-tu-vao-giao-duc-dai-hoc-va-nghien-cuu-bay-gio-chinh-la-thoi-co/20180809100832649p1c785.htm

Hayden, M., & Thiep, L. Q. (2007). Institutional autonomy for higher education in Vietnam. *Higher Education Research & Development, 26*(1), 73-85. doi:10.1080/07294360601166828

Hoang, L. (2018). Twin privatization in Vietnam higher education: The emergence of private higher education and partial privatization of public universities. *Higher Education Policy*, 1-22. doi:10.1057/s41307-018-0086-8

Khuat, H. T., Do, T. T., Nguyen, A. V., Vu, T. X., Nguyen, T. P., Tran, K., . . . Vuong, Q.-H. (2018). The Dark Side of Female HIV Patient Care: Sexual and Reproductive Health Risks in Pre- and Post-Clinical Treatments. *Journal of Clinical Medicine, 7*(11), 402. doi:10.3390/jcm7110402

London, J. D. (2011). Education in Vietnam: Historical roots, recent trends. In J. D. London (Ed.), *Education in Vietnam*. Singapore: Institute of South East Asian Studies.

NAFOSTED. (2018). Ký kết thỏa thuận tài trợ kinh phí trao giải thưởng Tạ Quang Bửu [Signing a sponsorship agreement for Ta Quang Buu Prize]. *NAFOSTED*. Retrieved from https://nafosted.gov.vn/ky-ket-thoa-thuan-tai-tro-kinh-phi-trao-giai-thuong-ta-quang-buu/

Napier, N. K., & Vuong, Q.-H. (2013). Serendipity as a strategic advantage? In Wilkinson (Ed.), *Strategic management in the 21st century (Vol. 1: The operational environment)* (Vol. 1, pp. 175-199). Westport, CT: Praeger/ABC-Clio.

Nature Index. (2018). Vietnam. *Nature Index*. Retrieved from https://www.natureindex.com/country-outputs/vietnam

Nelson, B. (2012). Business and science: In the market. *Nature*, 261-263. doi:10.1038/nj7406-261a

Nguyen, H. T. L., & Meek, V. L. (2016). Key problems in organizing and structuring university research in Vietnam: The lack of an effective research "behaviour formalization" system. *Minerva, 54*(1), 45-73.

Nguyen, H. T. L., & Van Gramberg, B. (2018). University strategic research planning: a key to reforming university research in Vietnam? *Studies in Higher Education, 43*(12), 2130-2147.

Nguyen, N., & Tran, L. T. (2018). Looking inward or outward? Vietnam higher education at the superhighway of globalization: culture, values and changes. *Journal of Asian Public Policy, 11*(1), 28-45. doi:10.1080/17516234.2017.1332457

Pham, L. T., & Hayden, M. (2019). Research In Vietnam: The Experience Of The Humanities And Social Sciences. *Journal of International and Comparative Education (JICE), S.1*, 27-40. doi:10.14425/jice.2019.8.1.27

Pisano, G. P. (2010). The evolution of science-based business: innovating how we innovate. *Industrial and corporate change, 19*(2), 465-482.

Publons. (2018). Global state of peer view. *Clarivate Analytics*. Retrieved from https://publons.com/static/Publons-Global-State-Of-Peer-Review-2018.pdf

On pilot renovation of the operation mechanism of public tertiary education institutions during 2014-2017, (2014).

Stevenson, H., Roberts, M., & Grousbeck, H. (1989). *Business ventures and the entrepreneur*. Homewood, IL: Irwin.

Tran, C.-D. T. T., & Villano, R. A. (2017). An empirical analysis of the performance of Vietnamese higher education institutions. *Journal of Further and Higher Education, 41*(4), 530-544. doi:10.1080/0309877X.2015.1135886

Tran, D.-N. (2018a). Impacts of international organizations on Vietnam's higher education policy: The good, the abad and the ugly. In L. T. Tran & S. Marginson (Eds.), *Internationalisation in Vietnamese Higher Education* (pp. 99-117). Cham: Springer International Publishing.

Tran, D. L., & Thanh-Tam. (2014). Kể về ngôi trường Đại học dân lập đầu tiên [Talk about the first people-founded university]. *Nhan Dan*. Retrieved from http://www.nhandan.com.vn/giaoduc/item/24780102-ke-ve-ngoi-truong-dai-hoc-dan-lap-dau-tien.html

Tran, T. T. (2014). Governance in higher education in Vietnam – a move towards decentralization and its practical problems. *Journal of Asian Public Policy, 7*(1), 71-82. doi:10.1080/17516234.2013.873341

Tran, V. N. (2018b). Khat vong Duy Tan [Duy Tan's ambition]. *Tia Sang*. Retrieved from http://tiasang.com.vn/-giao-duc/Khat-vong-Duy-Tan-11165

Van Noorden, R. (2017). Web of Science owner buys up booming peer-review platform. *Nature News.* Retrieved from https://www.nature.com/news/web-of-science-owner-buys-up-booming-peer-review-platform-1.22094

Vuong, Q.-H. (2019). Computational entrepreneurship: from economic complexities to interdisciplinary research. *Problems and Perspectives in Management, 17*(1), 117-129.

Vuong, Q.-H., Bui, Q.-K., La, V.-P., Vuong, T.-T., Nguyen, V.-H. T., Ho, M.-T., . . . Ho, M.-T. (2018). Cultural additivity: behavioural insights from the interaction of Confucianism, Buddhism and Taoism in folktales. *Palgrave Communications, 4*(1), 143. doi:10.1057/s41599-018-0189-2

Vuong, Q.-H., Napier, N. K., Ho, M.-T., Nguyen, V.-H. T., Vuong, T.-T., Pham, H. H., & Nguyen, H.-K. T. (2018). Effects of work environment and collaboration on research productivity in Vietnamese social sciences: evidence from 2008 to 2017 scopus data. *Studies in Higher Education*, 1-16. doi:10.1080/03075079.2018.1479845.

Vuong, Q.-H., La, V.-P., Vuong, T.-T., Ho, M.-T., Nguyen, T. H.-K., Nguyen, T.V.-H., Pham, H.-H., Ho, M.-T. (2018). An open database of productivity in Vietnam's social sciences and humanities for public use. *Scientific Data 5,*180188. Doi: https://doi.org/10.1038/sdata.2018.188;

Weiss, B. (2018). Meet the renegades of the Intellectual Dark Web. *The New York Times.* Retrieved from https://www.nytimes.com/2018/05/08/opinion/intellectual-dark-web.html

Closing remarks
Quan-Hoang Vuong, Trung Tran

As the global academic landscape is ever-changing, so is that of Vietnam. An emergent economy and a country considered to be in development still, yet at the same time, Vietnam is home to a rich, millennia long cultural identity that is fiercely present in every aspect of both the civil society and the scientific community. This contrast makes the case of this country well worth a look – and a long, hard look, at that, for all the unpredictability that often came with accelerated development. And so, the story is far from ending, even as we are nearing the conclusion of this book.

The first two chapters set the stage for later discussions with a panorama of academia in Vietnam, all of which is largely based on our updating database on SSH scholars of the country. As the economy prospered and the material needs of the Vietnamese people become satisfied, the country now aspired to thrive in equal measures in the world of knowledge creation, more specifically represented by scientific publishing. Vietnam has been lagging behind in this regard, which should not come as a surprise given how recognition for the importance of academic development has been a long process. The conjuncture has morphed, however, and shows positive signs of growing scientific productivity. On the part of policy-makers, this has been accompanied by the establishment of a national institution dedicated to scientific funding – the NAFOSTED – as well as the decree-based adoption of standards that match those of the international academic sphere. The picture could not be completed without initiatives on the side of the researchers themselves. Efforts to improve productivity and work quality are not limited to solely the technical aspect of doing science, but also in the networking among peers, both domestic and international. Indeed, accounting for a great portion of the rise in scientific production of Vietnamese authors are journal articles resulting from collaboration with foreign authors.

Going more into details, the three following chapters paint a more in-depth picture of the frontrunners, whose footsteps throughout the years from 2008 to 2018 have been recorded in our SSHPA database. Field-wise, of the 32 SSH disciplines in Vietnam, Health Care, Education and Economics make up the 'Big Three' in terms of publication counts as well as number of authors; each with their own remarkable attributes. Economics set the trend of interdisciplinary research, while Health Care was characterized by a clear tendency towards open access science; and whereas both of these lean towards collaboration, solo authorship prevailed in the field of Education. Author-wise, the most eminent researchers and their networks came under focus, revealing a highly skewed distribution of scientific output, where the top 10% most prolific scientists account for nearly two thirds of the entire country's scientific production during the decade in question. Male prevalence represents another imbalance in the community, a characteristic that is gradually changing with the rise of female researchers.

The last three chapters touch on more philosophical discussions regarding academic publishing in the emerging SSH fields of Vietnam. We address the matter of setting quality standards, with a particular focus on the growing competition between institutions of higher education both public and private. We note that principles matter especially where it involves policy-making, which is of particular importance considering the positive impact of Circular 08 on post-graduate training. In fact, not only did this policy kick into motion the scientific productivity nominally as evidenced by our data, it has also enriched public discourse with the subject of academia and its development. We raise ethics questions in doing research, especially where funding and sponsorship are involved. Beyond public grants and private compensation uss the self-funding potential of academic publication – the novel possibility of doing business and doing science in tandem. All of these issues, despite being common discourse in the international community, are playing out in the Vietnamese academic sphere at a promising speed.

This book shall not close without opening up a plethora of new questions. Our broad strokes could only cover so much of the the decade-long period of Vietnamese publishing in the fields of SSH. International publishing, especially in a nascent scientific community such as that of Vietnam, is not a painting but a motion picture – one that has moved at a modest pace in the past, but has been and will definitely be accelerating in the future. How would SSH develop in Vietnam? How would these developments look like when placed side-by-side with the growth of STEM fields, which typically receive more attention and appreciation? How would academic growth, open access and digitalization tendencies impact the country in other aspects, such as politics or legal domains – as did France with the law on the *République numérique* (digital republic)? As of yet, we do not have the answer. We, however, are certain of one thing: that we, as researchers, shall remain invested in this subject for years to come. We welcome you to join us on this journey.

APPENDIX A
Complete transcription of interviews

With the purpose of providing an objective view of Vietnam's social sciences and humanities, in the process of writing this book, we contacted many social scientists who are working in Vietnam and overseas. We were fortunate and grateful to the opportunities to speak to and become acquainted with many scholars through emails and Skype. This Appendix presents the entire transcription of the interviews we have made with 28 Vietnamese authors. The interviews were conducted in Vietnamese and translated into English. We sincerely apologize if our translations do not do justice to the original opinions.

A.1. Bui Thanh Huong
Dr. Bui Thanh Huong, Ritsumeikan Asia Pacific University, Beppu, Oita, Japan

1. Please tell us about the papers that you take the most pride in.
- Bui, H.T. & Le, T-A. (2016). Tourist satisfaction and destination image of Vietnam's Ha Long Bay. *Asia Pacific Journal of Tourism Research*, 21(7), 795-810.
- Yoshida, K., Bui, H.T. & Lee, T.J. (2016). Does tourism illuminate the darkness of Hiroshima and Nagasaki?. *Journal of Destination Marketing and Management*, 5(4), 333-340.

These articles were published in SSCI-indexed tourism journals. The first article belongs to a research project about Ha Long Bay, a famous but under-researched attraction in Vietnam. Many students find this article interesting and uses it as a reference in their research.

The second article became the 2016 Best Paper Runner Up of the *Journal of Destination Marketing and Management*. The paper proposes a new aspect in tourism research, which emphasizes on the impact of Asian culture in developing tourism.

2. What do you think about international collaboration in the current context of Vietnam?
I think international collaboration in Vietnam is still a mere façade and does not result in a ready product such as international

publications. The main reason is the level of expertise. To have a fruitful collaboration, both sides should have similar level of expertise, or at least each side possesses certain skills or resources that can complement each other. Currently, Vietnam's advantage is that we can offer many new interesting topics, but the Vietnamese authors lack writing and editing skills, and credibility in scientific publishing to convince the reviewers and editors of high-ranking journals. Therefore, most of the international collaborations that resulted in scientific publications are usually from personal efforts and connection.

3. What do you think about the role of interdisciplinary research in pushing scientific output and quality?
Interdisciplinary research is very necessary because the differences in expertise of people involved will offer new and fresh ideas about the research subject. Moreover, the methodology and the theory from different disciplines can support each other as well. Finally, interdisciplinary research is all about teamwork, and a team can produce more effectively than a solo player.

4. What do you think are the biggest challenges facing Vietnam's SSH?
I think a narrow local mindset is probably the biggest challenge that Vietnamese SSH is facing. Besides, Vietnamese science does not have a lot of funding and it directly resulted in the lack of resources like databases, scientific journals, or books to support the researchers in finding new results and theories. Finally, data analysis and writing skills are also challenging for Vietnamese social scientists.

A.2. Bui Thi Minh Hong
Dr. Bui Thi Minh Hong, Bath University, United Kingdom

1. Of your publications, which one do you take the most pride in?
I take pride in all of my works because I have put a lot of efforts in those studies. International publication is a ranking game, and in the United Kingdom, the game is even more competitive. However, I think any ranking is only temporary, while academia is a life-time work. I can see that the academic ranking game is

beginning in Vietnam too. Indeed, the game has certain positive aspects, but we cannot deny it also has negative aspects. If I must choose, I will choose the following two projects:
- o Tabvuma, V., Bui, T. M. H, & Homberg, F. (2014). Adaptation to externally driven change: the impact of political change on job satisfaction in the public sector. *Public Administration Review, 74*(3), 384-395.

The first one is a paper that provides a new approach to an old topic, which eventually gave us new interesting results (Tabvuma, Bui, & Homberg, 2014).

The second one is the research project about Learning organization between Vietnam and the UK. This is a self-financing project but the eventual outputs are 6 journal articles and a book chapter.

2. What do you think about the role of interdisciplinary research in increasing scientific output and quality?

I started thinking about participating in interdisciplinary research around 2011, 2012. I thought that interdisciplinary research would eventually take off, but at the moment, its development should be considered carefully. Generation gap is one of the issues that holds back interdisciplinary research because the older generation is still conservative and they rather focus on a narrow field, meanwhile, the younger generation is more open-minded. Even in the UK, the academic world is not especially fond of promoting interdisciplinary research. Another problem is when you know a lot about everything, you might not have an in-depth understanding about one subject.

Since 2016, I have participated in different interdisciplinary workshops such as energy, agriculture, healthcare, or immigration. As I was one of the few invited social scientists, I realized that new technology is often beyond the current comprehension of the society, thus, social scientists can play a role in building learning capacity for the government, and corporation. The beauty of interdisciplinary research is how we can help each other.

3. Can you share about your hardest peer review experience? How does peer review improve the quality of your work and your expertise on the field?

There is nothing called an easy peer review. I think publishing is hard work that has little joy and requires a lot of passion and effort. My most recent accepted paper will be published in a mid-tier journal, but I went through two rounds of review with four reviewers. However, the harder the review, the more you can learn. The question is whether the researcher wants to deal with the hardship or not? Unless you are a superstar, otherwise science is full of hardship, and often without glory. In the UK, the norms are already established, so everything is simpler. In Vietnam, the main goal is still to make end meets, so I can understand why research and science are underdeveloped, and I think being able to publish in an international journal is already a great endeavor from Vietnamese scholars.

In a particularly negative case, I was forced by an editor, whose research topic is similar with mine, to shift my paper toward his favored direction. I lacked experiences back then, so I decided to compromise. Moreover, I also know a lot of cases where reviewers reject a paper for non-academic reasons.

4. To have a good research in natural science, investment in laboratory equipment is a must. What do you think about the necessary investment for social sciences in order to increase scientific output and quality?
For a social scientist, it is necessary to be passionate. Other than that, raising the quality of collaboration is also necessary. Asian researchers have a lot of quality materials, but they lack the capability to elevate their studies, therefore, collaboration might address this issue. For young researchers, a mentor or co-authors will be good long-term development.

However, I'd like to point out that Vietnamese people are blindly fond of Westerners. There are many international conferences in Vietnam, which often prefer to invite foreign scholars, despite their research quality is not as good as many Vietnamese who are working oversea. I think Vietnam should make a good use of the Vietnamese who are doing research overseas. For instance, Hong Kong or Singapore is able to invite many professors from the United States to collaborate with them, but for Vietnam, the overseas Vietnamese scholars might be a wise choice for collaboration.

A.3. Giang Thanh Long
Dr. Giang Thanh Long, Institute of Public Policy Management (IPPM), National Economics University, Hanoi, Vietnam

1. Do you think funding is an issue that prevents the development of social sciences and humanities (SSH) in Vietnam?

The role of funding depends on the type of research. For instance, the research that is based on freely available, open access information would only need financial support for the working hours of the researchers, which is the salary. On the other hand, finance will be a major concern for a research project that requires a large-scale survey. In my opinion, researchers can still perform with a limited budget, they only need to be clear about what they can and cannot do in that situation. Therefore, it is perhaps an overstatement to say that the lack of budget is restraining the development of SSH.

2. Regarding organizing data and controlling the quality of data, do you think they are a problem in the current condition of Vietnamese society?

I agree that data-related issues can be a problem, because a cleaned and quality dataset (either primary or secondary) will play a major role in determining the quality of the research. A poor dataset rarely leads to a good research, regardless of the budget or human resources. On the contrary, high quality data only need a handful of good researchers to produce a high-quality study.

3. What are your criteria in choosing a research partner?

My prioritized criterion is the attitude of a potential partner: whether they truly want to work on the research project or not. Once we find the common ground, the problems of finding a shared topic, distributing resources can be solved easily. Hence, in the current context, it is necessary to build a network of researchers who shared the same direction.

4. Please tell us about the papers that you take the most pride in.
- o Teerawichitchainan, B., Pothisiri, W., & Giang, T. L. (2015). How do living arrangements and intergenerational

support matter for psychological health of elderly parents? Evidence from Myanmar, Vietnam, and Thailand. *Social Science & Medicine, 136,* 106-116.

The paper published in Social Science and Medicine that discussed the life of aging people in three countries with different levels of income: Thailand, Vietnam, and Myanmar. This paper has implications for policies that promote the mental health of the aging population regardless of the living standard.

- o Giang, L. T., Nguyen, C. V., & Tran, T. Q. (2016). Firm agglomeration and local poverty reduction: evidence from an economy in transition. *Asian-Pacific Economic Literature, 30*(1), 80-98.

The paper published in Asia Pacific Economic Literature that proved business development in a province will have positive effects not only on economic development but also poverty reduction. This will in turn raise the education opportunity for children.

A.4. Ho Huu Loc
Dr. Ho Huu Loc, Ho Chi Minh City University of Science, Ho Chi Minh City, Vietnam

1. Please tell us about the paper(s) that you take the most pride in.

- o Ho, H. L., Irvine, K. N., Nguyen, D. T. H., Nguyen, T. K. Q., Nguyen, N. T., & Shimizu, Y. (2018). The legal aspects of Ecosystem Services in agricultural land pricing, some implications from a case study in Vietnam's Mekong Delta. *Ecosystem Services, 29,* 360-369.

Of all the papers that I have published up until now, I like this paper for three reasons:
- Continuity. The content of this paper follows up from the results of another article that I have published. Since then, I have continued with this direction.
- Spontaneity. I did not plan to write this paper, but after chatting in a party with colleagues, I started writing the paper immediately. Honestly speaking, I feel very lucky!

- Practical application. The paper reviews the law carefully and points out some rules that can benefit from the empirical result.

2. What do you think about the role of interdisciplinary research in increasing scientific output and quality?
I think interdisciplinary research is very important and it is the inevitable trend in scientific research. Personally, I really enjoy collaborating with researchers from other fields. For example, I have been working with a biochemist and a *Hán-Nôm* researcher.

3. Do you think funding is an issue that prevents the development of social sciences and humanities (SSH) in Vietnam?
I think finance is an issue for every discipline, not only SSH. In natural science, you cannot buy chemicals or laboratory equipment without abundant financial resources.

4. What is your preferred methodology?
I am a natural scientist turning into a social scientist, so I don't have a defined 'style'. I usually learn from journal articles, and then apply what I learn to my own research.

A.5. Huynh The Du
Dr. Huynh The Du, Fulbright University Vietnam, Ho Chi Minh City, Vietnam

1. Please tell us about the papers that you take the most pride in.
- Huynh, T. D. (2015). The misuse of urban planning in Ho Chi Minh City. *Habitat International*, 48, 11-19.

I like this paper because of its practicality and generalization.

2. What do you think about international collaboration in the current context?
I think for international collaboration to be effective, we must focus on the substance, rather than the appearance. Some universities spend a fortune to organize international conferences, but the central theme of the conference has nothing to do with the university; we should keep practice like this from happening. I also think international collaboration should focus on specific individuals, research projects, or organizations.

3. What do you think about the role of interdisciplinary research in increasing scientific output and quality?
Interdisciplinary research is necessary, but we should refrain from having interdisciplinary studies that have very loose framework, which lead to products of no substance.

4. To have a good research in natural science, investment in laboratory equipment is a must. What do you think about the necessary investment for social sciences to raise the scientific output and quality?

I think social sciences and humanities research should focus on practical applications. We could also raise the level of competitiveness by require more publications in high-ranking journals.

A.6. Khuat Thu Hong
Dr. Khuat Thu Hong, Institute for Social Development Studies (ISDS), Hanoi, Vietnam

I don't think I can be qualified in the group of high-productivity scientists because publishing in international journals has not been my top priority in the past years. Although I knew this is something I should do, I do not actually work in an academic environment where publishing is one of the criteria for promotion. Publishing also requires significant time commitment whereas I am too occupied with other projects to be invested in. Only when the projects I work on require international publication of the research results would I do it. This is why I don't have many published works. Personally, I was not that concerned about authorship so I used to offer my colleagues the first-author position, especially overseas colleagues who need to improve publication records to get tenure. However, I have changed my mind about this and plan to dedicate more time to this.

As for your questions, my answers are below:
1. Of your published articles, which ones do you take the most pride in? Why?
I am most proud of the following three articles:

- Khuat, T.H. (1998). Study on sexuality in Vietnam: the known and unknown issues. *South and East Asia Regional Working Papers No. 11*. The Population Council. Available at https://www.popline.org/node/523255. Doi: 10.13140/RG.2.2.15215.84640.

While this is only a working paper, I think it has laid the groundwork for later research on this topic in Vietnam. I noticed that the paper has been cited quite often.

- Khuat, T. H., Nguyen, V. T., Jardine, M., Moore, T., Bui, T. H., & Crofts, N. (2012). Harm reduction and "Clean" community: can Viet Nam have both?. *Harm Reduction Journal*, 9(1), 25.

I like this article for it points out the contradiction between political will and actual understanding when it comes to drug use in Vietnam. The article offers glimpses into the politicization of grassroots-level community. The police force, which plays a critical role in the fight against drug-related crimes, in a way feeds into that politicization, and subsequently, is stuck in that trap.

- Phinney, H. M., Hong, K. T., Nhan, V. T. T., Thao, N. T. P., & Hirsch, J. S. (2014). Obstacles to the 'cleanliness of our race': HIV, reproductive risk, stratified reproduction, and population quality in Hanoi, Vietnam. *Critical Public Health*, 24(4), 445-460.

This article was written based on my ideas. It points out the Vietnamese's thought of eugenics is reflected in the language and reproductive health of people living with HIV. Deep down, the article raises questions about the humanity of such thought. The article is particularly meaningful for it pokes right at Vietnam's eugenic tendency as maintained in the so-called "population quality" – a term that is being discussed in the revised Population Law and may be passed soon. If this is passed, Vietnam will face harsh criticisms regarding human rights.

2. What are your opinions on international collaboration in the current context? What are its advantages and limitations?

International cooperation in scientific research is necessary. Frankly speaking, social sciences in Vietnam remain underdeveloped and severely limited because the local scientists were not trained properly and even lack access to the new materials and theories. Many of them are held back by the dogma of Marxism-Leninism. This is why the quality of social sciences research (with the exception of Economics) in Vietnam is low. International cooperation in conduction research will help correct for these shortcomings, filling in the gaps in research materials, theories, methodology, and publishing standards, etc.

3. Some of the biggest challenges facing Vietnamese social sciences

The biggest challenge for Vietnam's social sciences is without doubt the training of skilled human resources. Vietnam has a large number of social scientists with high doctorate degrees but only few of them can do research per international standards. The majority lack foreign languages and cannot access non-Vietnamese materials nor exchange information with international colleagues. Even the exchange and discussion of ideas within the domestic social scientist community remains limited. Those who do not know how to do research make up the dominant group and wield power, thus, the academic spirit of learning and criticizing in a professional manner is not truly encouraged. For this reason, a genuine academic space does not exist, or if it does, it is rather fragile and fragmented.

A.7. Le Quan

Dr. Le Quan, Vietnam National University Hanoi, Hanoi, Vietnam

1. Of your published articles, which ones do you take the most pride in? Why?

My interest is on corporate innovation in Vietnam because surveys have shown that over 500 businesses are lacking creativity/innovation. Other corporate shortcomings include insufficient financial investment for innovation, the absence of human resources devoted to research and development (R&D), short-term business plans, low-value-added operation chain, etc. This all shows that, in order to improve labor productivity in

Vietnam, businesses have to first change their mindset regarding innovation, upon which they can establish a culture and financial mechanism that support pro-innovation human resources.

2. What are the advantages of writing an article solo and what are the difficulties?

Doing research on your own is laborious because you have to do everything it takes to complete a study, including planning your ideas, constructing the theoretical framework, collecting and analyzing data, examining the results, drafting and writing up the manuscript. Such well-rounded and capable scientists are not everywhere. Therefore, scientists are better off working together to accentuate each one's strength. Particularly for Vietnamese SSH scientists who are not fluent in English and quantitative methodology, doing research in groups helps address the problem more effectively.

3. When picking a colleague to conduct joint research, do you have any particular criteria?

This depends on the research topic. There are research projects that require someone fluent with collecting and processing data. Some projects require someone with critical reading and writing skills. Other projects need someone capable of mobilizing resources for the research, etc. Nevertheless, the most important criterion is to search and build altogether a strong research team, to jointly grow and contribute. A published scientific article is only the final product, the output of a long process of collective research efforts.

4. If in natural sciences, a good research project requires investment in laboratories and measurement systems, then what do you think are the necessary investments in social sciences and humanities?

The two biggest barriers to SSH research are English proficiency and quantitative data collection and analysis methodology. International publication in SSH is in fact not beyond our ability because besides originality, the typicality of a research project can also yield fruitful results and worthwhile information for it to be accepted for publication. Rejection by a journal of international standards is often due to lack of reliability in research methodology.

A.8. Le Quang Thanh
Dr. Le Quang Thanh, Flinders University, Adelaide, Australia

1. Of your published articles, which ones do you take the most pride in? Why?

My research concentration includes macroeconomics and growth theory. During my research, I focus on both the theoretical and empirical aspects even though I prefer the theoretical side much more. This is simply a matter of preference. For every researcher, each research article has its own interesting and unique points for we all put our hearts and minds into it. Each article is the product of a deep intellectual journey, the result of repeatedly examining an issue, as well as the reflection of our hardship during the tortuous process of researching, publishing, and even post-publishing. However, if I have to choose one particular article, I would pick the following:

- o Le, T. (2008). 'Brain Drain' or 'Brain Circulation': Evidence From OECD's International Migration and R&D Spillovers. *Scottish Journal of Political Economy, 55*(5), 618-636.

This is an empirical study conducted and written solely by me and published in 2008. I like this article because it lays the groundwork for a new research direction at that time. Back then, and even many years before that, there were constant worries about the issue of brain drain due to the increased mobility of high-skilled laborers. Countries that have negative high skilled labor mobility were worried about falling further into disadvantages as the talents migrated away. My article at the time proposed a new method to quantify the benefits of having many skilled laborers overseas, through whom there can be spillover effects. The argument is, everyone is inclined to remember and contribute back to his or her homeland. The linkages between these overseas high-skilled laborers and their homeland are familial ties, friends, and colleagues. Through these connections, they transfer information, knowledge, and job opportunities that altogether bring big benefits to their homeland. For example, we can find in India many IT businesses that create jobs for thousands of local people; these businesses were formed thanks to the connections with high-skilled IT Indian engineers working in Silicon Valley.

There are many similar examples that we can find around us. Within a permissible parameter, the results enable a reversal of the brain drain theory because brain gains have accompanied the outward worker flows.

My work has attracted attention from other researchers, evidenced by the number of downloads and citations. Along this line of research, I have written some more research papers that focus more on international students – who make up one type of the high-skilled labor.

- Bodman, P., & Le, T. (2013). Assessing the roles that absorptive capacity and economic distance play in the foreign direct investment-productivity growth nexus. *Applied Economics, 45*(8), 1027-1039.
- Le, T. (2012). R&D Spillovers through Student Flows, Institutions, and Economic Growth: What can we Learn from African Countries?. *Scottish Journal of Political Economy, 59*(1), 115-130.
- Le, T., & Bodman, P. M. (2011). Remittances or technological diffusion: which drives domestic gains from brain drain?. *Applied Economics, 43*(18), 2277-2285.
- Le, T. (2010). Are student flows a significant channel of R&D spillovers from the north to the south?. *Economics Letters, 107*(3), 315-317.

2. What are your opinions on international collaboration in the current context? What are its advantages and limitations?

My answer to the previous question, together with my arguments in published works, has reflected some of my opinions on international collaboration in research. I believe that international collaboration, especially in research and training, is an inevitable and irreversible trend today. We all know that to have an international publication, especially in high-ranking journals, is not easy at all. Given that many universities and research institutes in Vietnam still lack the basic infrastructure such as laboratories, research equipment, e-library, etc., international collaboration will help us overcome such shortcomings. Additionally, international researchers could help us see more clearly where we stand in the global research landscape, thereby, allowing us to catch up faster with the world.

A big challenge of doing joint research is perhaps the gap in research skills: many Vietnamese researchers cannot yet meet the standards for international collaboration. It is possible that we need a longer period to smoothen this type of collaboration. Nevertheless, I believe that we can do this when an increasing number of high-skilled researchers who have received overseas training return home. Besides, many universities and research institutes have embarked on the path toward international integration, such as Hoa Sen University, Ton Duc Thang University, National Economics University, and Phenikaa University.

The second challenge is Vietnamese researchers are yet to be able to live on their meager research salary. They have to take part in lecturing at various places to make a living. This indubitably affects their research productivity.

Another issue is, many domestic researchers still lack the mindset of doing research for publication, let alone international publication. This is perhaps due to the inadequate recognition at home for internationally-published articles as well as due to the limited and small budget for funding research.

3. The NAFOSTED has a policy to invest in strong research groups, what are your thoughts on the organization of a strong and sustainable research group?

I highly value the government's efforts in supporting basic science and international publication via the NAFOSTED. The foundation will enable the formation of research groups intra- and international aimed at high-quality international publications. The publication of one such article requires a certain amount of budget, which would cover the experimental process, costs for organizing and participating in international conferences and inviting international scholars over. Funding from the NAFOSTED, despite being limited, allows domestic research groups to overcome financial difficulty to a certain extent.

A strong and sustainable research group is a group that has reached consensus in both the ways of thinking and doing research. That group must be comprised of many members who come from different generations: rich in experience, some experience though young, and passionate about research work. This combination will promote the strengths of every member and enable the group to positively exchange knowledge. Such research group must also be backed by abundant research funding. Although the development of information technology (emails, Skype, video conferencing, etc.) has somehow eased the differences in space and time, direct face-to-face interactions will nonetheless allow group members to better understand each other, and thereby, raising the efficiency of their research activity.

4. How do you assess labor productivity?
To calculate labor productivity, the simplest way is to divide total output by total input. However, this method has many problems. First, many jobs today allow laborers to engage in casual or part-time contract, thus, the aforementioned method can lead to miscalculation of labor productivity. Second, the method will also make it difficult to compare the productivity among certain sectors because each sector has different characteristics, structures, and inputs. For example, comparing labor productivity between agriculture and industry, or between industry and services, would be inaccurate. Third, this way of calculation will also obstruct comparison of labor productivity within the same sector over a certain period of time. For instance, it does not support comparing labor productivity in agriculture 10 years ago with today because much has changed today in terms of crops, equipment, technology, and climate, etc.

For these reasons, I think the best way that could rectify the above shortcomings is to divide total factor productivity over multi-factor productivity. Obviously, this method is not entirely perfect and remains limited by the selection of denominator for capital and labor as well as the problem of capacity utilization. Yet, it is believed to be the more optimal method. I often use this calculation in my research, especially the articles I have listed in my answer to the first question.

A.9. Le Van Canh
Dr. Le Van Canh, University of Languages & International Studies (ULIS) - Vietnam National University Hanoi, Hanoi, Vietnam

Publishing research results in international journals is a requirement for those working at universities and research institutes in most countries. However, for researchers in some developing countries, this requirement is a major challenge. For instance, the low rate of international publication in the social sciences in Vietnam has garnered much attention, with many explanations offered in the media. In response to the questions from the Editorial Board of this book, I would like to share some personal experiences as someone who has acted as both a published author and a reviewer for some leading journals in applied linguistics (TESOL Journal, TESOL Quarterly). I am now part of the Editorial Board of the Journal of Asia TEFL that is indexed in Scopus.

The ultimate requirement for publishing an article in a reputable international journal is academic quality. Academic quality is evaluated first and foremost based on the research results — whether they are novel and what the scientific community can gain from (readership), followed by the application of a new methodology or new theoretical framework to examine an issue that has been studied before. If the research uses a new method, the author(s) must present in details the advantages of the new method over the extant approaches.

To select a suitable journal to submit one's article is an important task but is equally difficult for those who lack experience. Therefore, it is necessary to do careful research on various journals before submitting one's paper. Researchers need to read "About the Journal" carefully, keeping track of the purpose and scope of the journal, the reviewing process, the reviewing criteria, the rejection rate, the journal's requirements for word limits and presentation, etc. Many requirements can be checked in the "Instructions for Authors."

The average rejection rate in social sciences is 70%, i.e. only three articles are accepted out of ten submissions, with the rejection rate in some journals as high as 90%. If an author wants to submit his/her work to a journal with a high impact factor (JIF), he/she has to modestly and seriously evaluate the research work to see if it would meet the requirements of the journal. Otherwise, it could be a waste of time.

One should also note that some journals may have high impact factors but low credibility because they operate under the open access model. It is important to remember that there is a large number of international scientific journals that are bogus/predatory, many of which are even indexed in Scopus. Differentiating between the genuine and bogus journals is not a simple task but one tip is to avoid journals that demand article processing charge and promise to publish the piece within weeks or months of submission and payment. Additionally, it is imperative to avoid sending one article to several journals at the same time. Below are some criteria for evaluating the academic quality of an international scientific journal that have been recognized by many universities worldwide:

- o The Editorial Board composes of top experts in their fields, with recognition at the international level
- o Members of the referee board are renowned international scholars
- o The journal publishes works by scholars from different countries
- o The journal has an appropriate rejection rate and impact factor
- o The journal has a large readership and high citation score.

Overall, to publish one's research works in prestigious international journals, the first step is to understand the type of journals that one wants to submit, and to select a journal that is suitable with one's research content, methodology, etc. If one wants to go far in academia, it is important to pick journals with high impact factors. If the purpose is to share one's personal experience with colleagues at the international level, selecting a 'normal' journal would be okay. In Vietnam, the State Council for Professorship Title recognizes articles published in journals that have ISBN code. Yet, for the international academic community, this code has no meaning in terms of academic value because it is only a sort of "identification card" for the book or journal to be circulated at a global scale.

A.10. Luu Trong Tuan
Dr. Luu Trong Tuan, Swinburne University of Technology, Victory, Australia

1. Of your published articles, which ones do you take the most pride in? Why?
I love all of my publications, even the very first articles that were published in lower-tier journals, for they nurtured my love for science. I think if we forget those first papers, the papers that we made when we were early in our career, then it is not so much different from forgetting friends who have been with us when we are facing hardship.

I still remember those first papers that I wrote in Vietnamese and published in Vietnam. The feeling of being able to publish for the very first time is unforgettable. I also want to share my gratitude with my teachers and friends who supported and gave me advice back then, such as professor Sununta Siengthai (AIT), my PhD supervisor, and Nguyen Quynh Mai (Faculty of International Management, Ho Chi Minh International University).

2. Can you share about your hardest peer review? How does peer review improve the quality of your work and your expertise?
I never take peer review lightly, even a positive one or a minor revision decision. I consider the reviewer's comments carefully in order to provide an answer that is better than reviewer's expectation, not just to merely satisfy him/her. For instance, if a reviewer asks me to state the limitations clearly because I did not use a certain data analysis procedure, I will re-run the analysis according to the reviewer's suggestion. In another situation, if a reviewer suggests that the paper should use a moderating variable in the model as both moderator and mediator, then I will rebuild my model, re-hypothesize, and find the evidence for the new model.

I think we can learn so much more by being humble and respecting reviewers' comments. A lot of young researchers feel upset when their papers get rejected or receive negative reviews. I think we should always be a student, and the reviewer is our teacher (even if we can be more famous).

The sincerity will eventually lead to new opportunity. For instance, I have a chance to work with professor Chris Rowley (Oxford University) because of our exchange via emails about one of my papers.

3. In your opinion, what is the toughest type of academic publications?

Publishing in high-ranking journals is always a dream of every researcher, the tougher it is, the more beautiful the dream. I think we should not feel satisfy with just being able to publish internationally, because the higher the ranking of a journal, the more readers will know about our works, and they can know about Vietnam.

Many Vietnamese scientists think that foreign scholars should find and translate their works in Vietnamese journal. This is a selfish way of thinking. I think we should always bring the image of Vietnam to the world, we should plant the seed and let it grow in the mind of scholars from around the globe.

I write and publish partly because I want the word "Vietnam" to be known by as many scholars as possible. This is a small contribution that I can do for Vietnam. In all of my publications, Vietnam is always an important keyword.

4. Can you share you experience in choosing a journal?

I always consider every aspect such as impact factor, time from submission to first decision, time until publication, or publishers carefully. However, I do not focus on the time for peer review because I think this is the time that we should be patient and careful. In that time, we can work on different research.

A.11. Nguyen Cao Nam

Dr. Nguyen Cao Nam, University of Adelaide, Adelaide, Australia

1. Of your published articles, which ones do you take the most pride in? Why?
- Bosch, O. J., Nguyen, N. C., Maeno, T., & Yasui, T. (2013). Managing complex issues through evolutionary learning laboratories. *Systems Research and Behavioral Science, 30*(2), 116-135.

I picked this article because it lays the groundwork for defining and applying "Evolutionary Learning Laboratory" – ELLab. ELLab is a very useful method in social sciences and is being adopted by many international researchers.

2. What are your opinions on international collaboration in the current context? What are its benefits and limitations?

If there are opportunities for international collaboration, then that's very good:
- Benefits: expand one's research network, research opportunities, learn and exchange research writing, methodology, and coordinate in applying for research funding
- Limitations: differences in languages, culture, and distance, etc.

3. What do you think are the biggest challenges to Vietnam's social sciences and humanities today?

- The complexity of social issues only heightens but research approaches in Vietnam's SSH still fall short of explanatory power and efficiency.
- There lack coordinated efforts among key partners as well as world's leading academic institutions in this regard.
- Vietnam lacks the ability to identity key SSH areas for priority development and investment.

4. If in natural sciences, a good research project requires investment in laboratories and measurement systems, then what do you think are the necessary investments in social sciences and humanities?

Considering the challenges I listed in answer no. 3, the conventional research methods and instruments are no longer effective. We need to invest in the application of advanced technology, systems, tools, and solutions that would bring about efficiency.

A.12. Nguyen Trong Chuan
Dr. Nguyen Trong Chuan, Institute of Philosophy, Vietnam Academy of Social Sciences, Hanoi, Vietnam

1. Please tell us about the papers that you take the most pride in.
I take pride in the book named "Một số vấn đề Triết học - Con người - Xã hội" (Problems in philosophy, human and society). This book is a collection of essays and presentations on philosophy of natural sciences. The Department of Philosophy from universities in the country have been using this book since 1976.

2. What do you think about international collaboration in the current context?
I think the current context has allowed international collaboration to thrive significantly:
1. More people are capable of using English.
2. The number of journals is rising.
3. There are also many policies that support international publications financially.
However, despite the conditions, the younger generation seems to miss the opportunity.

3. To have a good research in natural science, investment in laboratory equipment is a must. What do you think about the necessary investment for social sciences to raise the scientific output and quality?
There are many fields in social sciences, and the challenge to publish internationally is also varied among the fields. Thus, I think every researcher must be able to apply new methodologies that the world is using. The old methods are becoming obsolete very fast.
Scientific research is important a nation, however, Vietnam is still lacking the 'scientific'. This is even truer for research projects that use data. Many papers that I have read lack both a good theoretical framework and a quality dataset.

4. What do you think about the role of interdisciplinary research in increasing scientific output and quality?

30 years ago, I gave my remarks regarding interdisciplinary research in Vietnam. We have also invited experts to present about interdisciplinary research and methods. Social sciences and humanities in Vietnam need more of it.

5. Do you think economics and finance are the problems that restrain the quality of science in Vietnam?
They are definitely a problem, but not an unsolvable one. For instance, information is always available and easy to access. I think the larger issue is the determination. When there are still researchers expecting shortcut in every aspect, for sure we cannot expect the final product will be at the highest quality.

A.13. Nguyen Tai Dong
Dr. Nguyen Tai Dong, Institute of Philosophy, Vietnam Academy of Social Sciences

[This interview was transcribed based on our direct talk with Dr. Nguyen Tai Dong]

1. Of your published articles, which ones do you take the most pride in? Why?
I think that the works that I am most proud of are still ahead. But if I have to choose, I would pick "A Brief History of Vietnamese Philosophical Thoughts" [*Khái lược lịch sử tư tưởng triết học Việt Nam*] because the book provides comprehensive survey of Vietnamese philosophy and follows up on different generations of scholars at the Institute of Philosophy.

2. What are your opinions on international collaboration in the current context? What are its advantages and limitations?
International collaboration is a must and brings about many benefits. For instance, those who traveled overseas in ancient times excelled not merely in diplomacy but also brought back books and knowledge to the homeland. These people were extraordinary figures who also got to grow personally during the eye-opening overseas trips. Moreover, international collaboration helps us better understand our cultural depth for we can compare our own country with other countries. After the collapse of the Soviet Union, international collaboration in Vietnam took a hit for

some time, but we managed to return to international integration very quickly afterward.

In terms of limitations, anything excessive is not good. We still exhibit a mindset that is too dependent on French scholars, who are seen as having contributed significantly to Vietnam's social sciences. But we need to recognize the fact that the West does not necessarily understand Vietnamese thoughts and culture.

Another important point is the goal of social sciences research is to serve the motherland, thus, research works must answer questions pertaining to the motherland, the society, before addressing global issues. Therefore, ISI WoS/Scopus may be a standard in scientific research but is not the only criterion to evaluate one's skills and contribution to the nation.

For these reasons, I believe we can rephrase the purpose of international collaboration and international publication. We can promote images of Vietnam through publishing research articles internationally, thereby strengthening our soft power and national brand in cultural influence. Besides talking about oneself, one should provide materials so that outsiders can also conduct research on Vietnam. We need to open up for the world to evaluate and better understand Vietnam. For instance, doing research on Vietnam thoughts is not about introducing giant Vietnamese thinkers to the world but also about opening up our rich materials to foreign readers and scholars. Here, we need to promote the digitization of data and research materials.

3. What are your thoughts on the translation of works in social sciences?
There are many issues to this. Not only do Vietnamese need translation of foreign works to disseminate and be familiar with international standards, or vice versa, but Vietnamese also need correct translation of ancient materials by our predecessors so that we can maintain our ties to the past, to history.

A.14. Nguyen Thi Hien
Dr. Nguyen Thi Hien, Vietnam National Institute of Culture and Arts Studies

1. What are your opinions on international collaboration in the current context? What are its advantages and limitations?
In the current context, academic platforms such as international conferences for specific disciplines and major science funders such as Toyota Foundation, European Foundation, the Wenner-Gren Foundation, etc. have all encouraged scientists from different disciplines, schools, institutes, and countries to collaborate together. One of the reasons behind this collaborative expansion is the trend of interdisciplinary and cross-border research. On this basis, collaboration between scholars of different countries is important to social sciences research today.

The advantages are as follows. Some research topics truly require collaboration among scholars of different countries. For instance, when some foreign scholars do research on Vietnam, they need collaboration from Vietnamese scholars due to the latter's native language, understanding of Vietnamese culture, Vietnamese relationships and academic networks. These foreign scholars may be equipped with better research skills than Vietnamese, they are even more up-to-date in terms of academic developments. Collaboration between Vietnamese and international scholars can bring about many benefits in terms of specialization, thereby making the research more closely reflective of the reality in Vietnam. The result of this joint research could facilitate the writing process, the identification of analytical issues, and the overall academic discussion. In terms of language, jointly-written articles with international experts are better in presentation, style and scientific quality. Projects that mark the collaboration between Vietnamese and foreign scholars also help the former group become more confident in academia.

Limitations: Given the development of IT, foreign and Vietnamese scholars are now able to work together in a much more convenient manner even though they live in different countries. They only need to meet when it is truly necessary and when both time and finance permit. However, this is not to say there are no barriers. Some challenges include differences in languages, academic viewpoints, working style, research methodology, time allocation, and research writing in a foreign language. These shortcomings sometimes cause internal disagreements and a failure to complete the research project. To minimize such problems, researchers must maintain a collaborative spirit, be supportive of and respectful toward each other.

International collaboration on equal terms among different scholars can become a reality when their intellectual ability, knowledge, and experience converge on a similar academic plane. Frankly speaking, Vietnamese scholars are not fluent in foreign languages, while foreign scholars are not fluent in Vietnamese. If both sides lack experience, research skills, fail to update themselves with the latest research in their fields, then it would be very difficult for them to collaborate effectively and co-author an international publication.

2. What are the research methods you commonly use?
In order to write an article for international publication, a researcher first and foremost must have independent research skills, be equipped with all the necessary knowledge and skills for doing research. In my own work on anthropology, I most often use quantitative methods such as participant observation, in-depth interviews to collect data from the localities or subjects in question. In general, to write a good paper, a research has to "struggle," to gain real life experience, to directly participate in events, rituals and festivals related to the topics of research. Fieldwork research requires experience, skills, observational ability, data collection and mining ability, skills to approach and interview, etc. For certain difficult topics, it is important to thoroughly understand the essence of an event in order to truly write about it well. One such example is in writing about the Spirit Possession Ritual (*lên đồng*), a researcher necessarily has to let go of his/her ego and fully take part in the ritual like an insider. After that, the researcher must know how to leave the ritualistic act behind and return to the role of a scholar equipped with knowledge about the field's basic science. In other words, to write an article suitable for international publication, one must apply strong data collection methodology based on fieldwork research, rely on information from different sources, and be equipped with the theoretical basis and research methodology of that discipline. Another requirement that is equally important is having a logical

mindset, knowing how to write in a scientific manner, be sharp and up-to-date with on-going academic debates and concerns.

3. In your personal opinions, which type of research articles is the most difficult to write?

During my recent research, I found that articles submitted to the top journals of a discipline go through the most difficult peer review process. Some examples include the *Journal of Anthropological Theory*, *Journal of Contemporary Ethnography*, and *Journal of Folklore Research*, to name a few. Specialized journals demand authors to contribute something new in terms of academics and theory. In reality, publishing an article in an ISI-indexed journal is not as hard as people often think. There are many opportunities to publish in ISI-indexed journals because there are many options for authors to send their work to. As I have said, the trend today is interdisciplinary research, thus, the content of one article can be relevant to various journals. For example, I wrote one article on the cultural identity of the Vietnamese community in the United States through analyzing the practice of certain traditions. This kind of paper can be submitted to journals on cultural studies, anthropology, folk culture, Asian studies, Southeast Asian studies, overseas community, transnational studies, Asian-American studies, or Vietnam studies (a journal published by the University of California – Berkeley), etc.

A chapter in an edited book is basically an invitation by the editors to write, thus, as long as the piece is written well per the editors' guideline, then it will be published. Book reviews are often written at the invitation of the journals (unsolicited book reviews are not common), but reading a book and writing a review are not difficult. Some articles that have been presented at a conference can be revised and submitted to the conference organizers to be printed in the conference proceedings. I have never written a review article for any international journals, but writing this kind of piece is easier than writing a full-length research paper in a refereed specialized journal.

A.15. Nguyen Thi Thuy Minh
Dr. Nguyen Thi Thuy Minh, National Institute of Education of Singapore, Singapore

1. Among your publications, which one do you feel most satisfied with? And why?

My most satisfactory article is:
- Nguyen, T. T. M., Pham, T. H., & Pham, M. T. (2012). The relative effects of explicit and implicit form-focused instruction on the development of L2 pragmatic competence. *Journal of Pragmatics,* 44(4), 416-434.

As far as I know, currently, there are only seven journals related to the field of Pragmatics that are indexed in Scopus, and the *Journal of Pragmatics* is qualified as a Scopus - Q1 journal. My colleagues and I developed that paper from a university-level project, which cost around VND30 million.

I am satisfied with that article for the following reasons:
- The paper is a comparative study about the effectiveness between the explicit and implicit instruction methods in the development of second language proficiency, which is a vital matter in pragmatics. Our study has two new contributions to the literature. First, we employed the definition of implicit instruction more comprehensively than previous studies. Besides, we applied different types of analytical techniques to improve the robustness of the findings.
- Until now, this article is still the most cited paper of mine with 73 citations, according to Google Scholar. Some leading scientists in the Pragmatics even referred to it in their articles. For example, in state-of-the-art research published in the prestigious Language Teaching journal by Professor Lyster at McGill University, Canada and his partners, they mentioned our study as an excellent demonstration by using various types of analytical techniques and suggested later studies in Pragmatics to follow suit. My study was also cited in many studies by leading specialists and scientists in Applied Pragmatics and Second Language Pragmatics, such as Prof. Kathleen Bardovi-Harlig at Indiana University, Prof. Janet Holmes at Victoria University of Wellington, Vice Prof. Naoko

Taguchi at Carnegie Mellon University, and Prof. Carsten Roever at the University of Melbourne, etc.
- My colleagues in Vietnam and I also developed and learned new research skills after completing this research. Two colleagues in my research team later decided to pursue a PhD degree in Australia.

2. Can you share some thoughts about your most challenging peer-review? Could the peer-review improve your knowledge or the research's quality?

The most challenging peer-review that I've ever received was two years ago when my Vietnamese co-authors and I submitted to a leading journal in the field. Our paper got feedbacks from a reviewer who had an opposite perspective to ours. The reviewer seriously criticized our research method, but he also admitted that it would be unfair if the journal did not publish our paper, as many publications also used the same method. Therefore, they required us to improve the article by adding new information related to our research method and modifying some points to make our logic more concrete. On behalf of our team, I revised the manuscript and sent it back with an eight-page-long response letter to the reviewer. The reviewer seemed to agree with some points in the letter but still required us to modify some other aspects. Finally, after two rigorous rounds of review, the editor decided to publish our paper.

In my opinion, it is entirely reasonable to review the manuscript according to the suggestion of reviewers. However, that was the first time I faced a reviewer that had a completely different paradigm. To convince the reviewer and editor, we had to add many more citations of related studies. Thanks to that experience, I have learned a valuable thing that the author does not always need to satisfy the reviewer. Even though the peer-review was very helpful, and I personally felt thankful to that reviewer, it does not mean all feedbacks of the reviewer were plausible. The most important thing is to have a solid logic to back up our arguments so that the editor will give a fair decision.

3. The NAFOSTED has an investment policy to fund strong research teams, how should a sustainable and strong research team be organized?

I do not know much about the NAFOSTED, but to me, a strong research team needs to have not only a strong leader but also strong members. In other words, a strong team needs to have "internal strength." Because I think the dependence on "external strength," such as international collaboration, is not a sustainable solution, only a temporary one. I also believe that creating a strong team not only concerns scientists but also the scientific administration. The establishment of scientific grants and funds is necessary. In other countries, depending on the nature of the fund, the fund will prioritize a specific type of research, either applied research, interdisciplinary research, or theoretical research. Notably, a researcher with a good profile (having high quantity and quality publications) is always prioritized. I believe this is a great alternative for Vietnamese scientific management to adopt in order to increase the "internal power" of Vietnamese research teams. However, I want to emphasize that because I don't know what NAFOSTED has done, so my thought doesn't refer to NAFOSTED.

4. In your opinion, what are the biggest challenges in social sciences in Vietnam?
I have lived away from Vietnam for a long time, so I may not have a holistic view of this matter. Through newspapers and my colleagues in Vietnam, I think the biggest challenge in Social Sciences nowadays is the lagging behind in knowledge and research methodology. I don't know what the main reason for this is, either that we are lack of update on new knowledge, lack of motivation to learn new things or the management mechanism of social sciences is not adequate. Annually, many PhDs graduating from prestigious international universities come back to Vietnam and bring with them the most updated research method, but I don't know how many among those people keep doing high-quality research, and supervising high-quality PhD students. Hopefully, if there is a suitable management mechanism like developed countries, we can see positive changes soon.

A.16. Nguyen Thu Thuy
Dr. Nguyen Thu Thuy, Foreign Trade University, Hanoi, Vietnam

1. When selecting collaborator for scientific research, what are your criteria?
Personally, I don't think there are many options, as not so many international scientists are interested in research topics related to Vietnam. For that reason, it's already good if there is any collaboration.

As for collaboration within the country, I think it depends on the research topic, and people that have equivalent experience and capacity of conducting research will be prioritized.

2. Do you think there is any difficulty for organizing and ensuring clean and reliable data clean in the current Vietnamese social condition?
I think it takes a lot of effort and money to organize and keep data reliable and clean. It is necessary to have a team, and team members need to have strong research ethics.

3. What research method do you usually use?
I think it depends on the topic. For example, I usually use quantitative analyses in my research in Economics and Finance.

A.17. Nguyen Viet Cuong
Dr. Nguyen Viet Cuong, Institute of Public Policy Management, National Economics University, Hanoi, Vietnam.

1. Among your publications, what is your most satisfactory paper? And why?
There are two articles that I'm most satisfied with. One of them is:

- o Nguyen, V. C. (2011). Poverty projection using a small area estimation method: Evidence from Vietnam. *Journal of Comparative Economics, 39*(3), 368-382.

This study contributes to the projection method, especially for small area estimation method. The small area estimation method allows us to evaluate the inequality in a small geographical area, like district or commune. In the article, I explained how to augment the conventional estimation method to predict future poverty and inequality ratios using data in the past.

Another article is:
- Nguyen, V. C. (2018). The long-term effects of mistimed pregnancy on children's education and employment. *Journal of Population Economics, 31*(3), 937-968.

One of the significant findings of this relatively new research is that children born before their parents get married are less likely to receive higher education and employment opportunity than children born after the parents' marriage. This result is consistent for both high- and low-income countries. Even though parents of those children eventually got married, giving birth before marriage implies they did not have enough preparation of nurturing the children. My result suggests that a good preparation before pregnancy will contribute to the long-term educational development of children.

2. Do you find any difficulties and benefits of single-authorship?
Apparently, the creativity of a group of scientists is higher than that of a scientist alone, so I think the research written by a team will be more creative and it can provide various perspectives. Working as a team can also reduce the workload significantly for each team member compared to a solo author. In addition, collaborating with other people may help increase the responsibility of completing the research by motivating each other, but it sometimes reduces the responsibility of each team member due to the diffusion-of- responsibility effect. Co-authors often wait for each other, and if there is a busy member, who cannot finish his/her tasks, the work will not be completed by the deadline and the progress of the whole team will be slowed down.

3. In your opinion, what qualities define a highly credible researcher?
In my opinion, an academically prestigious person first needs to have multiple works of high credibility and impacts. Also, he/she has to contribute to the scientific development through supporting and collaborating with other scientists, especially young scientists.

4. In your opinion, what are the biggest challenges of social sciences research in Vietnam nowadays?

First, there are not many number of research teams and organizations. The experience of international publication usually stays within small research teams, and it does not get standardized. Second, I think conducting research based on international qualifications is neglected in our country. The number of funding agencies that require research projects to be qualified for international publication is limited. Other than NAFOSTED, I rarely see other funds setting international publications as one of their criteria for applicants. Even scientific promotion doesn't require any specific achievements in international publication.

A.18. Pham Si Cong
Dr. Pham Si Cong, Deakin University, Victoria, Australia

1. Among your publications, what is your most satisfactory paper? And why?
Honestly, it's hard to say which article is my most satisfactory one, but If I have to choose, I will select:

- Djankov, S., Freund, C., & Pham, C. S. (2010). Trading on time. *The review of Economics and Statistics, 92*(1), 166-173.

In this paper, I collaborated with Caroline Freund and Simeon Djankov. This was the first time I published with co-authors and they were quite famous at that time. Writing with other co-authors helped me learn how to contribute to the teamwork, especially when I was quite young and lack of seniority compared to my co-authors. The research topic also interesting to me, even until now.

2. Do you find any difficulty and benefit in single-authorship?
From my experience, writing a paper solo has the following difficulties. The author needs to acquire a very high responsibility and self-discipline because a solo author will not face any deadline pressure and receive any cross-checking from co-authors. However, writing a solo paper can, on the other hand, provide the author with the flexibility of time. And, if the article is published, it can prove their ability to work independently.

3. Can you share some thoughts about your most challenging peer-review?

The most challenging peer-review I've ever met was when I submitted my solo paper to the Journal of International Economics. I faced many obstacles during the peer-review period. The first struggle was my lack of experience and support from co-authors, as I just started my scientific career and did the research alone. The second obstacle was from Prof. Trefler, the editor of that journal. He had very stringent requirements on the quality and only gave me a short time to revise my work. One of his demands was to delete parts of the original version. Because of that, I had to restructure and rewrite most of the paper. Eventually, my work got accepted after three rounds of revision.

4. Do you think there is any difficulty for organizing and ensuring clean and reliable data in the current Vietnamese social condition?

I need to admit that I cannot get the question 100%, but let me answer the question according to my understanding. In the current social conditions of Vietnam, I think that the difficulty of organizing and ensuring the reliability of data might result from the negligence of Vietnamese scientists in organizing data as well as making the data accessible for peer-review and public replication after being published. Providing open access to data is now a common practice in leading Economics journals, so I believe it will be a scientific trend in the future.

A.19. Pham Van Ha

Dr. Pham Van Ha, Australian National University, Canberra, Australia

1. Among your publications, which one do you feel most satisfied with?

Among my research, my favorite is:

- o Pham, V. H., & Kompas, T. (2016). Solving intertemporal CGE models in parallel using a singly bordered block diagonal ordering technique. *Economic Modelling, 52,* 3-12.

It is published in the Special Issue on Recent Developments in Decision-Making, Monetary Policy and Financial Markets. This is the research that my colleagues and I pursued for many years with so much effort put in. Fortunately, we had a breakthrough in research direction. It allowed us to solve the Computable General Equilibrium models (for example, the model of the entire world economy) with hundreds of millions of equations. It also helped us solve dynamic Computable General Equilibrium problems for a period of hundreds of years. Previously, this problem had to be solved indirectly with an approximate result. We later expanded our research to develop a model that can solve up to half a billion equations (nevertheless, the result has not been published yet). Actually, the number does not say anything, because some people don't even believe in Computable General Equilibrium model. However, if someone wants to solve such a large-scale Computable General Equilibrium model, then our research can be helpful.

2. The NAFOSTED has an investment policy to fund strong research teams, what do you think about how to organize a sustainable and strong research team?
This is indeed not an easy question to answer, even though I have experiences in conducting research and research management in Vietnam. The most important thing is the goal, what is the goal of these research teams? If it's all about pouring money into a high-profile research team, which is not actually conducting impactful research for the community, there would be no difference from inviting the world's leading experts to conduct quality research. Once we run out of money, they'll leave. That is not sustainable. To build a sustainable science, in my opinion, it needs to be built upon the demand of universities, governments, and businesses. In the country where I am currently working, universities are very strong at conducting research. In Vietnam, I feel that universities concentrate more on teaching. A part of this is probably due to financial issues: funding or business revenue from conducting research is not enough to maintain sustainable research activities. In my opinion, NAFOSTED should experiment with supporting university-based research centers. I think it can be done under co-financing format: the funding partly comes from the foundation, partly from the school to make sure all parties are responsible. Likewise, it is feasible to follow the project-based funding

mechanism or even set a prize for teams that meet a specific set of goals.

I acknowledge that the above suggestions may have already been done more or less. Forming a strong group is, in essence, to solve the human resource problems: How to attract talented individuals for national science. In my opinion, that is the real purpose of the NAFOSTED. For this purpose, as I said above, there should be an extensive investment in schools and institutes to improve their research capacity through awards and supports for researchers to spend more time on research in strong research organizations. This might be better than only establishing a strong research team.

In fact, it's possible to form a strong research team, perhaps, as a consultant team, if there is actual demand. However, I think those teams should be given specific goals and functions. After achieving the given goals, the investors or owners of these teams have to carry on taking over the role. It is also crucial not to let a third party provide funding for the production and consumption to two sides at the same time. It's all about economics. Doing research, after all, must meet the actual demand. Yet actual demand also includes the affordability. If it is not affordable to conduct research, conducting research will become a burden and disrupt sustainability.

In short, no matter what will be done, I think the transparency needs to be the top priority. If necessary, recruitment should be publicized or even done through international recruitment agencies. In my university, all positions are recruited via international recruitment agencies. After being recruited, there will be performance reviews annually. The evaluation is based on international publication in journals within rank A, B, C according to international standards. This performance review system creates tremendous pressure on the researchers, which guarantees no one is wasting time or making excuses. Of course, such a demanding requirement must be associated with adequate payments. We're all human, and no one can be a superhero forever. It's up to society in terms of payment, and researchers also need to think of themselves when doing such a risky job.

3. Do you think there is any difficulty for organizing and ensuring clean and reliable data in the current Vietnamese social condition?

I'm not working with data from Vietnam at the moment, so it's hard to have a clear answer to this question. But as I remembered, when I was doing research in Vietnam, working with data was a real trouble. This is due to not only the limited accessibility but also the reliability of the data. Thus, I think that Vietnam should concentrate more on improving its collection and organizations of data in the future.

4. Do you think finance is a barrier to develop social science in Vietnam?

I don't really think so, the matter is how we can use available financial support to conduct the research efficiently. Specifically, it's about mechanisms and policies. Every society needs to develop scientific research step by step, along the way, it is natural to face financial challenges. The point is how to make the best use of money. I believe society will adjust by itself. If the mechanism and efficient investment in conducting research can lead to a positive change in production or business output, the cost of conducting research is no longer a concern.

A.20. Tran Dinh Phong
Dr. Tran Dinh Phong, University of Science and Technology of Hanoi (USTH), Hanoi, Vietnam

1. Which factors should be used to measure research productivity?

To measure research productivity, we should look at the research work itself, and in my area of concentration, this includes research programs, research projects and experiments. If the studies are done carefully, then questions about the level of skills, the volume of work, the nature of research problems are essential in assessing the productivity of a researcher or a research group. This is often a challenging task, especially, in the current context of Vietnam. For example, an ambitious research program's experiments tend to fail to produce positive results, then evaluating research productivity by counting the product output is not satisfactory. As such, it is very important for the leaders in scientific departments, institutes, or research centers to have a fair and balanced view. They should take into account factors that are hard to measure when evaluating research productivity. An easy (perhaps, too easy) way is to count the grant amount a researcher/a research group has managed to obtain. But clearly, this measure is not convincing.

Regarding the results of research, we can measure research results by scientific and technological products. Depending on the field, these products may vary; they could be patents, ISI papers, conference papers, etc. The research results of a researcher or a group should be put in comparison with results from other laboratories/research groups/scientists in the country, in the region, and in the top-notch countries. Taking this broad view, I believe the process of evaluation can become more balanced. Surely, there are typicalities for specific fields of research, yet, it may not be persuasive to conclude "in Vietnam, that is good enough. " <laugh>

Output/input density can be another measure. This is the measure of scientific products based on the level of investment (grant/facilities/ human resources) that the laboratory/researcher owned or received. To determine the appropriate quantity, we should be referring to international standards. When the output product does not have any breakthrough and the investment is big, we might say that labor productivity of the project in question is low. Consequently, it translates to low investment efficiency. This assessment is especially important for policymakers and science and technology leaders. It is absurd to ask a Vietnamese scientist to work as productively as a Singaporean scientist, who receives ten times the amount of investment.

2. What qualities define a scholar with high credibility?
- A leader of the research team conducting ambitious and prominent research programs/projects.
- Playing an essential role in international networks: being invited to discuss and provide input in building an international ambitious program, such as a substantially funded program (This sometimes is geopolitically influenced, but most of the times, it should reflect the leadership role of the scientist in the community)

- Regularly publishing studies or having a high level of scientific and technological contribution, being highly appreciated by the scientific community (a narrow discipline/major): For example, citation indexes can be used to gauge this aspect (Citation is, of course, not perfect as an indicator but still useful to certain extent at the present).
- Being invited to the editorial board of prestigious magazines, or board member of international conferences, giving a keynote speech at international conferences/seminars, participating in peer review for research projects, serving as a jury for academic recruitment, etc.
- Their trainees (PhD candidate, postdoc) develop well under them and show their abilities to be capable of working independently.

3. How to organize a strong and sustainable research team?

As mentioned above, evaluating a research group is not merely about counting the output products or how many grants they obtained but appropriately assessing their capacity. A strong research team must be able to carry out high-level studies, and must have a clear development path for a higher level: in my field, for example, the goal is to be capable of doing more experiments with high complexity. With that in mind, to organize a robust research team, we need:
- Human: Competent people should stay together for research purposes, for conducting high-level research. Highly-skilled researchers often have many choices. The difficulty now is how to guarantee that they can live as a research in a relatively comfortable way (middle class in society). If that is possible, talented people will be willing to come back without being guaranteed a "red carpet" career path.
- Senior research, postdoc: These are the leading researchers of a team. If you do not have the right kind of compensation, it is impossible to build a proper research team, not to mention a strong one. I personally think there are many potential grants and funds, if we really want to contribute more to research; for example, the fund of the Youth Union, or other associations, organisations. Nowadays the "image" is often prioritised: Funders want

to give X amount of money for some achievement instead of giving X /n monthly as a scholarship for a researcher who will work long-term (3- 4 years).
- Research equipment: NAFOSTED needs to invest in research equipment. Without a necessary investment, it will be difficult for researcg groups to improve their own capability with new experiments and new studies. Such development is vital since, without it, research ability would not improve much no matter how many international publications they conduct. Funders should also create technological platforms for research groups to share experimental resources. This is also a current trend: Sharing scientific resources in scientific cities. The NAFOSTED fund can negotiate a mutual investment with the hosts of strong research teams.
- Administration: It is challenging to do highly quality scientific research when you have to purchase right amount of materials and equipments right after submitting research proposals.
- Time: A research team needs 3-5 years to form and develop (it is also the reason why that Assistant Professorship usually takes 2x3 = 6 years). As such, people in manager position and investors need to be patient. If they keep the philosophy that with investment X, when the product should be sold to the market is the most important, that must be LOSS.

4. Is financial issue one of the factors that hinders the development of Vietnam's science?

The question has two aspects: the investment amount, and investment efficiency. High-level scientific research is certainly not cheap. Under the current economic condition in Vietnam, it is probably not possible to invest in all fields. There should be a national independent committee that specializes in identifying scientific fields that are worthy of ambitious investment. For example, Taiwan's semiconductor technology provides a valuable lesson. If we have one or two fields that reach the "top," it is better than having all fields being mediocre. Moreover, when the budget is limited, the efficiency of funding is critical. Unfair competition in accessing research funding is the factor we should be worried the most about at the present.

A.21. Tran Duc Vien
Dr. Tran Duc Vien, Hanoi Agricultural University, Hanoi, Vietnam

1. Please tell us about a paper or papers that you take the most pride in.

My most satisfactory articles are not the ones published in the last 10 years, but the previous ones, when I had not yet known about ISI, Scopus, IF or H-index; I did not publish in order to complete my graduate thesis, or to defend my dissertation, or to improve my profile for the title of Associate Professor or Professor. At that time, I wrote purely from my inner drive.

The article in my expertise that I am most satisfied with is:
- Ziegler, A. D., Giambelluca, T. W., Plondke, D., Leisz, S., Tran, L. T., Fox, J., ... & Tran, D. V. (2007). Hydrological consequences of landscape fragmentation in mountainous northern Vietnam: buffering of Hortonian overland flow. *Journal of Hydrology, 337*(1-2), 52-67.

This article along with a series of other articles explain the land degradation and protection measures for land resources on tropical slopes, employing longitudinal data from 1996 to 2008 on nutrient movement and soil erosion in a small basin along Da river.

But one of my most favorite articles is actually not within my expertise:
- Tran, D. V. (2003). Culture, Environment, and Farming Systems in Vietnam's Northern Mountain Region. *Japanese Journal of Southeast Asian Studies, 41*(2), 180-205.

The paper is published in Southeast Asian Studies, September 2003, a mid-range journal with low IF.

I also wrote / participated in writing many social sciences articles, such as "Decentralization in Forest management in Vietnam's Uplands: Case studies in three Communities", "Red Books, Green Hills: The impact of economic reform in the development of the midlands of Northern Vietnam", "Development Trends in Vietnam's Northern Mountain Region', 'Resources Management in the River Basin: Policy, People and Poverty", "Social organization and the management of natural resources: A case study of Tat hamlet, Vietnam," but, I still like that paper the most because it marked my journey to a new field: social sciences, the area in which I was totally a "newbie", and even now, I still think of myself as a "newbie". I stepped into social sciences, perhaps, partly because I have no fears.

2. What do you think about single-authorship, its difficulties and benefits?

In my opinion, a solo author possesses liberating ideas, and is willing to commit, innovate oneself, and listen to diverse opinions and perspectives in a responsible way, especially to those of young people. Besides, that person would respect and accept diversity.

A solo author would remain calm, show high self-respect, live realistically, enthusiastically and responsibly for his or her community and society. That person is admired and respected by their colleagues and students for his/her nature.

I also believe that a solo researcher reads a lot, knows a lot, studies a lot, has profound knowledge in his field, and even understands other relevant areas. He/she would be able to publish works that pave a new way. He/she might have the capability of doing something to change the community and gaining admiration by domestic and international colleagues for his quality of thinking, and scientific productivity.

He/she would have the ability to gather and build influential research organizations or research teams, because the era of individual work like in the generation of Newton is no longer. He/she knows how to create decent "jobs or opportunities" for his colleagues.

3. In your opinion, what are the biggest challenges of social sciences research in Vietnam today?

I think that social sciences in Vietnam are currently facing two main challenges.

The first one is from "outside" of the scientific community. We are living in a period when society only wants obedient people, there is no room for diversity and difference beyond the existing social framework. People usually say they "rather everyone dies than to live alone," or "rather all are equally bad than a few being good." Just look at how we vote for some awards, our society that only appreciates "good" staffs/officials, who would accept all kinds of constraints, whereas scientists with characters are not respected and even ignored. In my opinion, people with "real" abilities are often those who have their own ideas, their own idiosyncrasies, and ways of living. Having a character is the origin of creativity. I know a scientist who bitterly commented on the assessment and promotion of our researchers that we have tried very hard to remove the 'stamp' system (the stamp system during the subsidy regime), but then converted it into 'vote' system, which evaluates officials based on the majority of votes. Personally, I agree with him that keeping the system like that will take ages to really find a talented person! For example, Pyotr Kapitsa, a prominent Russian physicist, wrote in a letter to Khrushchev (then the General Secretary of the Soviet Communist Party) in 1961, explaining why the Soviet Union did not have "giants" like Lomonosov, Puskin, Tchaikovsky, Aivazovsky, etc. that Russia had previously given birth to: "If we only need an obedient society, we won't know how to accept individuals with different political views, so how to get talent?". Kapitsa, perhaps, also said: "The biggest stupidity of talented people is that they do not know how to grovel."

We really like to be flattered, we always want to be right, be the best in everything. As such, we cannot withstand criticism, countering or different ideas, and hardship. We want conformity in terms of ideas and ideologies. This leads to wrong perceptions of social values, using political promotion and the accumulation of tangible assets as the scale of all standards. With such misunderstanding, I don't know how long we need to wait until our society will acquire a Nobel prize, or classic works that are able to intrigue thousands of minds and hearts like what U-23 football team did in early 2018.

I also think that our society is mistaking between science and propaganda, so social sciences have been turned into a kind of royal activities, only reserved for ingratiation and groupthink. Within that scientific community, whoever has a contradicting political view will be isolated, discredited, even considered a disgrace. Yet, we all forget that among a group of monkeys walking on four legs, the first money walking on two legs was always isolated by other monkeys, but thanks to that monkey, humans started to exist on this planet!

Another challenge comes from inside the scientific community. I heard somebody said that the recent scientific community was more craven day by day, scientists did not dare to defend their own viewpoint, but live off other people in order to get promoted and become wealthy without any sense of shame; they could not update the latest scientific trend in an increasingly globalized world nowadays. I think those assumptions are dogmatic with no evidence, as I have never read any publication related to those assumptions. Not as bad as those assumptions, but I saw some cases with my own eyes explaining why many people are quite upset with some intellectuals in our scientific community.

One day during Tet holiday, I suddenly received an invitation to attend a New Year meeting with some intellectuals from a senior leader. I arrived on time, but a lot of people had already come earlier. Before the opening time, everyone gathered in three groups around the table and talk over tea and coffee. These guests whispered disparagingly about this leader, considered him to be unworthy. After the conference, the organizing committee expressed gratitude to the appearance of all the guests and asked everyone to come to the lobby for a commemorative photo. I saw our intellectuals rushed to stand up in the front, next to the official A who they had just whispered about. I believe many of them would have the photo taken with Mr. A enlarged, carefully photoshopped and put on the most beautiful place in their living room.

I know a senior official who is leading a big university in the capital, but because we have different expertise, I do not know precisely how influential as a scientist he is. Then he was nominated as one of the National Assembly delegates, appeared on TV talk-shows regularly discussing important policies. I admired him so much. Then once I saw his writing on VnExpress news outlet on how Vietnamese scientists need to sail to the "big sea" and how to publish internationally. Then I searched his name on Google Scholar, Scopus and ResearchGate, both in Vietnamese and English, but there was not even a single work showed up. I encountered this kind of thing not only once, but many times.

I also witnessed people exchanging money for research projects, and even professorship. Only a few people can keep themselves out of that "market", and maintain the mind and spirit of a "true scholar," reminiscing the ideals of intellectuals in the past generation. This is a sad fact.

Another difficulty for scientists in both Social Sciences and Natural Sciences I can think of is the "envelope culture", which has appeared during emergence of the "disbursement science." No one knows since when our society has formed and developed the "envelope culture," which leads to corruption in every single aspect of our society. Wherever and whatever we do, "envelope" is always necessary to guide and ease the way, otherwise nothing can be done. That makes true scientists lose faith; some even gradually become corrupted and get pulled into the vortex of that culture.

The "envelope culture" in Science and Technology management gave birth to the "disbursement science and technology," the lying science. If there is any field that needs studying in the world, Vietnam will have a similar research project a few years later. I even know that a "smooth disbursement" can mean the research is completed. All the objectives are achieved or exceeded, the applicability is confirmed by the provincial districts and communes. Only the country and the people are harmed, because no one actually needs most of the research and project results that are stored, except for when the authors need to complete their profile for the application of Professor and Associate Professor titles. I am sure that doing science like that has made many people wealthy from the bribery and corruption, we have created scientists who do not conduct research, but only talk about it.

In this country, everything is planned, including planning for the next leaders and managers; but apparently no one plans when, and how scientist X will become a leading scientist in the field Y, and the subject Z will become a world-class scientific field with a corresponding resource investment program.

Also, this country does not seem to consider universities as the potential pillar for the national science and technology like how developed countries had done and other emerging economies have wisely learned. Except for the two national universities and regional universities funded by the state, other universities had to take care of themselves, which means the university needs to find research funding independently. Meanwhile, funding for science and technology is given generously to provinces. Perhaps, policymakers in our country consider the provinces as the pillars of national science and technology, but not universities? Or is there any other unspoken reason?

As for the research budget of research institute system, it is usually used for salary payment and other regular expenditures, only nearly 30% of the budget is actually allocated for scientific research purposes. When can scientists in general, and social scientists in particular, overcome these challenges?

A.22. Tran Huu Tuan
Dr. Tran Huu Tuan, Hue University, Hue, Vietnam

1. Of your published articles, which ones do you take the most pride in? Why?
The work that I am most proud of is:
- Tran, H. T. & Navrud, S. (2007). Valuing cultural heritage in developing countries: comparing and pooling contingent valuation and choice modeling estimates. *Environmental and Resource Economics, 38*(1), 51-69.

This is my first paper in a prestigious international journal published by the European Association of Environmental & Natural Resource Economists in the field of Resource Economics and Environment. Successfully publishing in this Journal significantly gives me more confidence in the next international publications.

2. What is your opinion on the role of interdisciplinary research in boosting scientific quality and quantity?
Generally speaking, I think interdisciplinary research will help improve the quality and quantity of scientific works, especially in the fields that Vietnamese scientists don't have much experience, such as Social Sciences and Humanities. Therefore, interdisciplinary research will contribute considerably to the development of professional competence and publication skills, which in turn could raise quality and productivity of doing science in Vietnam.

3. Can you discuss the difficulties and benefits in publishing interdisciplinary work?
Advantages: For me, all of my international publications are products from my doctoral dissertation, international collaboration projects, and projects funded by national organizations.
Disadvantages: I find that seeking funding for international projects is increasingly difficult, and, the given research time is limited.

4. The NAFOSTED has an investment policy for strong research teams, how should a sustainable and strong research team be organized?
In my opinion, the policy of giving investment priority to strong research teams is necessary in order to increase the productivity and quality of science and technology activities, as well as to promote international publishing. However, the policy must be implemented in a very organized and flexible manner. It is advisable to use appropriate economic incentives, and to minimize unnecessary administrative procedures; this would attract and promote scientific research. If the policy is not implemented correctly, it will be taken advantage of by interest groups (rent-seeking groups).

To ensure the effectiveness of the investment policy, I think NAFOSTED also needs to leverage market mechanism by encouraging fair competition through open research calls. In that way, the mechanism will force researchers to form research teams strong enough to propose valuable research ideas that can compete against other proposals. Besides, it is necessary to continue to set higher criteria for principal investigators and co-authors involved with projects funded by NAFOSTED (qualified by publication in SCI, SSCI, Scopus, etc.)

A.23. Tran Nam Binh
Dr. Tran Nam Binh, RMIT Vietnam and New South Wales University, Sydney, Australia

1. Among your publications, which one do you like the most? Why?

For a researcher, each and every piece of work can be considered a child. Of course, for parents, comparing among children can be extremely difficult. But if I had to choose, perhaps I would like to nominate two articles: one on trade theory and one on cost compliance.

- Tran, N. B. (1985). A neo-Ricardian trade model with overlapping generations. *Economic Record, 61*(4), 707-718.

The article about my trade theory was published in 1985 on Economic Record, one of the leading economic journal of Australia. I remember it because this is the first study I published. Developing from the doctoral thesis that I had submitted a few years before, this article gave several suggestions which were contrary to mainstream normative trade theory; for example, trade without compensation that can be made may reduce the welfare of an overlapping generational society.

- Tran, N. B., Evans, C., Walpole, M., & Ritchie, K. (2000). Tax compliance costs: Research methodology and empirical evidence from Australia. *National Tax Journal, 53*(2), 229-252.

The paper on tax compliance costs I and co-authors published in 2000 on the National Tax Journal, which was the leading tax journal in the world. In this article, we discussed the notion of tax compliance costs, provided a method to estimate this cost, and applied the proposed method to determine the Australian federal tax compliance costs in 1995. This piece has been widely cited in studies of tax compliance costs.

2. What do you think are some of the biggest challenges of social sciences in Vietnam today?

My understanding of the current situation of Social Sciences in Vietnam is limited. From some working experiences in Vietnam, I

would like to give some subjective comments as follows:
- Teaching and researching social sciences in Vietnam are currently not consistent because of the distinction between universities and research institutes and between teachers and research teachers. In my opinion, the current teaching and researching model is not suitable for the long-term development of social science in Vietnam.
- Because of the research nature, social science in Vietnam is less globalized than the hard science. Therefore, many Vietnam Social scientists are still not entirely familiar with the modern format of presentation, citation, review and methodology.
- There are many different reasons for this, mainly because of the income. Only few teachers in the current social sciences sector have the opportunity to focus on research topics that they chose freely. When participating in "ordered" projects, whether they want it or not, researchers would lose the passion, objectivity and independence needed in research.

3. Can you share some experiences in choosing international journals for submission? For example, how do factors such as impact index, first decision time, publication time, review time, publisher, etc. affect the decision?

Let me begin with the presumption that a majority of Vietnamese social science researchers encounter many disadvantages when submitting articles to international academic journals. There are two main reasons. First, as I mentioned previously, the authors are lack of familiarity with the international publications structure and English writing ability. Second, editors of professional journals tend to be negatively biased towards new authors. When selecting an international journal, the author should consider the following points:
- Which journals published the articles that you cited?
- How do you evaluate the quality of your work (A *, A, B or C)?
- Do I need to publish early?

If the author has a good article, he should send it to high impact factor journal. These journals tend to have quite a long peer-review process and a high rejection rate, especially with new authors.

I also have a few suggestions for future authors:
- Young researchers should present their papers in conferences or seminars to consult with colleagues before submitting as journal articles.
- Do not send manuscripts to predatory journals that require very high submission fees and offer quick review (see also Beall's List of Predatory Journals and Publishers).
- Researchers should be active during the process of review, for example, researchers should directly contact the editor if they don't receive any updates about their manuscript after 4 months.

4. In natural sciences, to have a good research work, it is necessary to invest in laboratories, measuring equipment systems, so in your opinion, what factors should be invested in to increase the quantity and quality in social science?

In my opinion, we should invest more in the following areas.
- Scholarships for young, promising teachers to study in developed countries.
- Sponsoring foreign researchers and researchers of Vietnamese origin who came to collaborate, support or guide research projects.
- Organizing seminars to improve research skills and methods.
- Supporting teachers to access social sciences journals (e-journals) and international data resources.

A.24. Tran Quang Tuyen
Dr. Tran Quang Tuyen, (Economics University – Hanoi National University)

1. Of your publications, which one(s) are you most satisfied with? Why?

My most favorite paper is published in the Journal of Happiness Studies:
- Tran, T. Q., Nguyen, C. V., & Van Vu, H. (2018). Does economic inequality affect the quality of life of older people in rural Vietnam?. *Journal of Happiness Studies*, 19(3), 781-799.

The idea of that paper is to examine the effect of inequality within a fine-geographical-scale living area on the citizens employing techniques of quantitative analysis and two datasets from the Survey of the elderly and the Census of Agriculture, Forestry, and Fisheries in 2011. I think ideas and analysis techniques need to supplement each other to create a new and innovative contribution to science.

My research also points out an overlooked impact of socio-economic environment on citizens' lives: Socio-economic environment can cause both material inequality and mental inequality. In our analysis, we find inequality in terms of growth and poverty reduction, and mental conditions such as happiness and life satisfaction. This problem can cause adverse social effects, reduce social connectedness, and other negative mental conditions.

2. What difficulties and benefits do you find in single-authorship?
- Benefits: I think a solo author can prove that he/she has the ability to conduct research independently. He/she can enjoy the freedom to explore. He/she can also have a better chance to develop his/her abilities, explore new areas, and gain valuable experience and skills.
- Difficulties: However, I think writing a research paper alone is quite risky if the author does not have enough experience and skills. It is not easy to published a solo article in prestigious journals, especially in a new field. Without self-learning, self-reflection, and collaboration with other authors, a solo write may face difficulties in gaining new knowledge and skills.
- Collaborating with other authors provide many benefits: improving research productivity and the sharing of knowledge, technique, and ideas, especially, when each co-author specializes in a different field.

3. Can you share some thoughts about your most challenging peer-review experience? How does peer-review improve your knowledge or research quality?
The most discouraging and challenging peer-review that I have been through was the time I submitted a manuscript to the Journal of Happiness Studies (Q1 in Scopus and ISI indexes). I received

the comments from three reviewers. Two reviewers accepted after the second revision, but the editor still added one more reviewer for the third round of review. Only after the fourth revision, I could successfully convince the reviewers about plausibility of the technique I used and the originality of the paper. My study examines the impact of inequality on happiness in a small geographical scale (commune), unlike previous studies which often focus on the national level. Moreover, as we had to modified the model and the control variables many times to ensure robustness of the results, the research was accepted after 16 months of peer-review. However, four times of revisions definitely help me improve significantly the quality of the paper, especially in terms of logics and policy implications.

During the research, I learned a lot from my collaborators, Dr. Nguyen Viet Cuong and Dr. Vu Van Huong. The result of our study was later mentioned by two popular newspapers: "Tia Sang" and "DanTri."

4. The NAFOSTED has an investment policy to fund strong research teams, how should a sustainable and strong research team be organized?
In my opinion, in order to determine a strong research team, there should be different assessment criteria for different research fields. As for basic sciences or well-established fields such as Economics, I think NAFOSTED has to require publications in high ranking international journals (indexed in ISI, Scopus). As for application sciences, some requirements in the applicability should be added into the assessment criteria. Most importantly, we must distinguish between strong groups and the rest objectively, and avoid doing things for appearance's sake. A combination of "sticks and carrots" should be applied so that hard-working researchers are compensated adequately.

A.25. Tran Tuan Phong
Dr. Tran Tuan Phong, Institute of Philosophy, Vietnam Academy of Social Sciences, Hanoi, Vietnam

1. In your opinion, in social sciences and specifically in philosophy, what are the biggest challenges?

The biggest challenge for the discipline of philosophy in Vietnam is the shortage of careful translation of the world's classic works in the history of philosophy. This leads to two problems: a lack of background knowledge and a lack of unified terminology. Currently, the Vietnam Academy of Social Sciences is running the project making an encyclopedia, including a philosophical dictionary; I believe this project will somewhat help solve the two issues above.

2. In natural sciences, to conduct a good research, it is necessary to invest in laboratories or measuring equipment systems. So what do you think is essential for investment in social sciences to increase the quantity and quality?
In philosophy, I think investing more in translating philosophical classics will be very helpful. Currently, translators like Bui Van Nam Son have done very well, but the number of translated classic works is still insufficient, especially for modern Western philosophy. I think an adequate investment in translation will be very helpful for faculties and students.

3. What do you think about the role of interdisciplinary research in promoting scientific output and quality?
In my view, this is definitely necessary because science is systematic. In Vietnam, there is a distinction between natural and social sciences. However, science is holistic, so there is a need to doing research across fields, which means the trend of interdisciplinary research is inevitable.

A.26. Tran Van Kham
Dr. Tran Van Kham, University of Social Sciences and Humanities, Vietnam National University Hanoi, Hanoi, Vietnam

1. Of your publications, which one(s) is/are your favourite? Why?
Among my publications in domestic and international journals, the article published in March 2016 in Social Indicators Research:
- o Tran, V. K. (2017). Social construction of public intellectuals in vietnam: current situation and possible changes. *Social Indicators Research, 132*(2), 659-679.

The paper is my fourth paper published in ISI indexed journals and the second article in this journal. It is an article that I, myself, developed from an idea during a discussion regarding public intellectuals in Southeast Asia in a conference of the Southeast Asian Research Exchange Program (SEARSP) in 2014.

The article discussed multiple aspects: the interdisciplinary research studies, and the theory social construction, which the topic I had worked on before. Among my published articles, there are 2 articles in SSCI indexed journals. Even though this article is only published in a Scopus indexed journal, it is my most satisfactory article. Especially, I am very satisfied with the content of the article: the first study in Vietnam on the topic of cultural influence toward management published in a prestigious international journal indexed in Scopus. This research has built a useful leadership model in the Vietnamese political/cultural context. Other than that, the study is the first piece of work in my life that I was the first author and published in an international scientific journal.

2. What do you think about the role of interdisciplinary research in promoting scientific output and quality?
For me, interdisciplinary research is a necessary scientific trend for the current social sciences, because social issues cannot be defined, analyzed, explained and evaluated from only a standpoint, but multi-perspectives. Therefore, interdisciplinary research will obviously provide opportunities to collaborate with scientists in other fields, develop the ability to publish and share research results with scientists in other fields.

3. Can you share your experiences of choosing international journals to publish your work?
I personally do not have much experience in international publishing. At first, I was trying to submit my works to different international journals indexed in the ISI / Scopus, without taking into account the impact factor or publishing time. This is the strategy I used to familiarize myself with the requirements and standards set by journals. Later on, I started paying more attention to the publisher and the scope of my current research topic. I also pay attention to publishers that have a pre-published program, meaning an article can appear online first. This format can let my

research be shared early, rather than waiting for my paper to appear in print.

4. In natural sciences, to have a good research, it is necessary to invest in laboratories and measuring equipment systems. In your opinion, what factors should be invested in to increase the quantity and quality?

I think that it is necessary to invest in data-generating activities, for example, the access to databases of the General Statistics Office, original databases of state-level and ministry-level projects, and international databases. Moreover, I believe that we should invest in building a strong connection with international scientists and organizations to improve the interdisciplinary research capacity, to create scientific products rapidly, and to communicate research findings beyond the academic world. A good example is like the model of collaboration between NAFOSTED and Newton Fund in UK, Belgium, and Australia. Another area that might benefit from more investment is a supporting system for research methodologies, data processing techniques (especially quantitative analysis), as well as the latest scientific trends and findings.

A.27. Truong Dinh Thang
Dr. Truong Dinh Thang, Quang Ngai Teacher Training College, Quang Ngai, Vietnam

1. Of your publications, which one(s) is/are your favorite? Why?
My favorite study:
- o   Truong, T. D., & Hallinger, P. (2017). Exploring cultural context and school leadership: conceptualizing an indigenous model of *có uy* school leadership in Vietnam. *International Journal of Leadership in Education, 20*(5), 539-561.

2. In your opinion, what are the biggest challenges of social sciences in Vietnam today?
In my experience, most of the theses and dissertations in Vietnam are not qualified for international publications, especially in terms of methodologies. Professors and associate professors of social sciences in Vietnam, who are the direct supervisors for master's students and PhD candidates, do not have updated knowledge of

the most recent scientific trends, which results in low-quality social science research.

I believe that another challenge for Social Science in Vietnam is the shortage of experienced and proficient-English-speaking researchers. Overall, we can sum it up into the following equation: Low-quality research method + low English proficiency = Challenges for international publication.

3. What do you usually use to evaluate research productivity?

In my opinion, the assessment for research productivity in the world today is the quantity and quality of published scientific studies (articles, books, proceedings, etc.) that follows the slogan "Publish or perish". Therefore, a scientific research that is not published (or not publicized formally) and is not applicable will become a meaningless work, or at least, have a very limited impact. In this case, the purpose of scientific research is lost, which is to create new knowledge serving the common interests of humanity.

4. What are the challenges of self-organizing data? To ensure that the data are clean and highly reliable in current Vietnamese social conditions, what are the difficulties?

Currently, I find the most challenging problem of scientific research in Vietnam is that we do not have a professional and robust database to serve scientific research. Usually, documents published in Vietnamese are quite scattered and unfocused. Therefore, this is a gap for the "plagiarism" problem in the scientific conduct. I think only when we have a reliable and massive database, we can build an anti-plagiarism software for ourselves.

A.28. Tran Thi Ly
Dr. Tran Thi Ly, Deakin University, Victoria, Australia

1. Of your publications, which one(s) is/are your favorite? Why?

My most favorite article is:
- o Tran, L. T. (2016). Mobility as 'becoming': A Bourdieuian analysis of the factors shaping international student mobility. *British Journal of Sociology of Education,* 37(8), 1268-1289.

My study introduces a new concept: "mobility as becoming" to the field of student mobility. The article portrays the experiences and ambitions of students when crossing geographical, educational and cultural boundaries.

2. Is there any experience that you want to share about selecting international journals for submission?
For me, the journal's prestige and Impact Factor index in the field of my study and the relevance of the article topic with the scope of the journal are the most important factors.

3. What qualities do you think define a scholar of high credibility?
I think that authors must have several qualities at the same time: publishing in prestigious journals in his/her discipline, authoring articles that are practically and theoretically influential, and actively participating in assessment and building of research capacity in a specific scientific field or institute.

4. In your opinion, what are the advantages and disadvantages of single-authorship?
I think a solo author is quite lonely, and he/she has much higher workload than when he/she collaborate with other scientists.

References
Bodman, P., & Le, T. (2013). Assessing the roles that absorptive capacity and economic distance play in the foreign direct investment-productivity growth nexus. *Applied Economics, 45*(8), 1027-1039.
Bosch, O. J., Nguyen, N. C., Maeno, T., & Yasui, T. (2013). Managing complex issues through evolutionary learning laboratories. *Systems Research and Behavioral Science, 30*(2), 116-135.
Bui, H.T. & Le, T-A. (2016). Tourist satisfaction and destination image of Vietnam's Ha Long Bay. *Asia Pacific Journal of Tourism Research, 21*(7), 795-810.
Djankov, S., Freund, C., & Pham, C. S. (2010). Trading on time. *The review of Economics and Statistics, 92*(1), 166-173.

Giang, L. T., Nguyen, C. V., & Tran, T. Q. (2016). Firm agglomeration and local poverty reduction: evidence from an economy in transition. *Asian-Pacific Economic Literature, 30*(1), 80-98.

Ho, H. L., Irvine, K. N., Nguyen, D. T. H., Nguyen, T. K. Q., Nguyen, N. T., & Shimizu, Y. (2018). The legal aspects of Ecosystem Services in agricultural land pricing, some implications from a case study in Vietnam's Mekong Delta. *Ecosystem Services, 29*, 360-369.

Huynh, T. D. (2015). The misuse of urban planning in Ho Chi Minh City. *Habitat International, 48*, 11-19.

Khuat, T.H. (1998). Study on sexuality in Vietnam: the known and unknown issues. *South and East Asia Regional Working Papers No. 11*. The Population Council. Available at https://www.popline.org/node/523255. Doi: 10.13140/RG.2.2.15215.84640.

Khuat, T. H., Nguyen, V. T., Jardine, M., Moore, T., Bui, T. H., & Crofts, N. (2012). Harm reduction and "Clean" community: can Viet Nam have both?. *Harm Reduction Journal, 9*(1), 25.

Le, T. (2010). Are student flows a significant channel of R&D spillovers from the north to the south?. *Economics Letters, 107*(3), 315-317.

Le, T. (2008). 'Brain Drain' or 'Brain Circulation': Evidence From OECD's International Migration and R&D Spillovers. *Scottish Journal of Political Economy, 55*(5), 618-636.

Le, T. (2012). R&D Spillovers through Student Flows, Institutions, and Economic Growth: What can we Learn from African Countries?. *Scottish Journal of Political Economy, 59*(1), 115-130.

Le, T., & Bodman, P. M. (2011). Remittances or technological diffusion: which drives domestic gains from brain drain?. *Applied Economics, 43*(18), 2277-2285.

Nguyen, T. T. M., Pham, T. H., & Pham, M. T. (2012). The relative effects of explicit and implicit form-focused instruction on the development of L2 pragmatic competence. *Journal of Pragmatics, 44*(4), 416-434.

Nguyen, V. C. (2011). Poverty projection using a small area estimation method: Evidence from Vietnam. *Journal of Comparative Economics, 39*(3), 368-382.

Nguyen, V. C. (2018). The long-term effects of mistimed pregnancy on children's education and employment. *Journal of Population Economics, 31*(3), 937-968.

Pham, V. H., & Kompas, T. (2016). Solving intertemporal CGE models in parallel using a singly bordered block diagonal ordering technique. *Economic Modelling, 52,* 3-12.

Phinney, H. M., Hong, K. T., Nhan, V. T. T., Thao, N. T. P., & Hirsch, J. S. (2014). Obstacles to the 'cleanliness of our race': HIV, reproductive risk, stratified reproduction, and population quality in Hanoi, Vietnam. *Critical Public Health,* 24(4), 445-460.

Teerawichitchainan, B., Pothisiri, W., & Giang, T. L. (2015). How do living arrangements and intergenerational support matter for psychological health of elderly parents? Evidence from Myanmar, Vietnam, and Thailand. *Social Science & Medicine, 136,* 106-116.

Tran, D. V. (2003). Culture, Environment, and Farming Systems in Vietnam's Northern Mountain Region. *Japanese Journal of Southeast Asian Studies, 41*(2), 180-205.

Tran, H. T. & Navrud, S. (2007). Valuing cultural heritage in developing countries: comparing and pooling contingent valuation and choice modeling estimates. *Environmental and Resource Economics, 38*(1), 51-69.

Tran, N. B. (1985). A neo-Ricardian trade model with overlapping generations. *Economic Record, 61*(4), 707-718.

Tran, N. B., Evans, C., Walpole, M., & Ritchie, K. (2000). Tax compliance costs: Research methodology and empirical evidence from Australia. *National Tax Journal, 53*(2), 229-252.

Tran, L. T. (2016). Mobility as 'becoming': A Bourdieuian analysis of the factors shaping international student mobility. *British Journal of Sociology of Education, 37*(8), 1268-1289.

Tran, T. Q., Nguyen, C. V., & Van Vu, H. (2018). Does economic inequality affect the quality of life of older people in rural Vietnam?. *Journal of Happiness Studies, 19*(3), 781-799.

Truong, T. D., & Hallinger, P. (2017). Exploring cultural context and school leadership: conceptualizing an indigenous model of *có uy* school leadership in Vietnam. *International Journal of Leadership in Education, 20*(5), 539-561.

Yoshida, K., Bui, H.T. & Lee, T.J. (2016). Does tourism illuminate the darkness of Hiroshima and Nagasaki?. *Journal of Destination Marketing and Management, 5*(4), 333-340.

Ziegler, A. D., Giambelluca, T. W., Plondke, D., Leisz, S., Tran, L. T., Fox, J., ... & Tran, D. V. (2007). Hydrological consequences of landscape fragmentation in mountainous northern Vietnam: buffering of Hortonian overland flow. *Journal of Hydrology, 337*(1-2), 52-67.

INDEX

academic entrepreneurship, 7, 181, 182, 183
academic institutions, 102, 103, 134
academic publishing, 7
article processing charge, 135
articles, 3, 11
Bill & Melinda Gates Foundation, 132, 144
Brill, 98
British Journal of Psychiatry, 66, 73, 141, 151
Bui Thanh Huong, 8, 113, 122, 194
Bui Thi Minh Hong, 8, 195
Bulletin of the World Health Organization, 66, 67, 68, 73, 91, 93, 105

Business, 12, 47, 60, 61, 87, 88, 91, 92, 97, 102, 105, 150, 181, 188
business of science, 7, 174, 178, 180, 181, 182, 183, 184, 185, 186
Circular 08, 5, 23, 39, 133, 153, 154, 155, 158, 162, 166, 170, 171, 172, 173, 192
CiteScore, 121, 136, 137, 138, 139, 140, 148
co-authorship network, 118, 124, 125, 126, 127
collaboration networks, 7
conflict of interests, 27
Confucian society, 10
Confucian traditions, 73
công bố quốc tế, 55, 168, 169, 173

contribution point, 30
D.J.D. Price, 28
De Gruyter, 8, 98
Directory of Open Access Journals, 144
Do Quy Toan, 122
Do Truong Lam, 93
Dove Press, 99
Duy Tan University, 44, 47
Easter egg, 131, 139
Economics, 7, 12, 13, 43, 45, 46, 47, 60, 61, 62, 73, 81, 83, 87, 88, 89, 90, 91, 92, 94, 96, 97, 102, 104, 105, 114, 116, 128, 192
Economics University Hanoi, 46
education, 13, 25, 26, 40, 47, 57, 73, 74, 78, 79, 83, 150, 162, 163, 168, 175, 177, 178, 179, 183, 187, 188, 189, 192
Education, 3, 7, 11, 12, 33, 34, 45, 54, 56, 60, 61, 62, 73, 74, 75, 79, 80, 81, 83, 84, 85, 88, 94, 97, 102, 110, 114, 116, 153, 175, 187, 188, 189, 192
Elsevier, 28, 97, 98, 136
Emerald Publishing, 21, 98, 100, 104
Environment/Sustainability Science, 60, 61, 88, 111
Ernest Solvay, 132
European Science Editing, 30
female authors, 39, 40, 60, 111, 112, 114
female researchers, 7, 111, 114, 126, 192
financial funding, 7
first-authorship, 124
Fish and Fisheries, 142, 149

Foreign Trade University, 12, 45, 92, 102, 103
FPT University, 44, 47
GDP *per capita*, 19
gender gap, 40, 111
Gender issues, 111
Giang Thanh Long, 8, 9, 48, 122, 198
Global Environmental Change, 142
Global Health Action, 63
Ha Long Bay, 194, 250
Hanoi Medical University, 45, 46, 63, 93
Health and Demographic Surveillance System HDSS, 62, 63
Health Care, 7, 15, 16, 18, 60, 61, 62, 63, 64, 65, 71, 72, 80, 81, 83, 88, 97, 108, 114, 116, 192
healthcare, 57
high-productivity authors, 114
Hindawi, 99
Ho Huu Loc, 9, 123, 199
Ho Xuan Nang Science Foundation, 8, 176
Hoang Lan Anh, 122
Hoang Van Minh, 62, 64, 107, 113, 122
Hoang Viet Ngu, 122
homemade databases, 5
Huynh The Du, 9, 200
impact factor, 58, 59, 65, 74, 80, 90, 143, 147, 151
impact factors, 71, 79, 92, 121, 137, 138, 152
INDEPTH Network, 63
Inderscience, 99

institutional autonomy, 176
interdisciplinary networks, 96, 97
interdisciplinary research, 7, 32
international collaboration, 28, 31, 49, 50, 51, 52, 55, 65, 158
international collaboration networks, 50
International Journal of Drug Policy, 70, 73, 78
International Journal of Epidemiology, 141, 149
international journals, 52, 57, 58, 62, 135, 162, 166, 167, 179
international publications, 26, 27, 31, 36, 39, 47, 49, 55, 57, 73, 87, 106, 114, 158, 166, 167, 168, 169, 173, 174, 176, 179
International Relations, 13, 61, 96, 97
international standards, 26, 28
ISI Web of Science, 28
ISI/Scopus, 24
ISI/Scopus-indexed journals, 153
JIF, 10, 58, 64, 65, 66, 68, 69, 70, 71, 74, 75, 76, 77, 78, 79, 80, 89, 91, 92, 135, 136, 137, 138, 140, 142
John Wiley & Sons, 92
journal article, 28
Journal Citation Reports, 10, 135
JCR, 137

Journal Impact Factor, 10, 135, 136, 137, 138
Journal of Asian Business and Economic Studies, 167
Journal of Asian Business and Economic Studies (JABES), 100, 167
Journal of Cleaner Production, 91, 141, 149
Journal of Clinical Medicine, 66, 73, 187
Journal of Economics and Development (JED), 100
Journal of International Business Studies, 91, 92, 105, 140, 150
Khoán 10, 171
Khuat Thu Hong, 9, 201
Kim Bao Giang, 113
Kim Huong Trang, 92
Kim Ngoc, 171
Land Degradation and Development, 91, 92
Le Quan, 9, 203
Le Quang Thanh, 9, 205
Le Thai Ha, 113, 122
Le Thi Huong, 113
Le Van Canh, 9, 209
Little Science, Big Science, 28
low-quality journals, 145
Luu Trong Tuan, 9, 44, 107, 108, 109, 113, 123, 211
major policy changes, 6
MDPI, 99
Ministry of Education and Training, 7
multidisciplinary research, 117
multiple-authorship, 111

NAFOSTED, 3, 8, 10, 11, 22, 23, 25, 32, 55, 135, 150, 167, 173, 176, 187, 191
National Economics University, 8, 13, 43, 45, 46, 47, 100, 102, 103, 170, 198, 207, 223
National Foundation for Science and Technology, 22
National Foundation for Science and Technology Development, 8, 10, 98
National Science Foundation (NSF), 26
National University Hanoi, 11, 43, 44, 45, 134, 167
natural sciences and technology, 23
Nature, 26, 33, 54, 80, 84, 97, 118, 128, 129, 131, 132, 138, 139, 141, 146, 149, 150, 151, 152, 169, 176, 186, 188, 189
Nature Human Behaviour, 129, 140
Nature Publishing Group, 3, 11, 31, 80
network analysis, 30, 126, 127
Network of Vietnamese Social Scientists NVSS, 29
network theory, 118
new authors, 38
Ngo Viet Liem, 113, 123
Nguyen Cao Nam, 9, 213
Nguyen Dinh Tho, 122
Nguyen Duc Thach, 123
Nguyen Hoang Long, 113, 123

Nguyen Le Hau, 122
Nguyen Minh Ha, 122
Nguyen Ngoc Huong, 107, 108, 112, 122
Nguyen Quang, 92
Nguyen Tai Dong, 9, 215
Nguyen The Ninh, 123
Nguyen Thi Hien, 9, 217
Nguyen Thi Lan Huong, 113
Nguyen Thi Thuy Minh, 9, 113, 122, 220
Nguyen Thu Thuy, 9, 223
Nguyen Trong Chuan, 9, 214
Nguyen Trung Thanh, 93, 113, 123
Nguyen Van Thang, 123
Nguyen Viet Cuong, 9, 16, 48, 108, 109, 113, 119, 120, 122, 223, 244
Nham Phong Tuan, 122
of Circular 08, 7
of interdisciplinary research, 94, 117, 192
open access, 7
Open Access, 144
Open Science, 143, 144, 145
Palgrave MacMillan, 92
peer-review, 27, 142, 144, 145, 189
Pham Quang Minh, 109
Pham Si Cong, 9, 225
Pham Van Ha, 9, 227
Phan Chi Anh, 122
Phan Le Ha, 113
Phenikaa University, 3, 8, 11, 13, 44, 45, 47, 176, 207
plagiarism, 129, 145, 152
Plan S, 143, 144
PLOS Medicine, 65, 66, 73, 141, 149, 151

PLOS ONE, 69, 70, 73
PNAS, 139
pre-registration, 145
productive researchers, 7
publication output, 7, 37, 47, 57, 62, 63, 73, 87, 89, 107, 108, 112, 113, 119, 155
Publish or perish, 153
QS World University Ranking, 136
record-breaking individuals, 106
research capacity, 28
research culture, 175, 178, 183
research grants, 98, 133
research institutes, 31
research productivity, 5
Resolution 10, 171
School of Medicine and Pharmacy, 44
Science, 3, 10, 11, 12, 22, 33, 34, 53, 54, 55, 61, 70, 83, 88, 128, 129, 132, 135, 136, 138, 139, 150, 151, 152, 166, 173, 176, 179, 187
science communication, 147, 149, 180, 185, 186
science funding
   science funding policies, 25
Science since Babylon, 28
Sciendo, 8
scientific community, 28
Scientific Data, 31, 34, 56, 73, 75, 80, 84, 85, 190
scientific development, 146
scientific funding agency, 22
scientific impact, 117
scientific method, 146
scientific misconduct, 145, 149
Scientific output, 40
scientific papers, 29
scientific productivity, 27, 36, 37, 51
scientific publishing, 6
Scopus, 5, 7, 18, 20, 21, 24, 26, 28, 29, 32, 33, 34, 44, 45, 53, 54, 55, 56, 75, 100, 106, 128, 129, 133, 134, 135, 136, 137, 138, 140, 148, 150, 153, 167
Scopus-indexed journals, 7, 44, 106, 133, 153
sequence-determines-credit, 30
single-authorship, 74, 110
social sciences and humanities, 5, 23, 27, 34, 53, 55, 57, 83, 84, 87, 129, 130, 152, 181, 185, 190
SSH, 29
Social Sciences and Humanities Peer Awards, 5
Social Sciences and Humanitites SSH, 47
Sociology, 60, 61, 88, 114
Springer, 98, 189
SSH, 5, 6, 7, 10, 23, 25, 26, 27, 29, 30, 31, 32, 36, 37, 38, 40, 41, 43, 47, 49, 51, 53, 57, 61, 62, 64, 87, 88, 94, 95, 97, 106, 109, 111, 112, 116, 119, 124, 126, 133, 135, 142, 143, 191, 192, 193
SSIIPA, 5, 13, 98, 192
sustainable co-authorship, 127

Taylor & Francis, 63, 97, 98
Times Higher Education, 136
Total SciComm, 147, 149
Tran Dinh Phong, 9, 229
Tran Duc Thach, 107, 113
Tran Duc Vien, 9, 233
Tran Huu Tuan, 9, 122, 238
Tran Nam Binh, 9, 240
Tran Quang Tuyen, 9, 123, 243
Tran Thi Ly, 9, 113, 122, 249
Tran Tuan Phong, 9, 245
Tran Van Kham, 9, 246
Tran Xuan Bach, 63, 64, 93, 107, 108, 113, 122
Truong Dinh Thang, 9, 248
university, 31
University of Dong Thap, 167
University of Economics, 44
University of Economics and Business, 8
University of Economics and Business VNUH, 47
University of Economics Ho Chi Minh City, 45, 46, 47, 100, 102, 103, 167
University of Social Sciences and Humanities, 44, 134, 167
Vietnam Academy of Social Sciences, 44
Vietnam National University Hanoi, 43
Vietnam National University Ho Chi Minh City, 46
Vietnam National University of Agriculture, 93
Vietnamese authors, 7, 29, 37, 38, 51, 52, 57, 60, 63, 65, 71, 79, 92, 94, 98, 106, 158, 159, 160, 191
Vietnamese researchers, 27, 30, 34, 52, 53, 55, 57, 74, 124, 126, 129, 130, 147, 160, 186
Vietnamese scholars, 5
Vietnamese social scientists, 31, 52, 118, 124, 125, 126, 172
Vietnamese universities, 76, 77, 134
Vo Xuan Vinh, 109, 113, 122
Vu Duy Kien, 122
Vuong Quan Hoang, 64, 107, 108, 109, 113, 122
Vuong Thu Trang, 113
Web of Science, 10, 20, 21, 23, 32, 33, 49, 97, 100, 135, 136, 137, 138, 147, 182, 189
Web-of-Science, 5
Welcome Trust, 144
Wiley, 92, 98
World Trade Organization, 49
young researchers, 39, 142, 155

Bei Fragen zur Produktsicherheit wenden Sie sich bitte an:
If you have any questions regarding product safety,
please contact:

Walter de Gruyter GmbH
Genthiner Straße 13
10785 Berlin
productsafety@degruyterbrill.com